THE
KILLING
WINDS

THE KILLING WINDS

The Menace of Biological Warfare

by JEANNE McDERMOTT

ARBOR HOUSE

NEW YORK

Designed by Robert Bull
Manufactured in the United States of America

10 9 8 7 6 5 4 3 2 1

Library of Congress Cataloging in Publication Data

McDermott, Jeanne.
  The killing winds.

  Bibliography: p.
  Includes index.
  1. Biological warfare.   I. Title.
UG447.8.M34   1987   358'.38   87–1855
ISBN: 0-87795-896-3

To Ted

Contents

Acknowledgments

A book is always written with the cooperation of many people, too numerous to name, who answer questions, make suggestions, and challenge the writer along the way. They might not agree with what the author has written, but the book is far richer for their participation in the dialogue.

In particular, my thanks go to Richard Falk, Matthew Meselson, Julian Perry Robinson, Kei-ichi Tsuneishi, Susan Wright, and the Stockholm International Peace Research Institute for studies that have informed public discussion of a shadowy topic; to Ira Baldwin and Alexander Langmuir for recalling the history of biological warfare preparations; to Eddie Becker, Stanley Kutler, and Jay Peterzell for help with research; to Senator Kerry's office for responding promptly to a constituent's call; to Greg Rodriquez for the document at the beginning of Chapter Eight; to Richard Mooney for transcribing tapes; to the foundations which have supported and continue to support the Vannevar Bush Fellowship in the Public Understanding of Technology and Science at MIT.

Also, my thanks go to those whose support now and over the years has made a difference—to my immediate family: Julia Kramer, Ferd Kramer, Robert McDermott, Jane Mc-

Dermott, John McDermott, and Charlie McDermott; to friends and colleagues: Nancy Burson, Michael Congdon, Lew Frederick, Julia Freedgood, Karen Frenkel, Alice Markowitz, and James Raimes.

The people at Ten Concord and the Boston freelance writers who meet monthly softened the inevitable isolation of writing. Betsy Finch and my grandmother, Jean Wood, eased the headaches of travel with their hospitality.

Finally, heartfelt thanks to Ted Finch, my husband, for being there.

Foreword

By and large, you can't see biological weapons. You can't taste
them or feel them. And you can't do much to protect yourself
against them. They are poisons and diseases that steal through
the air, riding the winds, striking with a whimper, not a bang.
Imagine the Black Death, the plague, or any other dreaded
pestilence or poison wedded to sophisticated twentieth-century
military hardware and you have a feeling for how insidious biological warfare might be.

Before I embarked on this book, I knew little about biological warfare, military culture, or the politics of the Pentagon. I
came to it as a science journalist, familiar with how scientists
work, their laboratories, and the peculiar joys of pursuing
knowledge purely for its own sake. Since studying microbiology in college ten years ago, I believed that biological weapons
were, like slavery, an unsavory part of our past, forever banned
by international law, exiled beyond the pale of civilized behavior. They were noteworthy only as the one weapon that almost
the entire world agreed to purge from its arsenals. I considered
them dinosaurs—extinct. But in 1983, I began to pick up troubling hints that this might not be true.

A chance meeting sowed the first seed. Waiting in the Detroit airport to board an airplane for Boston, I sat next to a neatly dressed, curly-haired man in his fifties who was sorting through small black-and-white photographs in a manila folder. Since they had been taken through a microscope, I suspected that the man was a scientist and, like myself, returning home after the annual meeting of the American Association for the Advancement of Science.

"What are the pictures?" I asked. "Bee feces," he said, without a trace of a smile. Then, in a friendly way that assumed I knew more than I did, he proceeded to explain that Yellow Rain—the biological weapon that the United States believed Soviet-backed forces in Southeast Asia were using—looked just like the pollen-filled droppings of honeybees. Here were the pictures of evidence collected by the government and here were pictures of beeshit. Identical, no? Sure enough, they did look a lot alike.

By the time a voice announced that the plane was ready for boarding, I realized that I was talking to Matthew Meselson, a Harvard biochemistry professor, expert on biological warfare, and a man willing to tell his story to whomever would listen, including a curious stranger. As a reporter, crusades bring out my skepticism. I thought he had an interesting point of view, but I was not convinced.

A year later, I found myself, along with nine other science journalists from around the world, at the Massachusetts Institute of Technology on a Vannevar Bush Fellowship for the Public Understanding of Technology and Science. The fellowship was structured as a sabbatical year. We took classes and held seminars, often talking about the knotty problems of translating arcane and increasingly crucial scientific ideas for the public, which had to make decisions on the basis of experts' opinions. One of the speakers invited to the seminars was Meselson. For over an hour, he talked about Yellow Rain, laying out more reasons to question the administration's charge about its use in Southeast Asia.

After that, my skepticism turned into plain curiosity. I

knew that scientific experts often disagree, but that a consensus eventually emerges on many controversies. In this case, what was the evidence? What did the rest of the scientific community believe? Why had it become such a highly charged issue?

Very quickly, it became clear that Yellow Rain was a piece in a larger, more ominous puzzle, and I could not help but be drawn into wrestling with some very serious questions. Did this controversy signal the resurrection of biological weapons? Was this the dark side of the revolution in molecular biology? Would the spectacular scientific breakthroughs accomplished by genetic engineering unleash sinister new weapons? What peculiar horrors did biological warfare offer nuclear powers at a stalemate? Were biological weapons to be quietly included in our nation's military buildup? At the fellowship's end, I had the time and the inclination to find out for myself.

The desire to understand the dynamics, the crucial interplay, between science and the military outweighed my reservations about plunging into such a grim and chilling subject, and in a sense shielded me as I traveled around the country, talking to scientists, military officers, and bureaucrats, anyone whose work touched on the future of biological warfare. From Utah to Maryland, Alabama to Washington, D.C., I found a strange topsy-turvy world of cultured killers, a sort of deadly vapor trail where scientists pondered how the miracles of medicine might be marshaled toward destruction. I found growing budgets and active imaginations, galvanized by the newfound powers of genetic engineering. And I found an infatuation with what was now possible in the laboratory that blinded many to the reasons for banning biological warfare in the first place.

I did not answer all my questions in the year I spent researching and writing. The historical record, in particular, remains murky. Did the United States wage germ warfare in Korea? What really took place in the jungles of Southeast Asia? Others will have to answer more fully. I did discover something that gave me nightmares—that the world is taking the first frightening steps toward a biological arms race.

PART I

THE THREAT

ONE

In the Dog Days of August

In August, the nation's capital surrenders to the torpor of summer. Washingtonians flee the muggy, steamy swamp heat, leaving behind the tourists, museums, and monuments. Congress officially sanctions the ritual exodus by taking its summer recess as soon as politically possible. It is a wise move. In the nineteenth century, before the invention of air conditioning, rumor has it that the heat drove at least one diplomat to suicide.

In Mike Walker's office, a grandly styled, airless cubbyhole choked with files and set off a gloomy corridor in the Dirksen Building next to the Capitol, you would never guess the time of day, let alone the season of the year. Instead of windows, maps of the Middle East and other global trouble spots paper the walls. Walker works for the Senate Appropriations Committee and specializes in military affairs. His most distinguishing feature is not his sandy hair and mustache, nor his deceptively youthful face, but his ear, which seems permanently attached to the telephone.

For most of the day, Walker leans forward in a high-backed swivel chair, cradling the telephone on one shoulder, making notes with his free hand. "How's business?" he asks, a cordial Southern ring to his voice. "No kidding." He leans back, jotting a note. Without looking frenzied, he thrives on action, information, deals, and working, as he has done for Tennessee senator Jim Sasser since his election in 1976, behind the scenes.

Senator Sasser has been described as the rare politician who listens more than he talks, a moderate southerner with ties to all wings of the Democratic party, and a lawyer skilled at shaping compromises. He's never been known as a headline chaser nor an ironclad ideologue. As a ranking member of the Military Construction Subcommittee of the Senate Appropriations Committee, Sasser oversees the Department of Defense's brick and mortar decisions, a position that gives him a concrete view of military policy. He has spoken out when the Pentagon overstepped its bounds. In 1984, an on-site inspection of army bases in Honduras convinced Sasser that the army was constructing airstrips with money the Congress had never appropriated for that purpose, and he put a stop to it.

Mike Walker serves as Sasser's eyes and ears in the daily business of the Appropriations Committee, which includes handling "reprogramming requests." Between its annual requests for funds, the Pentagon sometimes discovers that it wants to shuffle money slated for one construction project to another. An obscure statute allows the secretary of defense to reallocate up to $30 million a year without going through the usual authorization process if the project is so vital to national security that waiting until the next year would risk the country's well-being. The Pentagon's comptroller just has to make a reprogramming request to the Military Construction Subcommittee in the form of a routine and informal letter and obtain the signatures of the committee's two ranking members.

On the eve of Congress's 1984 summer recess, a reprogramming request landed on Walker's glass-topped desk. It read like all the others:

Dear Mr. Chairman,

The Defense Components [meaning the armed services and other Pentagon agencies] have requested approval to reprogram, within available military construction funds, the amounts shown below:

The first project requested was an aerosol test laboratory at Dugway Proving Ground in Utah for $1.4 million. Ten more projects, including a physical fitness center, housing units, land acquisition, a heated parking garage, and an aircraft maintenance hangar, followed.

Your approval of the proposed reprogramming is requested. Additional details, including the source of the funds, are provided in the enclosures. Representatives of Defense Components are available to provide any additional information you may desire.

Sincerely,
John Quetsch
Acting Assistant Secretary of Defense
(Comptroller)

Seeing nothing out of the ordinary, Walker prepared to send back the standard five-line approval, and within three or four days Senator Sasser and the ranking majority member, Georgia senator Mack Mattingly, had both signed. "We turned that reprogramming around very quickly," Walker said later. "Too fast. The significance of the reprogramming escaped us." Like everybody else in Washington, Walker went on vacation and did not give the request another thought.

Two weeks after Labor Day, another reprogramming request crossed Walker's desk. This one was longer, listing twenty-nine projects. Between replacing a timber roof structure, renovating a gymnasium, and constructing a dining hall, the Pentagon sandwiched a request for a $7 million toxic-agent test support at Dugway Proving Ground in Utah. This time, something clicked in Walker's mind. Toxins. Dugway. Of the over seven hundred bases that the United States owns and operates around the world, Dugway staked an unusual claim in the history of modern warfare.

Wasn't Dugway the place the military once had tested biological weapons? What did the Pentagon want to build in the Utah desert? Why make an emergency request? What had the committee just approved? In 1969 the United States renounced biological weapons, purging them from the arsenal, and in 1975 most countries in the world signed a treaty banning their production, possession, and stockpiling. Was the ghost of biological weaponry rattling its bones? Was this a resurrection of a taboo technology?

Alerted by Walker, Senator Sasser called for a briefing on the Dugway facilities to learn why the army needed an aerosol laboratory. What Sasser heard troubled him. The army did not want an ordinary lab. It wanted one stringently designed to meet the highest safety standards for working with the most dangerous germs and toxins in existence. In the National Institutes of Health rating jargon, it was to be a BL-4 lab (biosafety level 4), a maximum containment facility created for genetically engineered organisms where scientists would do lab-bench experiments in totally contained spacesuits. Only four others like it existed in the United States, and one already belonged to the army's biological warfare researchers at Fort Detrick, Maryland.

This new one would be used to test the vapors of potential biological warfare agents, a list that reads like Mother Nature's Ten Most Wanted: highly potent toxins from Colombian frogs and cobras, the fragile viruses that cause the puzzling Lassa Fever, the rare Ebola and Marburg diseases, and a spectrum of other hemorrhagic fevers, most of which have a high fatality rate and no known cure.

Sasser blew the whistle. Although he had already given his approval, he took the unprecedented step of rescinding it. "There was no other alternative," says Walker. "The primary purpose was to put it in the public domain, to encourage other members of Congress to get involved with the issue." In a letter to Senator Mattingly, Sasser spelled out his qualms. "None of these projects have been debated and considered by the full Congress. It is my opinion that the Department [of Defense] has instead sought a reprogramming action under emergency fund statute in order to avoid the regular authorization and appropriations process of Congress. . . . The proposed expansion of test capabilities at Dugway raises an important question with regard to potential capabilities for testing and production of offensive lethal biological and toxin weapons, a capability which is presently prohibited by international treaty. I do not believe the proposed projects should go forward until the administration has provided the Congress with its plans and policies with regard to biological and toxin weapons."

When Sasser clued the public in, the story touched off debate and protest. Congressional staffers shook their heads knowingly; it was not the first time the military had tried to sneak a controversial project through the appropriations process. In an article in *Science* magazine, prominent molecular biologists asked why the army needed a BL-4 lab when information needed for defense could be obtained without it. David Baltimore, Nobel laureate and head of MIT's Whitehead Institute for Biomedical Research in Cambridge, said that even if the army's intentions were pure, the program was too elaborate, too open to ambiguous interpretation. Robert Sinsheimer, chancellor of the University of California at Santa Cruz and a biophysicist, found it troubling and capable of leading to an escalation of the arms race. Roy Curtiss, chairman of the biology department of Washington University, simply called the lab "overkill."

The army immediately denied any intention of going

around Congress or behind its back and explained the lab was planned several years ago, had been approved by the Pentagon in 1983, and would have been part of the routine 1985 budget request. But in light of the growing menace of Soviet activities in the arena of biological weapons, it seemed prudent to build the test lab as quickly as possible. When the reprogramming money became available, it put in for an emergency request.

Secretary of Defense Caspar Weinberger moved quickly to answer Sasser's concerns and quell his doubts, point by point, in a three-page letter. "There should be no misunderstanding of U.S. policy regarding biological and toxin weapons. Our policy in this area is unequivocal and has often been reiterated by the highest officials of the government. To summarize, the U.S. does not and will not possess biological or toxin weapons."

But the treaty does allow for defensive research, which by necessity demands the development of the suspected weapon. "We continue to obtain new evidence that the Soviet Union has maintained its offensive biological weapons program and that it is exploring genetic engineering to expand their program's scope," wrote the secretary of defense. "Developments in this area are driven by the Soviet threat. . . . To insure that our protective systems work, we must challenge them with known or suspected Soviet [toxic] agents."

To defend itself, the army wanted to experiment with the toxins and diseases that it either knew or suspected would be used against them. Was this legitimately justified in the name of defense? Or was this offensive work carried out under the cloak of defense? And would this escalation of activities be likely to lead to more?

Sasser's fellow committee members, including Utah senator Jake Garn, whose home state prospers by the military's spending, did not share his worries about the grim implications of building the aerosol lab. They took a vote and overrode his veto, rescuing the BL-4 lab from its legal limbo. As far as Congress was concerned, the army could go right ahead and experiment with exotic toxins and viruses in Utah.

If it hadn't been for Jeremy Rifkin, the army might have built its laboratory without any more fuss or fanfare. The newspapers, where Rifkin's name appears on a regular basis, usually give him the neutral and calming description of author and activist and occasionally mention that he is president of a self-styled public interest organization, the Foundation on Economic Trends. But such labels cloak his overwhelming sense of mission. Jeremy is a modern embodiment of Jeremiah, the pessimistic prophet in the Old Testament.

Rifkin titled his most recent book *Declarations of a Heretic* because he publicly dissents from the culture's unofficial dogma that technological progress is inevitably good. "I have been castigated as an obstructionist, a spoiler, a man dedicated to slowing, retarding or halting further advances of the human race," he writes in the book's preface. For good measure, he could have added zealot, fanatic, pariah, fear monger, and alarmist.

The new offices of the Foundation on Economic Trends occupy three modest rooms at a respectable address in downtown Washington, D.C. Visitors navigate folder-filled boxes stacked in the reception area while Rifkin's associate and co-author, Nicanor Perlas, answers the ever-ringing telephone. In the next room, Rifkin is surrounded by shelves that strain with multiple copies of his eight books. Bald, with a broad black mustache and comfortably dressed, he looks like a historian at a small college, not a gadfly with a ruckus-raising reputation.

"The first time I heard about Dugway was when Senator Sasser announced he'd been had," says Rifkin with rapid-fire delivery. "The DOD tried to pull a fast one when everyone was on vacation. They wanted to shift money from one project to another just to build an aerosol lab. Then Sasser said, 'What have I done? This could be a major change in policy.' He tried to raise questions, but other members of the committee put it through. Congress was powerless. It didn't want to open that can of worms."

Rifkin specializes in opening wormy containers and dumping their contents in the courts, a distinctly American way to place a concern on the agenda of public debate. Born in Chicago in 1945, he studied at the University of Pennsylvania, where he once described himself as a "rah-rah" fraternity member. Rifkin's political conscience awoke in 1966 when he saw some fraternity brothers beat up students protesting biological warfare. At the time, Penn was one of the major university centers for highly classified biological warfare research, exploring diseases to destroy the Vietnamese rice crop. (In response to protests in 1967, the university trustees voted to cancel the contracts.)

Rifkin got his master's degree from the Fletcher School of Diplomacy at Tufts University, then went on to organize antiwar rallies, work for VISTA, and generally practice liberal politics for the next twenty years. These days he worries almost exclusively about genetic engineering, a technological revolution without parallel in the life sciences. In the early seventies, molecular biologists had discovered ways to snip and clip the DNA, or genetic material, of one living creature and place it in another, short-circuiting the tedious process of natural evolution. In theory, the discoveries brought scientists to the brink of playing God, able to tinker with some of the fundamental mysteries of life.

How would scientists and engineers use the new tools? The answers are trickling in. Since 1980, when the Supreme Court ruled that genetically engineered forms of life could be patented, the biotechnology business has boomed. It promises and is even beginning to deliver better drugs to treat cancer, diagnostic tests for hereditary diseases, safer pills for diabetics, hormones for dwarfed children, hardier pest-resistant crops, and new processes to clean up waste and mine the earth.

But there is, inevitably, a dark side to all this good news. Where Rifkin leaves the pack of futurists is in his dogged insistence on examining the drawbacks to these technological changes and on holding social institutions responsible for weighing them. He is impassioned about the perils of the new biotechnology, which his critics say he overstates with inflammatory rhetoric and sensationalism. By taking strident, obstructionist actions, Rifkin has forced decisions about the use of genetic engineering and biotechnology into the arena of public debate.

"This is the first time anyone has tried to introduce questions before the technology happens. We can see the new technology has tremendous benefits, but it comes with a cost. If you can speculate about the benefits, you can speculate about the costs. We're committed to raising questions, and nowhere is that more important than in the military." He pauses as if he has said this many times before, sounding off for the media. Then frustration seeps into his voice. "A lot of industry says if I go away, the controversy will go away. We're at the crude beginnings of the new technology. Precedents are being set for what could be done for the next half millennium. I say, let's debate this. They say, you're an alarmist. Something happens, then they say, it is too late. The genie is out of the bottle."

In 1983, Rifkin went from proselytizing to prosecution, initiating over the next three years at least six lawsuits and two legal actions. He filed suit against the National Institutes of Health for approving the release of a genetically engineered bacterium without filing an environmental assessment; against the Department of Agriculture for introducing a human gene into a cow without filing an environmental assessment; another against the Department of Agriculture for mismanaging its germplasm and seed stock; a third against the Department of Agriculture for releasing a genetically engineered livestock vaccine. In almost all of his legal actions, Rifkin raised the question of safety, often in tandem with the specter of disaster that might result by releasing, deliberately or accidentally, a genetically engineered organism into the environment.

When it comes to deciding how safe it is to deliberately release an organism, scientists face a dearth of knowledge. There is no easy way to predict what will happen when a novel organism enters the environment. The assumption is that most die, unable to compete successfully with the millions of other microbes already there. But what about those that don't? What about the few bugs that, like starlings or the Kudzu plant or the gypsy moth, are introduced into a new environment and run riot? The potential is low but the consequences could be vast and disastrous.

When Rifkin heard about the army's proposed lab, he wondered what precautions were planned to insure its safety. Of the many Doomsday scenarios imagined about the new biotechnology, the deliberate creation and release of an organism designed to be a biological weapon is taken the most seriously. After all, it is the only scenario in which anyone has a vested interest in sowing destruction.

But Rifkin also had a clear-cut political agenda: He did not want to see genetic engineering used for the creation of biological weapons; he didn't want the development of offensive weapons to proceed in the name of defense without the public's consent and vigilance.

After Sasser failed to stop the army, Rifkin decided to intervene. He joined forces with Admiral Gene R. LaRoque, a retired navy commander who started and now heads the nonprofit Center for Defense Information in Washington, D.C., an organization of retired military officers that keeps a watch on the Pentagon. LaRoque had been a Pentagon war planner who supported President Nixon's decision to renounce biological weapons in 1969. "You could not aim them in the manner that you aim a rifle, missile, or plane. We didn't want them around ourselves," he explains. "Anyway, we've got nuclear weapons, who needs biologicals?" LaRoque joined the lawsuit, his first, because he thought that if the aerosol laboratory was not a violation of the treaty, it certainly appeared to be.

In turn, LaRoque put Rifkin in touch with retired Marine Corps general William Fairbourn, an associate director of the Center who happened to live downwind of the proposed Dugway lab. A veteran of World War II, the Korean War, and the Vietnam War, Fairbourn had worked for the Joint Chiefs of Staff as a senior strategic planner before retiring to his hometown, Salt Lake City. Although age tells in his gait and in the grid of lines that checker his forehead, his stern and commanding voice still carries. "Jeremy Rifkin called to ask me as a local person to join the lawsuit. It didn't take me long to make up my mind," says Fairbourn. "I've been a line-item budget sponsor and dealt with the transfer of funds. Technically, the army was within legal bounds. But it certainly was *not* the intent of Congress for the money to be used for this purpose."

In December, the environmental activist and the navy admiral (the marine corps general officially joined in the spring) filed a lawsuit against the Department of Defense, charging that it had violated the National Environmental Policy Act of 1971 by failing to study adequately the effects of the proposed laboratory on the environment and to consider safer alternatives. A month later, Rifkin agreed to postpone the suit when the army told him that it was about to complete an environmental assessment. But when Rifkin saw that the environmental assessment concluded the lab would have no significant impact on the environment, he resumed the legal action.

For the next two months, Rifkin's lawyers canvassed the community of molecular biologists, claiming that the army had safer alternatives, safer ways to shore up its defense. David Dubnau, a molecular biologist at the Public Health Research Institute of the City of New York, a private scientific research organization in Manhattan, had objected to Rifkin's political agenda in some previous lawsuits, but he shared his antipathy toward biological weapons. Dubnau specialized in *Staphylococcus* enterotoxins, the food poisoning toxins. During the Vietnam War, when the army had stockpiled food poisoning toxins as biological weapons and supported many academic researchers in their basic studies, Dubnau had refused to consider accepting money from the military.

In court briefs, Dubnau said that the army would be working with the most dangerous organisms known, in their most dangerous forms, and perhaps deliberately creating even more virulent species. While the BL-4 lab had been explicitly designed to avoid accidental releases, the possibility still existed and with very risky consequences. Dubnau said he would not want the lab in his backyard. "The intentional production and use of aerosols containing such organisms is extremely hazardous and the technology probably does not exist that can reliably insure that even extremely small numbers of pathogenic bacteria or viruses will not escape. It is my considered opinion that the proposed testing of substantial volumes of toxic biological aerosol agents represents a definite hazard to humans as well as to animal and plant life, including livestock and crops, in the neighborhood of the test facility."

Richard Novick, director of the Public Health Research Institute of the City of New York, argued that the army could pursue its defensive research with simulants—surrogate microorganisms that had all the salient characteristics of the real ones, except their pathogenicity, their ability to cause disease. For testing detectors and gas masks, the army could use killed microbes. Decontamination tests could proceed with live attenuated organisms, like those used in vaccines.

Furthermore, Novick questioned why the army needed to test for defensive purposes how persistent, infectious, and lethal an organism is. "If there has been an attack," he said in a court brief, "the attack area will be closed until it has been determined to be safe. This will require direct examination of live organisms, and prior knowledge of an organism's susceptibility to environmental factors will be of little or no use." The knowledge gained about germs and toxins from the course of natural diseases would be a sufficient defense. "The further analysis of the infectivity and lethality of a potential agent would be unnecessary for any imaginable, purely defensive purposes," he said. "Additionally, the filling of 'knowledge gaps,' suggested to be an important part of the program, arouses strong suspicions that new types of agents will be developed and tested for their potential as bioweapons."

The conclusion seemed obvious: use a stimulant, a dummy, a microbial stand-in. You don't need to crash a car with a real person driving to design safer seatbelts. Neither do you need to subject the army's gas masks and suits to every killer virus and microbe to know that they block the germs. It is the size of the germ, its surface tension, and other physical parameters that matter, not the presence of the germ itself.

But the army did not agree. "The plaintiffs paint a fictitious picture of the army's proposal and tend toward sensationalism by injecting the subject of recombinant DNA materials into their argument. Throughout their memorandum, plaintiffs speak of 'highly dangerous' and 'extremely toxic' biomaterials at Dugway. Nowhere in their memorandum, however, do they acknowledge that Dugway has been safely operating with these materials for over forty years with containment less stringent than would be the case with the proposed BL-4 facility. Nowhere in their papers do plaintiffs address the fact that the only proposed issue is one to construct a new, safer facility . . . to *continue* the same operations that are currently being undertaken."

As far as simulants were concerned, the army turned up its nose in disdain, arguing that the validity of simulant tests would always be dogged by a taint of uncertainty. What soldier wanted to use equipment that had not been tested on the real thing? Furthermore, it argued that it needed data on infectivity, symptomology, and lethality so detectors could be calibrated to sound the alarm bell when an infectious dose of microbes was present.

On April 26, 1984, U.S. District Court Judge Joyce Hens Green heard from three witnesses, two for Rifkin—Dubnau and Novick—who claimed the lab was unsafe and one for the army—I. Gary Resnick, manager of the lab at Dugway—who claimed it was. Rifkin pressed the army to declare its intentions about genetic engineering. Since the army needed the lab to prepare defenses against Soviet weapons, and in his letter to Senator Sasser, Defense Secretary Weinberger had already accused the Soviets of using genetic engineering, didn't that mean the army would create Soviet-inspired, genetically engineered organisms in its lab? The army denied any immediate plans without ruling them out in the future, adroitly sidestepping confrontation over what would be a highly charged issue.

One month later, Judge Green delivered her opinion. She refused to consider the legality of the army's reprogramming request and instead tackled the safety issues surrounding the proposed lab. An environmental assessment, she wrote, must "indicate that the agency has taken a searching, realistic look at the potential hazards and with measured thought and analysis, candidly and methodically addressed those concerns. Measured against these standards, the environmental assessment published by the army is clearly inadequate." She called it "an amalgam of conclusory statements and unsupported assertions of no impact." Just because other Class Four facilities operate safely did not let the proposed BL-4 Dugway lab off the hook. She likened that to arguing that once you have sited one nuclear power plant, you have sited them all, an approach she labeled "capricious and arbitrary." More critically, she wrote that "the possibility of an accident involving personnel or exposure to the outside environment, while low in probability, does exist." She cited the risks as "serious and far-reaching. Such an accident could produce extraordinary, potentially irreparable consequences." Rifkin won an injunction against the lab's construction.

The army went back to the drawing boards to prepare a

full-blown environmental impact statement. Utah's conservative politicians including Senator Jake Garn, burned, blaming the judge for getting out of her area of expertise and putting the lives of thousands of young men and women at stake. But General Fairbourn disagreed. "The facts are you don't have to use the actual agents to conduct the tests. There are simulants."

The plaintiffs believe that only the use of stimulants would insure the safe operation of the lab but more importantly that the United States must not set off a biological arms race or slide back into the business itself. "I consider this a major victory," says Rifkin, who has won most of his cases so far. "If they're not willing to accept simulants, we won't accept their environmental impact statement. There will be a long legal struggle." He stretches his arms. "I'm pretty convinced the citizens of Utah don't want Dugway to be known as the Los Alamos of the eighties."

TWO

Here Is What You Need to Know About Biological Warfare

"Armis Bella Non Venenis Geri"
(*War is waged with weapons, not with poisons*).
  —Roman condemnation of well poisoning

Identical copies of the treaty banning biological weapons reside in Moscow, London, and at the mammoth State Department building in Washington, D.C. The United States stores its treaties in a dim, almost shabby room, behind a massive, electronically controlled bank vault door, filled with scores of musty manila folders crammed together on rows of gray metal shelves. Here, the Convention on the Prohibition of the Development, Production, and Stockpiling of Bacteriological (Biological) and Toxin Weapons and on Their Destruction is nothing special, just one of thousands of international agreements on everything from wheat to whaling, seabeds to outer space.

Genevieve Bell has been the treaty librarian since 1969, the year Nixon renounced biological weapons. Dressed in a green corduroy suit and a green blouse for Saint Patrick's Day, she welcomes the infrequent visitor. In the age of instant Xerox, few people care to see the originals anymore. "It's not too often

18

at all that I bring out the Biological Weapons Convention," she says. "If a party wants to see it, yes, sure, we have an obligation to show it. But I can't say I've had many requests."

The Biological Weapons Convention, or BWC, as it is usually abbreviated, has the feel of a noteworthy and honorable modern document. It is bound with a simple, blue leather, folio-size cover; typed on creamy, gold-edged paper; decorated with a delicate red and blue ink border; held together with a red, white, and blue ribbon that threads through punched holes in the paper and binder.

The treaty itself is written in five languages: English, Chinese, French, Spanish, and Russian, and followed by thirty-five pages of official and often ornate signatures. To date, over a hundred countries have signed the Biological Weapons Convention, the most recent being China, which the State Department welcomed with a small ceremony.

The text of the treaty has fifteen articles, but the first and second express the heart of the agreement. The first says:

Each State Party to this convention undertakes never in any circumstances to develop, produce, stockpile or otherwise acquire or retain 1) microbial or other biological agents or toxins whatever their origin or method of production, of types and in quantities that have no justification for prophylactic, protective or other peaceful purposes; 2) weapons, equipment or means of delivery designed to use such agents or toxins for hostile purposes or in armed conflict.

The second article reads:

Each State Party to this Convention undertakes to destroy or to divert to peaceful purposes, as soon as possible, but no later than nine months after the entry into force of the Convention, all agents, toxins, weapons, equipment and means of delivery specified in Article I of the Convention, which are in its possession or under its jurisdiction or control.

The treaty specifically bans biological weapons, those made with disease-causing germs such as anthrax, and toxin weapons, those made with poisons produced by living organisms such as botulinum. It does not ban chemical weapons, those made with synthetic chemicals such as nerve gas. (Another treaty, the Geneva Protocol, bans the use but not the production or stockpiling of chemical weapons.) Despite the differences in their legal status, chemical and biological weapons are often lumped together, abbreviated in discussions within military circles as CBW. What the weapons have in common is the fact that they are invisible killers that travel through the air.

For historians, as well as students of arms control, the Biological Weapons Convention represents a daring landmark and a milestone in detente. It was the first treaty, and remains the only one in existence, to ban outright an entire class of weapons, prohibiting not only the use, but also the manufacture and stockpiling of the weapons. No other arms control treaty has aimed to be so comprehensive or ambitious, and in the last few years, no other treaty has found itself at the center of so much controversy. With the passage of time, the State Department retires some international agreements to the National Archives, simply to make room for newcomers. But those treaties that provoke accusations and counteraccusations—such as the Biological Weapons Convention—stay inside the vault.

The Biological Weapons Convention bans one of the oldest and least respected forms of warfare—the use of poison and disease. Since Greco-Roman times, poisons have figured not so much as weapons of war but as tools for assassination. Although the use and preparation of poison was a shrouded, clandestine art, it seems clear that the Greeks and Romans knew about the toxic qualities of hemlock, hellebore, rhubarb, the castor bean, and the amanita mushroom. In the imperial courts, professional poisoners tried to outsmart the cup bearers and food tasters, and often succeeded, the best-known example being Agrippina, who is thought to have poisoned her husband, the Roman emperor Claudius. Some historians claim that Pope Alexander poisoned his way to power, that during the Italian Renaissance, the powerful Borgias picked off their rivals with poison, and that the plotting in the courts of Louis XIV and the Russian czars involved tainted potions.

Until the invention of the microscope and the germ theory of disease, diseases could not be spread in the sophisticated ways that poison was. One technique was to dump a corpse in the enemy's well or water supply. But then, as now, the attacker ran the risk that the disease would strike his own troops.

Possibly the earliest, and one of the few, recorded accounts of biological warfare took place in the spring of 1346 when the Mongols laid seige to Kaffa, a walled city on the Crimean coast. After three unsuccessful years in which their own soldiers were dying of the plague, the Mongols tried something new. According to an eyewitness, "The Tatars, fatigued by such a plague and pestiferous disease, stupefied and amazed, and observing themselves dying without hope of health, ordered cadavers placed on their hurling machines and thrown into the city of Kaffa so that by means of these intolerable passengers, the defenders died widely. Thus there were projected mountains of dead, nor could the Christians hide or flee or be freed from such a disaster." While Kaffa filled with plague, some of the survivors fled, carrying the disease with them to Constantinople, Venice, Genoa, and other European ports. Within three years, the Black Death (spread by less heinous activities as well) swept Europe, killing a quarter of the population.

In another often recounted case, the British commander-in-chief in the American colonies, Lord Jeffrey Amherst, set out to destroy the American Indians with disease after an Indian rebellion in 1763. "You will do well to try to innoculate the Indians by means of blankets," Amherst told his subordinates, "as well as to try every other method that can serve to extirpate this execrable race." At his request, two blankets and a handkerchief from a smallpox hospital were given as presents to an Ohio tribe. A few months later, smallpox broke out, and, lacking immunity, the Indians were ravaged by disease.

By the twentieth century, disease ceased to be explained by mysterious miasmas or elemental imbalances of humors. Microscopic organisms—bacteria, fungi, and viruses—were gradually identified as the culprits, isolated, cultured, and studied. At the same time, the molecules responsible for the toxicity of so many plants and animals were extracted, concentrated, and purified by methods more reliable than making incantations under a full moon. During World War II, scientists around the world began to devise ways to incorporate invisible germs and poisons into conventional military hardware.

To the modern soldier, the various types of biological weapons developed since then do not look like anything very special. In fact, they look like conventional weapons—a bomb dropped from an airplane, a canister and shell fired from a rocket launcher or howitzer, a missile, a drone, and even bullets. The weapons are designed to be hurled, fired, or dropped. The weapons can also be in the form of a spray, spread by a low-flying airplane like a crop-dusting pesticide. While the bomb and the spray tank became standards, a few unusual efforts also emerged—like long-range balloons carrying feathers infected with anticrop spores, bombs filled with disease-carrying insects, and a deadly aerosol spray can shaped like a whisky hip flask.

What distinguishes one biological weapon from another is not so much the hardware but the fillings, which contain the deadliest organisms nature ever concocted, all too small to be seen with the naked eye. Some are bacteria and fungi, living creatures only one cell big. Others are viruses, even tinier, ephemeral entities on the threshold of life, made of chunks of

DNA, which replicate only by invading and taking over a cell. And finally, some are toxins, the poisonous molecules secreted by plants and microbes, sprayed by insects, or injected by snakes to destroy their own enemies.

In nature, the microbes, viruses, and toxins that cause disease are everywhere, lurking in the soil, the water, the air, your food. Physicians battle these primordial public enemies daily, trying to prevent their growth, treating those people who fall prey. The creation of a biological weapon, in fact, begins with the knowledge gained by doctors of medicine in the process of treating disease. Instead of applying that knowledge to save life, the practice of medicine is perverted, turned inside out, upside down, in violation of the Hippocratic Oath to do no harm.

From the enormous roster of the world's diseases and toxins, which grows each year as new diseases evolve or are discovered, almost all have been considered as potential biological weapons. But many have not been seriously studied because they are not hardy, swift-acting, reliably infective, or easily spread through the air—qualities that a weapon designer wants. From 1943, when the United States launched its biological weapons program, until 1969, it experimented with the following human and animal diseases and toxins: anthrax, botulinum, brucellosis, chikungunya, cholera, coccidiosis, dengue, dysentery, food poisoning toxin, influenza, melioidosis, plague, psittacosis, Q-fever, Red Tide poison, Rift Valley Fever, Rocky Mountain Spotted Fever, Russian spring-summer encephalitis, shigellosis, smallpox, tularemia, typhoid, Venezuelan equine encephalitis, and yellow fever.

It also experimented with the following crop diseases: wheat rust, rice blast, tobacco mosaic, corn stunt, potato yellow dwarf, Fiji disease (which attacks sugar cane), hoja blanca (which attacks rice), rice blight, corn blight, sugar cane wilt, coffee rust, maize rust, rice brown-spot disease, late blight of potato, powdery mildew of cereals, stripe rust of cereals.

Of all the countries in the world, only the United States

admitted to amassing a stockpile of biological weapons, and when the Biological Weapons Convention was signed, only the United States publicly destroyed its arsenal. It had had an active biological warfare program for twenty-five years and had produced and/or standardized ten different biological and toxin weapons, selecting them for a constellation of practical characteristics. The list included:

Anthrax: The renowned bacteriologist Robert Koch first cultured the single-celled bacterium, *Bacillus anthracis,* in 1877, which under the microscope looks like a football. It lives in the soil in many parts of the world, where it forms an almost indestructible spore resistant to disinfectants, rapid freezing and thawing, even boiling. Anthrax infects goats, sheep, horses, cattle, elephants, hippos, and many other animals, including people. If you touch the spores, the bacterium can enter through a wound in the skin and form a small lesion or pustule that eventually turns coal black. (Anthrax is from the Greek word for coal.) Fever, chills, malaise, nausea, and vomiting follow. Even without adequate treatment, almost everyone recovers.

While the cutaneous form of anthrax is the most common today, in nineteenth-century England the inhalation form of anthrax was widespread. It was known as wool-sorter's disease because factory workers fell sick after reaching into bins full of wool and shaking the wool out. The motion unleased a cloud of anthrax spores into the air which the workers then inhaled. Within two to three days, they died from suffocation, the result of a toxin released by the anthrax bacterium.

The spores clung not only to sheep wool but to many other animal products as well. A vaccuum cleaner assembler caught it from revolving horsehair brushes, a man who cut piano keys from an elephant's tusk, and a tourist from a hide-covered bongo drum brought back from a Caribbean vacation. If untreated, the inhalation form of anthrax kills almost everyone exposed to it. While anthrax remains a negligible livestock concern in this country, cases of inhalation anthrax have all but disappeared since the passage of stricter sanitation laws. The military concentrated on the inhalation form of anthrax as a weapon, particularly during World War II. But the spore is so indestructible that once unleashed it permanently contaminates an area, denying it to both defender and attacker. Despite these drawbacks, the United States continues to view anthrax as a potential biological weapon.

Botulinum: Botulinum is a toxin that takes its name from the Latin word for sausage because it was first identified in 1793 when thirteen people in a small German town fell sick after eating the same sausage. The bacterium, which secretes the toxin, was isolated a hundred years later when band members in a small Belgian town fell sick after eating a ham. Shaped like a stout rod, *Clostridium botulinum* commonly and harmlessly grows in the oxygen-free surface layers of the soil, particularly in California, and for reasons unclear, produces botulinum, the most potent neurotoxin known. The microbe only causes problems in improperly canned or cooked food, of which a mere nibble can kill. The toxin takes effect within twelve to seventy-two hours, leaving the victim headachy, dizzy, and (if the dose is sufficient) ultimately dead from respiratory paralysis. About a hundred people succumb to botulinum each year worldwide, and of these 30 percent die. The U. S. Army produced twenty-thousand botulinum-tipped bullets and also planned to spread the toxin as an aerosol until it became clear that sunlight degrades it and destroys its potency.

Brucellosis: Found in wild animals like antelope, reindeer, caribou, and hares, brucellosis was a common livestock disease in the United States until eradication programs began in the 1960s. Today, this country has about one hundred-fifty cases each year, mostly among abattoir workers, farmers, and veterinarians who are exposed to the blood of the infected animals. The disease is caused by several strains of the *Brucella* bacterium. After a four- or five-day incubation period, the infected person has a low-grade fever, and a tired, rundown feeling that gets progressively worse. Over the next two to three months, he or she loses weight, feels depressed, and suffers an intermittent fever. Once diagnosed, brucellosis is treated with tetracycline. Explored by the army as a weapon in the early days of the program, it was dropped in the 1950s in favor of diseases that act and incapacitate more quickly and more uniformly.

Q-fever: Q-fever is short for query fever. When first discovered among abattoir workers in Queensland, Australia, no one knew what it was. The disease hits suddenly, triggering severe headache, stiff neck, chills, sweats, and a lack of appetite, like a severe case of the flu. Within seven to ten days, it subsides. Nobel laureate F. McFarlane Burnet isolated the cause, a single-celled microbe that changes from the shape of a rod to that of a bead, and named it *Coxiella burnetii. C. burnetii* is highly infective and very persistent, able to survive in sheep's wool for seven to nine months. It spreads by aerosol, ticks, mice, bedbugs, and fleas. In Italy, the passage of a flock of sheep through a narrow street was enough to start an infection. Employees at a commercial laundry caught it from handling the unsterilized clothes of lab workers who studied it. Only one to ten microbes are needed to infect. Q-fever strikes sheep, goats, and cattle worldwide, but the infection often escapes notice in both animals and people. Doctors in the United States see one hundred to two hundred cases a year in people, but suspect that a milder form is more common and probably mistaken for the flu. For the military, Q-fever was attractive because it is stable, infective, and quick to act. The army continues to research it today.

Saxitoxin: Throughout many of the world's oceans, single-celled plankton called dinoflagellates bloom in the summer months, tinging the water red, creating what coast-dwellers call

Red Tide. Clams, mussels, oysters, and other filter-feeding bivalves eat the dinoflagellates. People eat the molluscs and occasionally die as the result of ten or more deadly and paralyzing toxins, including the extraordinarily powerful saxitoxin, produced by the dinoflagellates. In 1974, there were 1,600 cases worldwide of paralytic shellfish poisoning and 300 deaths. Death, when it occurs, takes place within thirty minutes after the meal, as the lips, tongue and face start to burn and tingle. As the feeling spreads to the legs and arms, paralysis sets in. The throat closes up. Until the respiratory muscles cease all movement and suffocation occurs, the victim stays calm and conscious. There is no specific antidote. In the 1950s and 1960s, Detrick scientists prepared over 30 grams of shellfish toxin by harvesting, collecting, and grinding up a vast number of Alaskan butter clams and other shellfish. The toxin was used in the suicide pill carried by Francis Gary Powers, the pilot who flew the secret U-2 plane over the Soviet Union in 1960.

Staphylococcus enterotoxin: Staphylococcus is a ubiquitous, beach ball–shaped bacterium that comes in many strains. Some are harmless and some, like those that cause toxic shock syndrome and food poisoning, are not. The food-poisoning strain wreaks havoc by secreting an enterotoxin. Although the organism is killed by normal cooking temperatures, it can multiply very rapidly, producing enough toxin to make you sick in two to three hours. Severe nausea, vomiting, and diarrhea hit within half an hour to four hours after eating and last for one to two days. The CIA chose the toxin for its immediate and fierce action and stockpiled a form resistant to the chlorine in city water supplies. Since the freeze dried form of the toxin is stable and can be stored for up to a year, the military planned to spray it over large areas.

Tularemia: Tularemia resembles the plague. Discovered in Tulare County, California, in 1911, tularemia is carried by squirrels, rabbits, field voles, mice, shrews, and ticks. The disease exists in all countries north of the equator. In Utah, Wyoming, and Colorado, it occurs most frequently during rabbit-hunting season. Caused by the bacterium *Pasteurella tularensis,* it strikes two to seven days after exposure—usually in the course of skinning the rabbit. The victim starts to feel achey, with chills and a fever as high as 105 ° F. If inhaled, which happens infrequently in nature but would be the case in a biological war, it causes a cough, chest pain, and difficulty breathing. If untreated, 5 to 8 percent of the people who get tularemia die. For inhalatory tularemia, as many as 40 percent may die. Doctors treat it with antibiotics, but the U.S. military developed a strain of tularemia that was resistant to streptomycin. There are 250 to 300 cases in the United States each year. At the time of the arsenal's destruction, the government had a large stockpile of tularemia and considered it a useful weapon.

Venezuelan equine encephalitis (VEE): VEE is a mosquito-borne virus first found in horses in Venezuela, and later across South and Central America, including Nicaragua, El Salvador, and Panama. In 1970, the mosquito harboring VEE crossed over the Rio Grande River into Texas, but the feared spread of the disease was contained by eradicating the insect. Within twenty-four hours of injection, the virus produces a headache and fever from which most recover in three days. The virus spreads to the nervous system in 10 percent of the cases and is fatal in 1 percent. The United States was increasing its stockpiles of VEE in the late 1960s.

Yellow fever: Yellow fever is a disease with a notorious legacy, responsible for killing the slaves on the slave ships and probably for destroying the crew and passengers of the legendary *Flying Dutchman.* It is caused by a virus carried by mosquitoes found in a belt just above and below the equator. It strikes three to six days after the mosquito bite, with a fever and often liver damage, which brings on a yellow color—hence the name. As part of an "entomological warfare" program started in the early 1950s, Detrick labs produced half a million mosquitoes a month, and in tests, planes dropped infected mosquitoes over a residential area in Georgia and Florida. In addition to yellow fever–infected mosquitoes, Detrick grew mosquitoes infected with malaria and dengue; fleas infected with plague; ticks infected with tularemia; flies infected with cholera, anthrax, and dysentery. By the late 1960s, yellow fever was not considered a weapon of choice.

The United States also stockpiled two anticrop diseases:

Wheat rust: In April of each year, the Romans held a ceremony, sacrificing a red dog to keep the gods from unleashing the red rust disease on their wheat crop. Like fire, the rust streaks the leaves and stems, sometimes even reddening the soil. Once it takes hold, the rust can destroy more crop in less time than any other disease. It is caused by a fungus, *Puccinia graminis*, which forms a tough, windblown spore that grows under humid conditions. Rust can kill the plant outright or shrivel and stunt it.

Rice blast: Caused by the fungus *Piricularia oryzae*, rice blast also spreads as a windblown spore, growing under humid conditions. If it attacks during an early stage of the plant's growth, the plant fails to produce rice. Some American planners considered dropping rice blast on Vietnamese rice paddies during the war but the plan was never approved by senior officials. It would have proved difficult to implement since the Vietnamese planted so many different strains, each becoming susceptible at slightly different times.

Outside of isolated sabotage incidents, biological and toxin weapons have seen remarkably little use in the twentieth century, or rather, remarkably little use that everyone can agree on. No one disputes that the Japanese used germ warfare against the Chinese during World War II. But opinions are divided on two notorious and widely publicized incidents. Did the United States wage germ warfare against North Korea and China during the Korean War? Did the Laotians and Cambodians use Soviet-made toxin weapons in Southeast Asia in the late 1970s and early 1980s?

Pound for pound, and penny for penny, biological weapons excel in packing the deadliest punch of any weapon. According to an army field manual written in 1966, a single fighter plane spraying a lethal biological agent could cause 50 percent mortality over an area of 300 square miles; that is, it could kill half the people in a city the size of Dallas or New York. That is ten times the area that would be devastated by the same amount of nerve gas.

Biological weapons come relatively cheap. A panel of experts told the United Nations in 1969 that in a large-scale operation against a civilian population, casualties might cost $2,000 per square kilometer for conventional weapons; $800 for nuclear; $600 for nerve gas; $1 for biological weapons. For the price, one gets a brutally versatile weapon. Biological weapons can be weapons of mass destruction, capable of wiping out huge civilian centers; they can blight a country's breadbasket while leaving the industrial infrastructure intact; they can be sprayed on people ill-equipped to defend themselves in order to drive them off the land; they can be spread in unconventional ways—on the wings of birds, through infected ticks, mosquitoes, fleas, flies, and tourists. They are, however, most uniquely suited to sabotage, terrorism, and covert operations since they are invisible, small enough to carry in a pocket, and, without careful monitoring, can be indistinguishable from natural occurrences.

Why, then, did President Richard Nixon, a political realist who approached foreign policy as if it were a chess game, give up such a good thing? The reason is simple: Biological weapons provoke far more trouble than they are worth. In the modern theater of geopolitics, their very attributes create horrendous liabilities. Consider this fact: biological weapons are so cheap and powerful that they have been dubbed "the poor man's atomic bomb." By condoning and furthering the development of biological weapons, the United States created an arms race that would only hurt it in the long run.

The United States is a rich and powerful country, one of the richest and most powerful in the world. One way it maintains military superiority is by spending money on the development and stockpiling of weapons. Very few countries are wealthy enough to keep up. It is in the best interest of the United States and the other superpowers to keep war expensive. The more expensive it is, the fewer countries that can pose threats. It was, therefore, not in the best interest of the United States to develop a cheap and powerful weapon like biological weapons. That was the fundamental logic behind Nixon's decision.

Other factors contributed to the American renunciation of biological weapons. There is no credible defense against an all-out biological attack. No devices will even give reliable advance warning. Even if such devices existed, what steps could be taken? People can be vaccinated against some diseases, but these work only if taken weeks before the attack. Even then, experts doubt their protective value against the onslaught of aerosol germs in a biological weapon, or that an attacker would choose a weapon for which the country had prepared an effective vaccine. Gas masks would help, but few civilians have their own. Lacking genetic resistance to a particular disease, crops and livestock are defenseless.

In 1969, the U.S. military was reluctant but willing to give up biological weapons. Troop commanders had never heartily approved of them, in part because they had a disreputable air that never quite fit the military's self-image of what an honorable warrior should be asked to do. For battlefield operations, the advocates of biological weapons never proved them superior to conventional or even chemical weapons.

A host of practical problems bedeviled biological weapons. They did not behave in a straightforward way. In the field, commanders found them too complicated, too demanding, too quirky. They spread like killing winds. For each disease, the symptoms, incubation, duration, and treatment varied. Coupled with the way the vagaries of the wind, temperature, and terrain influenced the weapon's stealthy drift, the commander had a lot of variables to juggle and few guarantees. Although the army subjected biological weapons to hundreds of tests, it never had enough data—for the obvious ethical reasons—on what real weapons do to real people. What good is a weapon that you can't test? In the end, the military decided it wasn't good enough to keep.

In 1969, three years before the two superpowers signed the Biological Weapons Convention, the United States gave up BW, as biological weapons are usually abbreviated, altogether. Nixon renounced not only biological weapons but also toxin weapons, which occupy a gray area, somewhere between biological and chemical weapons. Although the two had been developed in tandem at Fort Detrick, the U.S. center for biological warfare research in Frederick, Maryland, toxins behave more like chemical weapons on the battlefield. The only difference between a toxin and a chemical weapon is that one is synthesized by nature and the other concocted by man. Both are inert molecules, acting in minutes to hours, and toxic in micrograms or milligrams, not picograms like biological (or germ) weapons. By contrast, germ weapons are living creatures that grow and multiply, taking their toll in days.

Nixon did not renounce chemical weapons, nor did the subsequent international ban include them. Chemical weapons are deployed like biological weapons—in bombs, from spray tanks—but instead of spreading live organisms, they disperse toxic chemicals, such as nerve gas, tear gas, herbicides (like

Agent Orange), mustard gas, and other harassing and incapacitating chemicals. The United States, the Soviets, and now a number of other countries continue to stockpile chemical weapons, and the Iraqis are currently using them in their war against Iran. The Reagan administration lobbied hard to build a new generation of nerve gas weapons, but the Congress consistently blocked appropriations for that purpose until September 1986, when Congress finally gave its okay.

While it is illegal to produce and use biological weapons, it is not illegal to produce chemical weapons. (It is illegal to *use* them.) Chemical weapons remain a legal component of the world's stockpiles in part because they are not as cheap, potentially powerful, nor as unpredictable as their biological counterparts. They draw on a longer, more successful tradition within the military, and have a more powerful constituency than biological weapons. After all, they had been used in World War I and the Vietnam War, with arguable success. They have also served a useful function as a deterrent: the United States could give up biological weapons with an easy conscience because it could always retaliate with chemical weapons.

But chemical weapons also raise a prickly question from an arms control perspective. How can you distinguish between industrial chemicals and chemicals of war? What if you ban one but not the other? Since World War II, the creation of insecticides and nerve gases have marched hand in hand. Gerhard Schrader, a German scientist working at I. G. Farben, discovered an organophosphorus compound in 1936 that killed insects in seconds. Under a law that decreed that any industrial invention with military potential should be shared with the Wehrmacht, Schrader's finding led to the development of nerve gases. Today, a plant that produces the pesticides malathion or parathion could be used to produce nerve gas.

Many other chemicals are less toxic, but just as lethal and widespread as organophosphate pesticides. When a 1984 accident at the Union Carbide pesticide plant in Bhopal, India, released methylisocyanate into the air, five thousand people died. In a magazine interview, the Bhopal mayor said, "I can say that I have seen chemical warfare. Everything so quiet. Goats, cats, whole families—father, mother, children—all lying silent and still. And every structure totally intact. I hope never again to see it."

When the Biological Weapons Convention officially went into effect in 1975, it left the impression that every trace or consideration of biological weapons utterly disappeared from the world's military establishments. That was not the case. By keeping chemical weapons legal, military establishments maintained an institutional infrastructure familiar with the equipment, training, doctrine, and insidious action of invisible weapons. While the United States burned its germs and toxins, scrapped its weapon hardware, dismantled and converted its mass production facilities, it retained the books, reports, studies, and test data accumulated over the twenty-five-year existence of the biological-warfare program. According to one Pentagon official, it would take the United States (or any other country that dismantled its full-fledged offensive program) two to three years to get back into the biological weapons business IF the president of the United States renounced the treaty.

As allowed by treaty, research continues around the world. The systematic study of nasty germs and toxins has not stopped. In the United States, it takes place on a largely unclassified basis and in the name of defense. Fifteen years after the renunciation, the list of germs and toxins studied at Fort Detrick bears little resemblance to those studied in 1969. These new agents have been identified, grown, studied, analyzed, assessed, evaluated, and, if Dugway builds the BL-4 lab, will be tested. But they have not been developed into weapons, that is, mass produced or loaded into hardware—two steps that would clearly violate the treaty.

Since the Reagan administration took office in 1980, the budgets for both biological and chemical weapons have skyrocketed. Compared with the cost of building an F-16 fighter plane, the budgets dedicated to the subject of biological warfare still look small, but it is important to bear in mind that biological research costs relatively little. In 1987, the total budget for biological warfare defense was $71.2 million. Compare that with what was spent on research and development at Fort Detrick at the height of the Vietnam War in 1969. Then, it was $19.4 million—or if you adjust for inflation, $55.6 million. In other words, the United States is spending more on BW research than it did when it had an offensive program.

What this jump in budgets means is that the military is again talking about biological warfare. "Up until three or four years ago, we weren't talking on the subject [of biological weapons] at all," says Major Dick Ziegler, a Pentagon spokesman. According to the Department of Defense, the Dugway lab is essential for preparing a defense against the mounting Soviet threat. The Pentagon and the Reagan administration point to a mysterious outbreak of anthrax in Sverdlovsk and to Yellow Rain in Southeast Asia as evidence of the Soviet's disregard for and violation of the treaty.

In conservative circles throughout the nation, the two events are already taken as proof that the Biological Weapons Convention has failed. Like the clock in Shakespeare's *Julius Caesar*, the treaty is an anachronism, some say, out of step with the times. But others vehemently disagree with that conclusion. They stress that the evidence for treaty violations at Sverdlovsk is open to question and that cited for Yellow Rain has failed to stand up to scrutiny.

THREE

A Mysterious Outbreak of Anthrax

"Russia's Secret Germ Warfare Disaster!" shouted the October 26, 1979, headline in *Now!*, a now defunct British weekly that has been described as a cross between *Time* and the *National Enquirer.* A similar article had run earlier in *Possev,* a Frankfurt journal published in Russian for about two thousand Soviet émigrés and linked to the People's Worker's Alliance, a revolutionary anti-Soviet group said to be heavily infiltrated by both the CIA and KGB. With differences here and there, the stories told of an accident in June 1979 at a secret biological weapons research facility in Novosibirsk, a newly built "science" city in Siberia, that killed hundreds and injured thousands with a dread disease.

Subsequently, *Possev* ran another article that corrected the date, place, and many of the details. The accident struck Sverdlovsk, not Novosibirsk, and on April 3, not in June. According to émigrés, people ran very high fevers, over 107° F, and died within hours of being hospitalized. It was said that relatives received the bodies of the dead in sealed coffins, and that those who managed to glimpse the corpses saw them covered with brown patches. During the month-long epidemic, the city launched mass vaccination programs, and still the death toll climbed to a thousand.

Such a grim picture disturbed the U.S. government. In the sour aftermath of the Soviet invasion of Afghanistan, many were ready to believe the worst. But cooler heads prevailed, at least temporarily. On March 17, 1980, while the United Nations convened its first review of the Biological Weapons Convention in Geneva (every five years nations meet to discuss the status of the treaty), U.S. diplomats privately communicated concern about the reports of a disease outbreak through the usual diplomatic channels.

The next day, before the Soviets had a chance to respond, administration insiders leaked the story to the Western press, which cast the event in bleak terms. The State Department announced that "some sort of lethal biological agent" might have been involved. On March 20, the Soviets answered the query tersely. They privately acknowledged that anthrax had broken out in Sverdlovsk in April. It was gastric anthrax, caused by eating tainted meat, and they labeled any other notion "propaganda," skulking off with little more to say. But the Soviet Foreign Ministry did take the time and trouble to do something it had rarely done: it contacted Western media correspondents in Moscow to deny any wrongdoing.

The Americans did not buy the story. On March 28, the *New York Times* published an article written by journalist Richard Burt, now ambassador to West Germany. The paper reported, "The Carter Administration has concluded on the basis of new intelligence information that an outbreak of anthrax in the Soviet Union last year did not result from natural causes but from an accident at a biological weapons facility, government officials said today." Carter was apparently told that, based on the reported death toll, that tens of kilograms of anthrax had been released into the air, an amount so large that it confirmed the suspicion of germ warfare activity. Only later did officials recalculate that the amount probably came closer to one gram—at least 10,000 times less. But by that time, the U.S. government could not easily back off. Years later, an arms control official would say that any possibility for rapprochement "was blown by the way it was publicized."

For many years, chemical and biological weapons analysts had watched Sverdlovsk, an industrial city of about one and a half million people in the gently rolling hills of the Ural valley, 850 miles east of Moscow. The Institute of Microbiology and Virology clearly showed up on satellite photographs. According to a Defense Department official who requested anonymity, the presence of smokestacks, refrigeration facilities, animal pens, special venting outlets, sentries, and double barbed-wire fences led him to suspect that it was a biological research facility serving military purposes. The additional construction of revetments (explosion-proof barricades) deepened his suspicions. When he heard about an unusual outbreak of anthrax, it was easy to believe that it came from an explosion in the Institute's Compound 19.

The Defense Department official calls anthrax his choice as the ideal biological weapon. Anthrax enjoys the dubious distinction of being the granddaddy of biological weapons, foreseen as a distinct military possibility by Winston Churchill in 1925 and envisioned by Aldous Huxley in *Brave New World*. It took the British until the summer of 1942 actually to turn fiction into hardware. Researchers at the Porton Down Microbiological Research Establishment exploded the first anthrax bombs on a rocky outcrop of the island of Gruinard off the northwest coast of Scotland. They knew it was a success when sheep tethered in concentric circles died within days. The next summer, a bomber flew over the island and neatly dropped another anthrax bomb on target. Anthrax spores can survive for over fifty years, so to this day, the island remains off limits and contaminated.

After those trials, American researchers at Camp Detrick—the U.S. center for biological warfare research—cranked up a pilot production line to produce five thousand anthrax bombs, and in 1944 military strategists drew up a con-

tingency plan to drop them on six German cities. But satura-
tion bombing with anthrax never came to pass because the war
ended. If the bombing had taken place, the cities of Berlin,
Hamburg, Frankfurt, Stuttgart, Aachen, and Wilhelmshaven
would probably still be contaminated today. In fact, the
United States phased anthrax out of its arsenal of biological
weapons in the early 1960s because it lurks in the soil indefinitely, denying the area to friend and foe alike.

In the spring of 1980, a group of experts from the CIA, the
National Security Council, the State Department, and the
Joint Chiefs of Staff, as well as several outside consultants, met
to review the Sverdlovsk incident. They heard from no direct,
firsthand witnesses and so resigned themselves to secondhand
reports, satellite photographs, classified communications, and
press accounts. The group spent a lot of time looking at wind
rosettes, meteorological maps that tracked where the wind was
likely to blow anthrax spores. They heard that anywhere from
ten to a thousand people died over four to six weeks.

Was the outbreak man-made or natural? To the experts,
the reports of swift death had to mean inhalation anthrax,
which kills within two to three days. According to Philip
Brachman, the United States's anthrax expert at the Centers
for Disease Control, "It didn't seem reasonable from my
knowledge that it could have been due to eating contaminated
meat." But Brachman is the first to admit that his knowledge of
this type of anthrax lacks the backing of experience. "We in
the United States have never had a confirmed case of gastrointestinal anthrax," he says.

Since inhalation anthrax occurs only when some force
propels the spores into the air, the group focused on identifying
that force. Did an explosion occur during the production of an
anthrax vaccine? It didn't seem likely since the United States
believed the Soviets used an avirulent strain of anthrax for
their vaccine. The unscheduled arrival of the Soviet defense
minister in Sverdlovsk shortly after the outbreak and a satellite

photograph of a building at Compound 19 that reportedly showed it had been abandoned one year later lent credence to the theory that an explosion had occurred in this biological research facility, as did reports that the military performed the type of cleanup operations typically used to decontaminate surfaces covered with an infectious aerosol.

"Yes, there was an explosion. Yes, it was at a BW research facility," says Admiral Stansfield Turner, President Carter's director of the Central Intelligence Agency. "There was more activity than warranted by treaty." The group of experts hypothesized that the explosion led to a number of deaths—some believe the number to be between forty and one hundred—within the first three days from inhalation of the anthrax spores.

Still, that left the reports of a month-long outbreak unexplained, so the group suggested that the spores settled on nearby farmland, contaminating the grazing pastures. The livestock were then slaughtered, sold, and eaten, causing an outbreak of gastric anthrax that extended the epidemic for a month or longer.

But many puzzling details rocked that scenario. In contradiction to stories told by émigrés, satellite photographs reportedly showed that streets had not been repaved around the suspected BW research facility, a precaution that might have been taken to get rid of anthrax spores. In addition, a meat factory next to Compound 19 appeared to have stayed open and operating throughout the epidemic, which would have been unlikely if a major accident had occurred there. Regional papers published articles at the time advising readers to avoid buying or eating black market meat because of the dangers of anthrax. But the most telling and perhaps damning information came from an innocent bystander. While Sverdlovsk is usually described as a "closed" city, physicist and Northwestern University professor Donald Ellis, along with his wife and two children, happened to be visiting Sverdlovsk on an exchange program in April when the outbreak occurred.

Fluent enough in Russian to read the newspapers and understand the radio or a street corner conversation, Ellis registered shock that the U.S. government believed a massive epidemic had taken place. His family lived in the center of the city and bought food in the local market. He did not observe any unusual precautions, mass vaccinations, or quarantines, nor did he hear any talk or rumors, which there surely would have been if the epidemic had killed 1,000 people in a city of 1.2 million. If there had been an enormous accident at a military facility, would his hosts have let him stay? And if there had been a coverup, would they have allowed him to return as he did in June for another four-week stay? It seemed unlikely.

At least two members of the expert group, both of whom had access to classified information, did not believe that the anthrax outbreak in Sverdlovsk involved an explosion at the Institute. Admiral Thomas Davies, assistant director of the Arms Control and Disarmament Agency, suggested that if the outbreak had been anything but anthrax, the suspicions would not have hardened so quickly. "The average intelligence officer seeing anthrax would think BW," he says. But based on Ellis's account and the plausibility of the Soviet explanation, "I concluded it was a nonevent." Professor Matthew Meselson, a Harvard biochemist and authority on biological warfare, joined his dissent but even more emphatically. "I was totally unconvinced," he says. "It is more plausible that it was an outbreak of gastrointestinal anthrax."

Zhores Medvedev, a biochemist at the National Institute for Medical Research in London and a leading Russian dissident, also found the Soviet explanation to be fully possible. While there was reason to believe that the Sverdlovsk facility engaged in biological-warfare research (which is permissible), and even that an explosion had occurred, it would not be unusual for the Soviets to deny and cover up what might have been an innocent problem. For example, when eighteen plague-infected rats escaped from a military medical research facility north of Moscow, the director raised no alarm for fear he would be held responsible for the mistake. (Fortunately, nothing happened.) Medvedev had little interest in protecting the Soviet regime, since before his emigration he had been imprisoned in a Soviet mental hospital and diagnosed as an "incipient schizophrenic with paranoid delusions of reforming society."

While the Soviets' refusal to discuss the anthrax outbreak did little to help their claim, the open literature supported it. Although the Soviets publish few public health statistics, they face more problems with anthrax—or Siberian Ulcer, as they call it—than any other developed nation. Each year, two million vaccinations are given, many presumably in Sverdlovsk, where the spores linger in the soil. Unlike their American counterparts, Soviet doctors have not only seen but reported on cases of gastric anthrax, many of which were deadly. In 1923, a Soviet medical journal reported an outbreak in Yarovslavl in which twenty-seven people who ate contaminated smoked sausage got anthrax and died. Between 1923 and 1940, Soviet medical literature reported ten outbreaks of gastric anthrax, figures that might suggest they are common, occurring once every two years. In an article submitted for publication before the United States broadcast its concerns, two Soviet physicians noted that the symptoms of gastric anthrax mimic inhalation anthrax: The gastric form can act as swiftly, and be as deadly, as the inhalation form, a confusion that led some physicians to propose dropping the distinctions between the two.

According to the Soviet version, the Sverdlovsk outbreak probably originated with privately-owned sheep and cattle eating naturally infected fodder. Ignoring regulations, some citizens slaughtered their diseased animals and sold the unbranded meat on the black market. People ate the meat, ingested the anthrax spores, and over a period of six to eight weeks got sick and died. An article that appeared in a Russian medical journal after the outbreak put the death toll around twenty.

It is entirely possible that there could have been an explosion in one of the laboratories at the research facility and anthrax-tainted meat sold on the black market, but that the news was exaggerated or embellished when it reached the West. In July 1980, *Russkaja Mysl*, an émigré journal published in France for eight thousand readers without apparent subsidies from foreign governments, wrote that the first anthrax vaccines supplied by the government to counteract the 1979 outbreak came from a bad lot and didn't work. The people of Sverdlovsk had to be vaccinated twice, first in mid-April, and then at the end of April. An ineffective vaccine could have induced the disease, a tragic mistake that could lead to wild rumors.

The House Subcommittee on Intelligence, chaired by Wisconsin representative Les Aspin, concluded its own investigation in June 1980, hearing from officials of various U.S. government agencies and interviewing Mark Popovsky, a science writer and TV commentator in the Soviet Union who had immigrated to the United States in 1977. Popovsky had never been in the compound, and, reportedly, most of his impressions came from one letter sent by a Soviet dissident.

Although the committee took the Soviets to task for failing to abide by the clause in the Biological Weapons Convention that stipulates cooperation when questions arise over treaty compliance, it emphasized that the Soviets were not producing weapons in violation of the treaty. Rather, the committee concluded, the Soviets were conducting research and development in contradiction to the spirit and intent of the treaty. Despite the lack of hard information, a common scarcity when dealing with the Soviet Union, the committee took a pessimistic view, mirroring the analysis of the expert group. "Whether or not there were cases of gastric anthrax in Sverdlovsk, the salient fact is that there is evidence that there was an epidemic of inhalation anthrax. Information links the outbreak to an explosion at a military facility long suspected of housing biological warfare activities," it reported.

That opinion became current in Washington, D.C. The

true cause of the anthrax epidemic in Sverdlovsk is still shadowed with doubt. It came at a time when relations between the United States and the Soviet Union had hit a dismal low. The Soviets' wall of secrecy hardened the suspicions of those inclined to believe they had no regard for the treaty, and it unsettled those who had faith the two superpowers would recognize that their best interests lay in supporting the treaty in actions both large and small. And, in the final analysis, it lit the first fire under the Biological Weapons Convention.

FOUR

Something Happened

If the Sverdlovsk incident persuaded some members of the U.S. government that the Soviets kept biological weapons alive with a far more active research program than they believed to be sanctioned by the treaty, then subsequent events in Southeast Asia convinced many more that the Soviets actually used them. Alexander Haig, then secretary of state, spoke before the Berlin Press Association in Berlin on September 13, 1981. Mindful of sensitivities over the imminent introduction into Europe of Cruise and Pershing missiles, Haig wanted to reassure U.S. allies of the need to meet the Soviet threat. In his speech, "The Democratic Revolution and Its Future," he contrasted the accountability of open, highly visible, democratic societies with closed ones like the Soviet Union's. Few journalists would have paid attention except for Haig's unexpected and shocking announcement. He accused Soviet-backed Communist forces in Southeast Asia of using a novel toxin weapon.

"For some time now, the international community has been alarmed by continuing reports that the Soviet Union and its allies have been using lethal chemical weapons in Laos, Kampuchea, and Afghanistan," he said. "We now have physical evidence from Southeast Asia which has been analyzed and found to contain abnormally high levels of three potent myco-toxins, poisonous substances not indigenous to the region and which are highly toxic to man and animals."

The government's announcement rested on the analysis of one leaf and one stem, very slim pickings for such a solemn charge. (Haig had called the mycotoxins chemical weapons. Since mycotoxins are made by fungi and covered by the Bio-logical Weapons Convention, they are more accurately identi-fied as biological weapons. But, in many circles, toxins fall into a gray area, and Haig's statement reflected the confusion.) But backed by accounts from refugees, eyewitnesses, aid workers, medics, defectors, and classified intelligence data, the leaf and stem had compelled the U.S. government to go public. With historic words that would be later echoed by the president, the vice president, and the Joint Chiefs of Staff, Haig made clear that the Soviet Union had violated not just one but two inter-national arms control treaties: the Geneva Protocol of 1925, which bans the use of toxin and biological weapons in warfare, and the 1972 Biological Weapons Convention, which bans their stockpile and manufacture. If pressed, one could argue that no nations had legally declared war in Southeast Asia, a condition of the Geneva Protocol, but no such superlegalistic arguments could be tendered about the Biological Weapons Convention. If true, Haig's charges meant that the Soviets had brutally and cynically disregarded international law.

The timing of Haig's announcement intensified its drama. As the use of chemical weapons escalated in the war between Iran and Iraq, press accounts reported that over fourteen countries, up from five in the 1960s, had stocked chemical weapons in their arsenals. (The United States, the Soviet Union, France, and Iraq are known to possess chemical weap-ons. The suspected newcomers include Egypt, Libya, Syria, Is-rael, Ethiopia, Thailand, Burma, China, Taiwan, North Korea, and Vietnam.) In the midst of preparations for the Strategic

Arms Reduction Talks, the Reagan administration already seemed skittish about negotiating with the Soviets. Now after this charge of toxin warfare, the wariness strengthened to reluctance. The Soviets had apparently acted in such a ruthless, duplicitous way that the future of arms control agreements would have to be reappraised. Haig's charge also resurrected the idea that biological weapons hold a worthy position in a modern military arsenal, and that perhaps the U.S. prohibition had been hasty and unwise.

Before we embrace these judgments, the story of what has come to be known as Yellow Rain bears sharper scrutiny. It begins in Southeast Asia in the high mountain jungles of Laos. As in the Marabar caves in E. M. Forster's *A Passage To India*, something happened in the Laotian highlands in the late 1970s. Viewed from a westerner's perspective many likely explanations emerge. But the official explanation is not one of them.

Even though Laos, along with Burma and Thailand, forms part of the opium-rich Golden Triangle, it is one of the world's poorest countries. In the late nineteenth century, the Hmong emigrated to Laos from China, driven out by the government, which wanted their land to grow opium. Opium remains the cash crop of the Hmong, who live a hard life, farming poppies, along with corn and rice, by slashing and burning the mountain forests and then moving on every five or so years when they exhaust the soil. Perhaps as a result of this nomadic life elaborate family ties, embodied within twenty-four ruling clans, bind the Hmong.

The Hmong live in primitive, hardscrabble circumstances where the average life spans thirty-five years, child mortality runs high, and curable diseases such as malaria, malnutrition, diarrhea, dysentery, TB, and cholera are rampant. Despite this, the Hmong are sick only when they cannot eat, drink, or get out of bed. And then shamans treat them by chasing away bad spirits with magic and herbal medicine. Few Hmong read, write, or follow the Western calendar—and indeed the language lacks precise medical terms for illness—but their world is rich with storytelling.

Caught up in the United States's war in Southeast Asia and civil strife within Laos, the Hmong suffered twenty years of turbulence. In the early 1960s, the Royal Laotian government ruled the country from the lowlands, but weakened until it became ineffectual and unreliable. The Communists known as the Pathet Lao grew strong in the highlands, which cover two-thirds of the country.

To keep Vientiane, the country's capital city in the lowlands, from being overtaken by the Communists, the United States intervened in a way and on a scale it had never attempted before or since. In 1964, the CIA organized a secret army, recruiting thirty or forty thousand people, half of whom were Hmong. Over the next ten years, the CIA funneled $5–15 *billion* to fight the war in Laos—supporting the army that rescued downed American servicemen, made raids on North Vietnam, and fought the Pathet Lao forces. By all accounts, the Hmong fought fiercely and loyally. But the secret army failed to stop the Pathet Lao forces and in 1975, when the United States pulled out of Vietnam, the CIA pulled out of Laos, and the army collapsed.

The years of civil war evenly divided the Hmong: one-third fought with the Communists, one-third fought with the CIA, and one-third stayed out of it all together. When the Communists took over in 1975, most of the CIA-allied Hmong fled to Thailand, but some stayed, holing up in and around Phu Bia mountain, the highest peak in the country. In subsequent years, the Hmong emigrated. Accustomed to air drops of food, clothing, and medicine from the Americans and faced with a disastrous drought in 1977 and a devastating flood in 1978, which brought two consecutive years of crop failure, many of these Hmong died from starvation and malnutrition. In 1978, the Pathet Lao conducted a military campaign to drive out the remaining supporters of Vang Pao, the general who commanded the clandestine army.

As a result of the campaign, another large Hmong exodus took place, beginning in February and March of 1979, after the opium harvest. After a 150-mile journey that for some of them lasted as long as six weeks, dodging armed border patrols and swimming the Mekong River, they arrived at refugee camps in Thailand with harrowing stories of atrocities, including death that rained down from the skies. The Hmong used several different words for what westerners translated as poison gas, and they described the color of the poison as yellow, red, white, and green. But mostly they called it yellow and said it fell pitter-patter like a sticky rain and dried to a powder. In this way, the story came to be known in the Western press as Yellow Rain.

In Indochina, westerners had heard tales before of poison gas dropped from the sky. In fact, some carried a kernel of truth. For the last decade of the Vietnam war the United States dropped two million tons of bombs on Laos, or two tons for every person in the country. At the same time, the Americans sprayed the herbicides Agents Orange, White, Purple, and Blue to destroy crops and strip the jungle and sprayed more than 10 million pounds of tear gas to drive the Viet Cong out of hiding. (In open air, tear gas is not usually lethal, but it can be so in a closed cave.) In 1971, the United States sprayed poppy fields to destroy the Laotian opium crop.

But kernels of truth are often hard to extract when the stories grow out of a cultural framework that differs sharply from the Western one. In the early 1970s, Vietnamese Montagnards also told stories of massive deaths in their tribes, blaming it on Agent Orange and other herbicides sprayed by the Americans. At the same time, lowland Vietnamese, who had been exposed to the same spraying, told no such tales. Despite possible dangerous, long-term health effects, herbicides do not seem to provoke immediate death. A study done by the

National Academy of Sciences in 1972 suggested that the Montagnards linked naturally occurring diseases and deaths with the fact that an airplane flew overhead and discharged herbicides.

In the camps, Hmong refugees told many stories—some wild and atrocious—to willing listeners. They told of a rifle made from giant magnets that pulled weapons out of enemy hands and of Western doctors who gave poisonous injections. But journalists in Thailand picked up the poison gas stories. In the fall of 1976, the *Bangkok Post* reported on an attack against the Hmong, citing napalm and gas bombs. One year later, the same newspaper reported on a campaign of heavy attacks that lasted two months, using poison gas. Two French relief doctors working in Laos until they were expelled in mid-1978, Marie-Noelle and Didier Sicard, claimed that the poison gas resembled one used in World War I.

By late summer of 1978, the reports filtered out to American diplomats and European readers. With a Bangkok dateline and a UPI by-line, the *International Herald Tribune* reported on fighting in Laos in which the Communists crushed resisters with poison gas. The one-column, four-paragraph article cited an American researcher named Thomas Stearns, who had interviewed Hmong tribesmen describing gas attacks.

"Thomas Stearns" turned out to be one of several aliases for a man named Robert Schwab, Jr., an Atlanta-born adventurer. In 1985, he disappeared from sight while traveling down a river in the Philippines. He turned up eighteen months later, released by the Vietnamese government after attempting to rescue the fiancée he had left behind during the Vietnam War. Dick Childress of the National Security Council, an old friend, went to Vietnam to get Schwab personally. In his book *Yellow Rain*, journalist Sterling Seagrave calls Schwab Jack Schramm and describes him as "one of the Americans who stayed in Asia after the fall of Saigon in 1975. He had more in common with a Seventh-Day Adventist or a Mormon Missionary than he did with any secret agency." Yet Schwab was not the only mysterious character to play a role in the Yellow Rain story.

The Yellow Rain reports landed on Ed McWilliams's desk. A foreign service officer in his thirties with a background in military intelligence and experience at the embassy in Vientiane, McWilliams covered Laotian and Cambodian (Kampuchean) affairs stateside. He dispatched cables to the field, asking many people, including Leo Moser, the chargé d'affaires in Vientiane, Laos, to look into the stories. Although diplomatic restrictions kept Moser from traveling much beyond Vientiane, he said, "We regularly raised the issue to the Lao government. They regularly said there is nothing to it." "Marketplace intelligence," or the gossip that Americans heard from the Hmong and Lao in the marketplace, lent no support to the stories. But the reports prompted other countries—eventually including Britain, Australia, Sweden, West Germany, Canada, France, and Israel—to inquire and investigate.

If Vientiane turned up no leads, the American embassy in Thailand could also clarify little. With refugees pouring out of Kampuchea, brutalized by the Khmer Rouge regime, it had its hands full. Besides, a potentially embarrassing question cropped up. What if the poisons turned out to be chemical ordnance—tear gas or vomiting agents—left over by the Americans? Tim Carney, head consul in Udorn, a town in northern Thailand near the largest Hmong refugee camp, offered to help, as did C. Dennison Lane, a military attaché at the embassy in Bangkok. Although Washington, D.C., desk officers rarely venture into the field, McWilliams spoke Lao and knew the country's politics so well that he flew to Southeast Asia to see what he could find out. Carney, Lane, and McWilliams did the investigations on a shoestring budget. In contrast to the solemn weight and publicity given to the charges, Dr. Amos Townsend, an air force colonel and relief doctor working in refugee camps says, "the whole thing was a penny-ante game."

McWilliams and Carney traveled to the Ban Vinai refugee camp to conduct the first official interviews with Hmong refugees. The camp is a semipermanent settlement, now full of a generation of people who have never known any other type of life. Established in 1975 largely for the remnants of the CIA's secret army, it houses about 40,000 people, including the largest population of Hmong in the world, and is run by the first cousin of Vang Pao. Highly politicized, surrounded by barbed wire and patrolled by Thai police, it is a scary place. However, not all of the refugees eagerly seek resettlement in America, having heard stories of the high cost of living, alien customs, and even barbaric practices. They make a living by selling quilts sewn by Hmong women, and though it is a subject rarely raised, perhaps by selling opium.

"We didn't know what we were grappling with," says McWilliams, who in 1986 was posted to Afghanistan. But the refugee camp leaders knew that the official visitors arriving in cars had come to hear about poison gas. Camp doctors selected some of the people for interviews while McWilliams and Carney interviewed the rest by wandering through the camp. Almost half of those interviewed had been soldiers. Although a number of the Hmong soldiers spoke English or French, McWilliams and Carney also relied on an interpreter, a rough process since the Hmong refer to Yellow Rain with at least five rather vague terms—*ya bua*, *ya peet*, *chemie ai peet*, *chemie ya peet*, or simply *chemii*. When McWilliams and Carney left, they sensed they were on to something. They estimated that seven hundred to a thousand people had died after being sprayed with a yellow substance that fell like rain, but they could not identify what it was.

Six months later, the army rounded up a team of medical specialists knowledgeable about the effects of chemical and biological weapons. Dr. Charles Lewis, chief of dermatology at Brooke Army Medical Center at Fort Sam Houston in San Antonio, Texas, led the group because many Hmong refugees complained of skin problems. They went to Ban Vinai, met with leaders of the camp, and asked to meet with people who had seen or been injured by Yellow Rain. They grilled each person for two to three hours, using the same questionnaire that McWilliams and Carney had prepared. From forty-three interviews, they tried to fit the symptoms with known chemical weapons. The reports of tearing and itching suggested tear gas. The symptoms of muscular convulsions fit nerve gas. But no conventional agent could explain the reports of massive internal bleeding.

To solve the mystery, the Americans needed to analyze as many samples as they could get. The word spread through the grapevine and samples arrived at the embassy in the hundreds, some bartered at the Laotian border and some delivered by refugees who had just crossed the Mekong River. Plastic bags, paper bags, aluminum foil, and glass vials carried scrapings, bark, twigs, leaves, stones, even a cobweb. No one knew their exact source or their precise pedigree, but they got shipped to the United States for analysis.

None of the standard chemical or biological agents in the American arsenal showed up in laboratory tests performed by the army's Chemical Research, Development and Engineering Center (CRDEC) in Edgewood, Maryland. The negative findings centered attention on the army's hypothesis that an unknown agent had been used. Pressure built. Until the U.S. government identified the active ingredient in Yellow Rain, it could not act.

The Yellow Rain investigation swung into full gear when Ronald Reagan took office at the beginning of 1981. After two years of what some politicians considered to be merely polite, well-intentioned concern from the Carter administration, the Reagan administration demanded hard answers. Admiral Stansfield Turner, Carter's CIA director, says, "I'm one of those not fully persuaded by Yellow Rain. I didn't see any conclusive evidence when I was in the CIA." His successor,

William Casey, made the collection of information a new priority. Iowa representative Jim Leach, who had helped negotiate the Biological Weapons Convention in Geneva, pressed for
political action. In response to American requests, the United
Nations launched an investigation.

The Reagan administration was genuinely troubled by the
reports of illness and death from Southeast Asia. But it also
had a strong motive for pushing the Yellow Rain investigation:
a fervent desire to expose the Soviet Union as an untrust-
worthy partner in arms control agreements, especially one like
the BWC, which had no provision for verification. "The Reagan administration felt at the highest political levels that it
could be used as an issue to attack the Soviets on activity in a
forbidden area, as a violation on agreements, to convince
countries that the U.S. position on verification was correct,"
says Stuart Schwartzstein, a former foreign service officer who,
at the State Department's request, spent two years working on
the Yellow Rain investigation as a voice from the private sector.

The United States organized an interagency Yellow Rain
task force, a group of about twenty-five people from the State
Department, Defense Department, CIA, Defense Intelligence
Agency, Arms Control and Disarmament Agency, Office of
Management and Budget, and the White House National Security Council. To the army fell the task of solving the identity
of the mysterious toxic agent. Sharon Watson, an intelligence
specialist with a doctorate in toxicology who worked for the
Armed Forces Medical Intelligence Center at Fort Detrick in
Frederick, Maryland, had a hunch. The symptoms of internal
bleeding sounded like mycotoxin poisoning. She had done her
thesis on the subject.

It was an unusual but not unlikely idea. In 1979 or 1980,
Fort Detrick had started a research program that focused on
naturally occurring, low-molecular-weight toxins that might be
useful as biological weapons. In addition to frog toxins and

pufferfish toxins, mycotoxins "had been perceived as a threat, I think by both the U.S. and U.S.S.R. in years past," says Lieutenant Colonel David Bunner, head of the program at Fort Detrick.

Mycotoxins are any toxin produced by fungi. The most infamous is ergot, produced by a dark purple mold that grows on bread. In medieval times, it was known as St. Anthony's Fire because it left the victim with such a burning pain. Outside of the military, farmers had recognized a class of mycotoxins called trichothecenes as troublemakers. In 1972, scientists discovered that certain *Fusarium* fungi that grow on wheat, millet, and barley can produce trichothecenes that contaminate the grain and poison the people or livestock who later eat it. While not wildly toxic, there are more than forty different trichothecenes compounds, some of which can cause vomiting, some of which can cause bleeding, and some of which can cause the skin to blister. In fact, in Khrushchev's memoirs, he describes the terrible winter of 1943 when, in the wartime chaos, Russian farmers allowed the wheat and barley to stand in the fields until spring. Millions later died from eating the grain. Soviet medical literature described the syndrome as alimentary toxic aleukia.

The chance to test the trichothecene mycotoxin hypothesis came when one leaf and one stem were delivered to the embassy in Bangkok twenty-four hours after an attack in Kampuchea. (By November 1979, the guerrilla forces of the Khmer Rouge had reported that the Vietnamese used chemical agents against them.) Looking for trace amounts of trichothecenes is no exercise for a freshman chemistry class. Even veteran chemists throw up their hands. The analysis can take anywhere from sixteen to twenty-four hours. You need scrupulous technique and a tried and true extraction and identification method.

In 1981, a handful of laboratories in the world possessed the expertise to accurately detect tiny amounts of trichothecenes. The army's lab at Edgewood was not one. Through a colleague of Sharon Watson, the leaf and stem went to a plant pathologist at the University of Minnesota who had been testing feed grain for trichothecene mycotoxins since 1963. His name was Chester Mirocha. Because university regulations do not allow employees to do classified work, Mirocha was not told anything about the origins or suspicions surrounding the sample.

When Mirocha received the samples, he opened them with scant enthusiasm. He usually analyzed feeds, grains, and cereals, not leaves. But he made an extraction, placing the sample in a gas chromatograph where it was heated into a gas and allowed to separate chemically. After running the components through a mass spectrometer, he got a spiky readout on a long strip of graph paper, a chemical fingerprint whose peaks and valleys matched the trichothecenes.

Specifically, Mirocha reported 109 ppm (parts per million) nivalenol, a substance that can produce skin lesions; 59 ppm vomitoxin, which can cause vomiting; and the most potent, 3.17 ppm of the toxin known at T-2 which can cause internal bleeding in laboratory animals. He thought the combination unusual, especially on the surface of a leaf. Odder still, Mirocha had never seen trichothecenes in such high concentrations in a natural sample. Only several months later, when he read about Yellow Rain in the press, did Mirocha realize that the government considered his findings to be the "smoking gun."

At a meeting in August, the Yellow Rain team discussed whether to make Mirocha's findings public. While the intelligence agencies worried about compromising their sources, others found the scientific evidence compelling. Apparently, the group had few if any qualms about going public on the basis of a single and problematic laboratory analysis. Following customary protocol in chemical analysis, the army had split in two the sample it sent to Mirocha, spiking one-half with a known quantity of T-2 toxin and leaving the other half unaltered. Mirocha looked not only for T-2, but for three other mycotoxins. If the spiked and unspiked samples came from the same leaf, one would expect him to find at least the ratio of the other mycotoxins to be identical in each sample. But Mirocha's ratios were different, a troubling result that cast doubt on the reliability of his analysis.

The possibility that the press might scoop the government tipped the decision. Journalist Sterling Seagrave, who had learned of the trichothecene hypothesis from CIA connections, was about to publish it in his book, and he had also passed along the word to *Time* magazine, which had a story pending. Rather than let the press go out on a limb, the government decided it would. Richard Burt, then head of the State Department's Bureau of Politico-Military Affairs and a former *New York Times* journalist, did not want to be beaten. He lobbied for an announcement. The decision would later prove to be embarrassing. Before the facts came in, the administration had boldly committed itself to a position that would gradually collapse.

The media couched the Yellow Rain story with restraint— after all, the government had based its charge on the analysis of only one leaf and stem. (The one exception was the *Wall Street Journal*, whose editorial-page writers were vigorously questioning the future of arms control.) NBC science correspondent Bob Bazell called up professor Matthew Meselson for his opinion as a biological weapons expert. Meselson did not know any details about Yellow Rain. In fact, the interagency team had just invited him to a briefing that would be held in a couple of weeks. With a note of caution, he said that the presence of mycotoxins alone proved nothing. The *Fusarium* fungi, which produce them naturally, grow worldwide. The spot aired and, without any explanation, a member of the task force canceled Meselson's briefing. In retrospect, it was the first hint of the government's lack of appetite for any critique.

In over twenty years of consulting to the government on biological and chemical weapons, Meselson had said many times that, without careful analysis, the government could one day find itself in hot water. In a set of hearings before the Senate Committee on Foreign Relations in November 1981, Meselson advised against jumping too hastily to any conclusions of wrongdoing. After reviewing the scientific literature for information on mycotoxins, he found some things that contradicted the government's statements. First, there was some evidence that the fungi that produce the mycotoxins found by Mirocha grow naturally in the Asian tropics. Second, he questioned the government's claim that these mycotoxins cause rapid hemorrhaging. A paper co-authored by Chester Mirocha was entitled "The Failure of Purified T-2 Mycotoxin to Produce Hemorrhaging in Dairy Cattle." (Mirocha would later say that the title was not in fact accurate, but his co-author had persuaded him to use it. "As a project leader, you have to satisfy a lot of people," he explained.) Third, with the lack of adequate controls, how could anyone be sure that the reports of trichothecenes were not due to error or contamination? And finally, he brought up the story of the Montagnards who mistakenly attributed naturally caused deaths to planes spraying herbicides.

But all caution vanished in the momentum of events. In 1982, Yellow Rain became a cause célèbre, an issue of international stature. The State Department released an exhaustive thirty-two-page white paper, detailing the attacks, the evidence, and the rationale. Between 1975 and 1981, attacks had taken place in Laos—some two hundred of them at Phu Bia, where more than 6,000 people were killed. One hundred twenty-four attacks had taken place in Kampuchea, leaving 1,000 people dead, and forty-seven occurred in Afghanistan, killing over 3,000. Although the United States charged that chemical agents were used, specifically riot-control chemicals and "probably incapacitating agents," it emphasized, and only provided evidence for, the use of trichothecene mycotoxins.

Independently, Joe Rosen, a food scientist at Rutgers University, confirmed Mirocha's findings of trichothecenes. In a sample said to have been scraped off a leaf in Laos and given to him by an ABC-TV documentary team, Rosen found the trichothecenes deoxynivalenol (DON), diacetoxyscirpenl (DAS), and T-2, in concentrations of roughly 50 ppm. He also found an industrial chemical known as polyethylene glycol, which to many people clinched the charge that the toxins had an unnatural origin.

The House of Representatives Committee on Foreign Affairs held hearings at which Richard Burt testified, making Yellow Rain sound like the neutron bomb. "Principally these weapons are designed to destroy communities, to move people off the land, to deal with the whole insurgency problem," he said. Others testified in the same vein, except for Fred Schwartzendruber, a Mennonite aid worker and one of the few Americans who had been in the Laotian countryside at the time of the alleged attacks. He said it was very difficult to travel in north-central Laos, as he had, and believe there was massive biochemical warfare taking place. New York City Congressman Stephen Solarz reacted with scathing disdain and disbelief. "I suspect that short of being hit on the head by Yellow Rain, nothing would convince Mr. Schwartzendruber that it was going on."

Later, Schwartzendruber would recall that when he and his wife, Jan, traveled through Laos from 1979 to 1981 in the course of working on aid projects, they often flew and took many pictures of aircraft, airstrips, and facilities. At one of the "bases" from which Yellow Rain flights were alleged to have taken place, Schwartzendruber says security was minimal. "I never saw or heard anything which would've suggested either CW in progress or an extermination campaign against the Hmong."

The media hedged on the Yellow Rain story until the fall of 1982, when the State Department released another white paper report, this time charging the Soviets with using mycotoxins in Afghanistan. The Soviet invasion of Afghanistan had aroused great anger, and the American public and press were ready to believe the Soviets capable of the most heinous behavior. As the *Boston Globe*, a newspaper not known for its conservative bent, summed it up: "The Soviets appear to be on the road to convicting themselves of egregious violations of civilized norms, both the Geneva Protocol of 1925 and the 1972 Biological Weapons Convention."

As in the Sverdlovsk incident, the Soviets did little to help plead their case. To the charges, they sent only one public rebuttal, a humdinger of a theory so apparently contorted by the propaganda-makers that not even the skeptics took it seriously. They explained the mycotoxins by pointing out that the United States had deliberately defoliated the jungles in Vietnam. After defoliation, elephant grass began to grow. The *Fusarium* fungus grew on the elephant grass, and the wind blew the spores into Laos and Kampuchea.

The Great Bee Caper

Disquieting developments soon clouded the government's Yellow Rain case. The four members of a United Nations team led by Ezmett Ezz, an American-trained Egyptian doctor, were denied visas to enter Laos. Furthermore, they found how hard it was to analyze for trichothecenes. The team sent samples— one control and one blank—to three top labs in three countries. In two labs, scientists found no trichothecenes, even in the spiked samples. In the other, they found trichothecenes in all samples, including the blank. The UN could neither confirm nor deny what the United States charged: "While the group could not state that these allegations had been proved, nevertheless, it could not disregard the circumstantial evidence suggestive of the possible use of some sort of toxic chemical substance in some instances." The accusations died there, never to be taken up by the United Nation's Security Council, the forum envisioned by the Biological Weapons Convention for settling disputes over violations.

No mycotoxin-tainted canisters, shells, grenades, rockets, or weapon fragments had been turned in to the U.S. embassy in Bangkok, despite a reward advertised in *Soldier of Fortune*. That left open the possibility that Yellow Rain had been delivered by airplane spray tanks. But, like crop-dusters, the planes would have to fly no more than 300 feet above the ground, which the refugees had not observed.

If indeed Yellow Rain was sprayed from an airplane, there were other bothersome inconsistencies. Trichothecenes are solids that vaporize only at high temperatures, and thus could not have been sprayed as a gas. It is possible to dissolve them in an appropriate solvent and spray an aerosol or a mist of particles small enough to penetrate the alveoli of the lungs. But that would dilute the already weak action of their poison. And aerosol spraying would make no discernible sound. According to an article co-authored by Christopher Green, a CIA physician who investigated Yellow Rain, "aerial attacks, usually by spray, dispersed yellow to yellow-brown liquid or semi-solid particles that fell and sometimes sounded like rain."

Some Westerners doubted the literal truth of the Yellow Rain stories. Jerry Barker Daniels, who had worked closely with the Hmong during the CIA's secret war, qualified as one of the most informed Americans on the Hmong. Before his mysterious death in Thailand in 1982, he had helped relocate Hmong refugees in the United States. Some colleagues say he expressed skepticism that Yellow Rain was a novel weapon of war.

Lacking sophisticated lab equipment in the refugee camps, as well as expertise, relief doctors and nurses had no way to decide if their patients had been exposed to mycotoxins. Their opinions varied considerably on whether the symptoms and complaints they saw could be explained by the toxin warfare charge. They saw the question as more political than medical. "Most UN organizations did not want to be perceived as being involved in anything political," explains McWilliams. In some camps very few if any refugees claimed to be victims of Yellow Rain attacks, while in others many said they had been attacked. If the Laotians and Kampucheans had used Yellow Rain so extensively, no one could explain why the stories came principally from the Hmong in the Ban Vinai camp.

Two aid workers with the American Friends Service Committee, Jacqui Chagnon and Roger Rumpf, had worked in Laos between 1978 and 1981. A husband and wife team, they traveled in the alleged attack areas and saw nothing unusual or suspicious. They only heard one reference to an airplane that dropped Yellow Rain, and that was on the Voice of America. After returning to the United States for a speaking tour, audiences asked so many questions about Yellow Rain that Chagnon and Rumpf decided to investigate. "If the stories were true, we had to *do* something," says Chagnon. "And if they weren't, we had to *do* something."

For six weeks in 1983, Chagnon and Rumpf traveled in Southeast Asia, first visiting the Hmong refugee camps in Thailand. At Ban Vinai, they heard a variety of Yellow Rain stories, but none at another camp, Ban Nam Yao. Inside Laos, they tried to cross-check stories heard at Ban Vinai. They found an official, named by a refugee as the investigator of an alleged attack, who attributed deaths to Yellow Rain in 1981 but made no mention of planes or warfare. After interviewing others, they found that Hmong remaining inside Laos, as well as ethnic Lao, were familiar with Yellow Rain, described it as a yellow powder on the ground, believed it caused bloody diarrhea, dysentery, and death but did not report seeing planes or link it with warfare.

Back in the United States, Saul Hormats, who until his retirement in 1973 directed the development of chemical warfare munitions for the army, ridiculed the military utility of mycotoxins. In comparison with the most lethal chemical agents in the arsenal, T-2 is not very toxic. (In aerosol form, the army estimates that it takes 35 milligrams of pure trichothecenes to kill a 75-kilogram man—a dose forty to sixty times greater than the comparable lethal dose of VX nerve gas.) He calculated that it would take twenty to thirty thousand shells fired for two hours by a full Soviet artillery division or 8,000 tons of bombs or 3,000 tons of agent to destroy twelve to twenty families in a village. Why go to the trouble of standardizing such a weapon when agents that were much more toxic existed?

Although Mirocha's initial findings of trichothecenes, in what seemed to be relatively high concentration and unusual combinations, had led Haig to charge the Soviets publicly with violating the treaty, further research indicated that the results did not necessarily mean the trichothecenes came from an unnatural source. The National Academy of Sciences released a study that reported that trichothecenes had been detected in nature at 25, 31, 40 parts per million, close enough to the range of figures obtained by Mirocha to challenge the conclusion that high levels of trichothecenes automatically meant a weapon had been used.

Independently, Sweden, Australia, Canada, France, Britain, and, reportedly, Israel and West Germany, made laboratory analyses of Yellow Rain samples. But some odd findings turned up. The British said their samples contained pollen. When the Australians, Canadians, Thais, and Americans examined their samples, they found pollen too, but no one could explain what purpose the pollen served in a supposed weapon of war.

In October 1982, several army scientists made a trek to Joan Nowicke's laboratory, asking her to identify the pollen grains in electron micrographs of Yellow Rain. Nowicke is a palynologist, an expert on the pollens of flowering plants, who works at the Smithsonian's Museum of Natural History in Washington, D.C. You get to her office by turning right past the snake skeletons in the museum's bones-and-fins exhibit and entering the flower morgue, a room with hundreds of white lockers storing flower and pollen specimens from all over the world. Serious and unaccustomed to visitors, she said a thorough analysis would take months but right off the top, she recognized pollens from the daisy and grass families. The news disappointed her visitors, who had hoped the pollen left a botanical fingerprint pointing unequivocally to Moscow.

While Sharon Watson and others in the government speculated that the pollen served as a clever and novel carrier for the mycotoxins, the news bewildered Meselson. Why go to the bother of putting pollen in a weapon? In his twenty years of analyzing biological and chemical weapons, he had never heard the faintest suggestion of such a thing. "I knew for sure, in the way a scientist has a hunch, that pollen was not a component of a chemical weapon," he says.

In the spring of 1983, Meselson organized a conference, inviting members of the Yellow Rain task force, the United Nations investigators, anthropologists, toxicologists, aid workers, micrometeorologists, arms control experts, and anyone else who wanted to solve the Yellow Rain riddle. The two-day conference was organized as a think tank, a brainstorming session. In retrospect, it proved to be the last time any of those professionally interested in the issue of Yellow Rain hoped for a common ground of agreement.

Peter Ashton, director of Boston's Arnold Arboretum and a forest botanist who had lived for fifteen years in Southeast Asia, first broached the notion that would later divide the participants so sharply. He began to think out loud about the pollen. Since it was too dense to have been windblown, and since it came from indigenous trees visited by bees, perhaps bees had something to do with the pollen. Perhaps they had regurgitated it? Could Yellow Rain be bee vomit?

At the end of the conference, a still puzzled Ashton went back to Meselson's office, where he called Tom Seeley, a Yale biologist and one of the world's few experts on the bees of Southeast Asia. Was there anything in the behavior of honeybees that would leave little yellow pollen spots in the forest? Seeley, who is methodical, slow to excite, and given to Yankee understatement, said, "That's a perfect description of their defecation patterns." The State Department's explanation was not the "most parsimonious." Honeybees do eat pollen, digest it, and, in northern climates at least, take mass defecation flights after the winter's hibernation. On the other end of the telephone line, Seeley heard laughter. What? Beeshit?

Later Meselson pumped Seeley with questions. Like most newspaper readers, Seeley believed Yellow Rain to be a biological weapon. But after two or three long, probing telephone calls, another possibility emerged. Meselson and Seeley found that the size of bee droppings, the typical area covered, the color and texture—all matched the size, coverage, color, and texture of the samples of Yellow Rain. In the first rough analysis, in all aspects except for the presence of mycotoxins, the samples of Yellow Rain matched the samples of bee feces.

In the spring, Meselson and his colleagues collected bee droppings in and around Cambridge, scraping them off windshields and plants to make further comparison. Except for the presence of mycotoxins, the samples of Yellow Rain continued to match the samples of bee feces. The corcordance encouraged Meselson, Seeley, and Nowicke to go public. At a meeting of the American Association for the Advancement of Science in May 1983, they unveiled their hypothesis, well aware of the impact it would have. "I realized that one of the reasons I was asked to go was to lend credibility as someone not involved in discussions of chemical weapons," says Seeley.

A State Department spokesman labeled the theory "The Great Bee Caper" and made little attempt to address the contradiction it raised. While other newspapers had let the Yellow Rain issue fade, the *Wall Street Journal* carried a steady stream of articles on its editorial page. According to William Kucewicz, the editorial writer who wrote most of the Yellow Rain stories, someone in the administration had asked the *Journal* to keep the issue alive after Haig made his announcement. The *Journal* believed in its importance and "took it on as a cause." Nearly one year after Meselson and Seeley advanced the beeshit theory, the *Journal* dismissed it, declaring that the idea that "mycotoxin residues in attack areas are actually only bee droppings is too ludicrous for serious discussion." In fact, Meselson and Seeley never claimed to explain the mycotoxin findings.

For the better part of a year, Nowicke analyzed the pollen in the Yellow Rain samples, not for the government but as an independent researcher whose curiosity had been piqued by the controversy. Despite her initial tendency to believe the government's charge, she found herself swayed by the evidence she gathered. The spectrum of pollen matched that found in Southeast Asia. It showed no signs of homogeneity but varied in each sample the way it would if it had been gathered and dropped by local bees. Finally, and most convincingly, it showed signs that it had been digested. As Nowicke and others wrote in an article that appeared later in *Scientific American,* "It would seem that in order to accept the chemical weapons theory of yellow rain in the face of this evidence, one would have to imagine an enemy so devious that its chemical weapon is prepared by gathering pollen predigested by honeybees."

The presence of pollen cast a shadow on the mycotoxin analyses. In another attempt at reconciliation, Schwartzstein, the former State Department foreign service officer, invited Meselson, Mirocha, and Rosen to dinner at a Thai restaurant in New York City. (After his initial findings, Mirocha had continued to analyze Yellow Rain samples for the government—environmental samples scraped off the ground, and biomedical samples of blood and urine from alleged victims.) For the entire evening, Schwartzstein sat silent while Meselson grilled Mirocha and Rosen about a report in *Science* magazine that the government had tested over sixty environmental samples for trichothecenes and only five turned out to be positive. (Rosen's one sample had not been included in that tally.) Who did the five, Meselson asked. "I certainly had not realized that all of the five were from Mirocha and that he had only looked at six," says Meselson. "The army had never found any positives. That to me was a stunning development because it seemed incredible that one lab could find it nearly all the time

and another lab never finds it." As one journalist later phrased
it, the "smoking gun," the mycotoxin evidence heralded by
Richard Burt, had the combined weight of less than a large as-
pirin.

The army's negative findings put the Edgewood lab on a
political hot seat. When Mirocha first performed his analysis in
1981, the army's Chemical Research, Development and Engineering Center (CRDEC) had the equipment but lacked the
experience or knowledge to identify trichothecenes. Emery
(Bill) Sarver, chemist and head of the analytical laboratory,
spent over a year developing reliable protocols, quality controls, and methods for handling unknown samples. From 1981
to 1986, the lab spent an average of $300,000 a year on the
analysis of Yellow Rain samples. Sarver, who staunchly de-
fends the accuracy of his methods, refuses to discuss, much less
publish his results. He politely deflects questions to Joe Vervier, associate director of research at CRDEC, who refuses to
divulge the total number of samples the lab has analyzed. Most
people believe it to be well into the hundreds. He will only explain that "internally we've elected not to get involved." Formally or informally, it appears that the lab has buried findings
that contradict the government's position. The CRDEC loyally
backs the Reagan administration's charge, but the scientists
have not offered a shred of evidence to confirm it.

The failure of the government's own laboratory to corroborate the mycotoxin hypothesis led Meselson and others to
hammer away at other types of evidence gathered. The more
people prodded, the faster the government's case broke down.
The evidence for mycotoxin weapons in Afghanistan rested on
two contaminated gas masks. But the evidence evaporated
when tests showed that toxins contaminated the exterior of one
gas mask but not the filter, as would be true if a soldier had
worn the mask in the presence of the weapon. On the second
gas mask, the traces of mycotoxins found by one laboratory
could not be confirmed by another laboratory. In 1986, even a

report prepared by the army's Defense Science Board dismissed the claim that mycotoxins were ever used by the Soviets in Afghanistan.

More revelations made the charges in Southeast Asia also look wobbly. Thoy Manikham, a Lao pilot who had defected and described firing rockets on Hmong villages, was called "one of the most interviewed refugees we have had." Yet some military experts doubted that he had used toxic gas. Nguyen Quan, a Vietnamese artillery officer, and defector from the Kampuchean civil war, claimed to have fired chemical shells on Kampuchean villages, but retracted part of his story, complaining that he had cooperated in exchange for a promise that was not kept, that he could immigrate to the United States.

Canadians disputed the American results of a 1982 autopsy performed on a Khmer Rouge soldier named Chan Mann who died one month after he said he had witnessed a Yellow Rain attack near the Thai border. When Mirocha and Rosen received tissue samples from Mann's autopsy, they both found T-2: Mirocha reported 88 parts per million in the intestine and 25 ppm in the stomach. Rose found 2,010 parts per billion in the intestine and zero in the stomach. But the Canadians found nothing, and attributed Mann's death to kidney failure, adding that they could not rule out the possibility that he died from Blackwater Fever, a complication of chronic malaria. More important, they believed that symptoms of other casualties from the Tuol Chrey attack did not fit those produced by mycotoxins, as a result of which they suspected some other type of chemical.

In the first extensive media investigation of Yellow Rain, Lois Ember of *Chemical and Engineering News* reported in January 1984 on irregularities and inconsistencies in the chemical analyses. In a sample said to be taken from a March 1981 aerial spray attack on Phu Bia Mountain, Mirocha reported 143 ppm of T-2, the highest level found in any sample. A year later, when the toxin should presumably still have been present, Sarver analyzed the same sample and found no T-2, only pollen. In the same sample, scientists at the British Defense Ministry found no T-2.

Mirocha also found trichothecenes in eighteen out of sixty blood and urine samples taken from alleged victims one to ten weeks after Yellow Rain attacks. But evidence cited by the State Department in its 1982 white paper suggests that myco-toxins disappear from the body within twenty-four to forty-eight hours of exposure. Detrick researchers now believe that some reservoir in the body releases the toxins slowly over time, a hypothesis that has yet to be proven. In addition, the myco-toxins did not show up in samples from forty people who claimed to have been attacked. How to explain this contradiction?

According to Richard Kenley, an analytical chemist at Baxter-Travenol Laboratories in Chicago and an army reserve officer who has specialized in CBW intelligence over the last decade, one problem might have been that Mirocha made tri-chothecenes in the same lab in which he analyzed for them. "I think he had false positives and contamination in the lab," Kenley says. At the parts per million, parts per billion level, it does not take much to skew the results. "You can have residues in the inlet ports [of your analytical instruments]."

In the winter of 1984, the McArthur Foundation awarded Meselson a $250,000 "genius" grant, recognizing in part his lifelong efforts to curb biological and chemical weapons. When the unexpected call arrived, Meselson put the receiver to his chest and whispered one word to his secretary. "Money." Shortly thereafter, he and Seeley flew to Thailand to resolve the remaining questions about the bee feces hypothesis. It was Meselson's first trip to Southeast Asia since 1970, when the American Association for the Advancement of Science sponsored a scientific investigation into the ecological and health effects of herbicides, a trip that led the United States to stop spraying Agent Orange.

In Bangkok, they met up with Seeley's friend and Thai bee expert, Pongtep Akratanakul, rented a Land Rover, and stayed in small roadside hotels, never sleeping more than three or four hours a night. Even though Seeley had lived in Thailand, he had failed to notice if bees defecated in anything approaching a rainlike shower, the one constant thread running through the refugees' varied descriptions of the yellow stuff. He had simply never paid attention.

They traveled to bee nest sites in Thailand's national parks and found tiny yellow specks on the leaves and rocks that matched the descriptions of Yellow Rain. But the most compelling experience took place on the last day of the journey, when they examined two tall trees—one with thirty bee nests and one with fifty, with tens of thousands of bees clinging to the outsides of the nests—in the village of Khua Moong. At 5:17 P.M., many of the bees left the nest and flew off in a big curtain.

The scientists stood by their Land Rover, elbows propped on the hood, watching the bees through field glasses. The sky looked clear. Then the insects defecated, showering Meselson, Seeley, and Akratanakul with yellow spots. None of them could hear or see the bees. "It fell everywhere—on us, on the Land Rover, on Tom's glasses," says Meselson. They were astounded, delighted, and laughing.

If the Hmong failed to associate Yellow Rain with bees, then it explained why they might, sometimes, associate yellow spots with airplanes flying overhead. To the Ban Vinai camp, Meselson and his colleagues brought branches dappled with bee feces and asked sixteen groups of refugees met at random to identify the yellow spots. Thirteen groups said they could not, and three groups called the spots *chemii*, one of the Hmong words for the Yellow Rain poison.

In another encounter, one Thai villager recognized the yellow spots as the residue of a chemical weapon, and said those who failed to do so were ignorant because they had not gone to classes given by the Thai border patrol on how to recognize Yellow Rain. The scientists concluded that the Hmong refugees do not know beeshit when they see it, and some mistakenly believe it is a biochemical weapon.

"The truth of an idea," William James wrote at the turn of the century, "is not a stagnant property inherent in it. Truth happens to an idea ... by the process ... of its verification." Outside of the analyses performed by Mirocha and Rosen, the international scientific community looked for but found no laboratory evidence to back the claim that Yellow Rain is a mycotoxin weapon of war. In the spring of 1986, the British Ministry of Defence acknowledged that it had never detected trichothecenes in any of its biomedical or environmental samples of Yellow Rain. It did, however, find pollen. After analyzing blood samples from Thais who were *not* exposed to Yellow Rain attacks, Canadian investigators found trichothecenes in five out of 272 samples. The five lived in three different villages, all remote from alleged attack sites. The implication was that trichothecenes occur naturally in Southeast Asia, probably infecting the food. Other allies remained silent.

Even as the U.S. government's case desperately faltered, the refugee accounts lingered. From more than a thousand accounts, of which the government released summaries of about two hundred interviews, the impression of suffering is impossible to ignore. No one doubted that the Hmong suffered, but the earlier reports of massive slaughter now appear to be an exaggeration. "I think the accusation of a genocidal campaign against the Hmong is easily repudiated," says Robert Cooper, a British anthropologist with the United Nations High Commission for Refugees in Geneva. During the three years he worked with the Hmong in Laos, from 1980 to 1983, he reportedly never heard Yellow Rain stories, despite the Reagan administration's assertion that attacks went on.

Anthropologists and sociologists fault the government for naiveté in structuring refugee interviews. Where is the evidence that refugee stories were cross-checked and cross-referenced, either internally or with other available outside sources? While the investigators felt they went in without bias, the way they set up the interviews, the types of questions asked, and their frame of mind often presumed that a chemical attack had taken place and that the task at hand was to identify the compound. For example, when Canadian investigators went into the Thai village of Ban Sa Tong in 1982 to investigate allegations of an attack, they used a questionnaire that asked about activities at "the time of the attack" and symptoms felt "upon exposure."

Jeanne Guillemin, a medical sociologist at Boston College, participated in a critique of the interviews, initially at the request of Stuart Schwartzstein. She argues that the interviews should have been conducted in a group, not one on one, because of the importance of clan relationships among the Hmong, and stressed the importance of knowing the speaker's social identity and relationship in the group. "If a clan leader decides this is what we are doing, a younger or poorer man would follow what the leader framed as reality," she says. And she emphasizes the etiquette in Southeast Asian cultures of verbal accommodation, of agreeing with strangers.

The question of how many people died, and of what causes, remains alive. Like most observers of the Yellow Rain story, Guillemin does not believe that the Hmong invented the story completely out of the blue. The symptoms reported by the Hmong were vague—like headache, vomiting, bloody diarrhea, weakness—but are characteristic of endemic diseases like fungal infections, cholera, and malaria. After two devastating years of crop failure, many Hmong were chronically malnourished, a condition that complicates and exacerbates many of these infections.

It is clear that the Hmong witnessed a military attack in 1978. "We know there was fighting between Pathet Lao and pro–Vang Pao Hmong, who ended up making a last-stand defense around Phu Bia, and that Vietnamese troops were called in to assist," says Fred Schwartzendruber. "Aircraft were used to hit pockets of resistance that were proving difficult to over-run by ground forces. Could chemicals have been used in such attacks? The situation makes sense tactically and there cer-tainly were leftover stocks of American ordnance which in-cluded CS, a tear agent, and perhaps DM, a vomiting agent. I don't know that this happened but it seems a plausible sce-nario."

CS, or tear gas, falls as a very fine powder and causes the eyes to burn and tear, and the skin to itch and sometimes blis-ter. It is a myth that tear gas presents no harm to human health. If sprayed heavily, or in an enclosed, unventilated space, if inhaled by the very young, the very old, or the very sick, it can be lethal.

In all of its official accounts, the U.S. government insisted that attacks in Laos, Kampuchea, and Afghanistan took place not only with mycotoxins but other chemical agents. Accord-ing to a State Department White Paper, the Vietnamese made "limited use of riot control chemicals against Kampuchean guerilla forces in 1978–1979." Meselson agrees that CS was used in Kampuchea. But oddly enough, the U.S. government has never revealed the evidence to support its chemical warfare charge.

Recently, a government official who asked for anonymity, conceded that the majority of investigated attacks in Southeast Asia and Afghanistan involved the use of chemical weapons, presumably tear gas. Only a small percentage actually involved mycotoxins, he said. Was this the government's face-saving retreat when confronted with a scientifically untenable posi-tion?

In any event, the military campaign against the Hmong stopped in 1978. But the Yellow Rain stories, which continue to this day, tapered off only in 1983. Like all good tales, per-haps Yellow Rain became an amalgamation of several uncon-nected events that took place at the same time—a military

campaign, mysterious yellow specks that fell like rain, and un-
explainable deaths—spun again and again by those in search
of a better life, solicited by willing listeners.

In the spring of 1986, the *New York Times,* in a lead
editorial, urged the Reagan administration to admit its hasty
mistake. "The Administration can admit that Yellow Rain is
bee excrement and that it has made an intelligence blunder, or
it can doggedly march on, unsupported by its own Army, or
allies, with the thesis that Yellow Rain is an agent of biological
warfare. It has so far found retreat too preposterous to contemplate. But its posture is more so."

Even though a State Department official acknowledges
that "Yellow Rain is a very awkward matter," the Reagan administration sticks to its original charges that the Soviets were
behind the use of mycotoxins in three different countries. It
grants that scientists have proven many environmental samples
to be bee feces. It grants that mycotoxins were not widely used.
It even grants that mycotoxins do not make very good weapons.

Instead, the government's case rests on refugee reports, investigations pursued by other unnamed and silent countries,
and classified intelligence. The investigations pursued by Canada, Australia, and England, three countries with whom the
United States has historically had an exchange agreement in
the arena of biological and chemical weapons, contradicted the
charge, and France, Sweden, West Germany, and Israel are
not yet talking. The value of the classified intelligence, like a
wild card in poker, is known only to its holder. At the moment,
it is a card that the United States refuses to play.

Dismissing the scientific controversy as inevitable, irre-
solvable, and too abstruse for the person in the street, the Reagan administration is using the conflict to emphasize the threat
and menace of biological weapons. "We're headed toward a
more dangerous era, designing weapons whose chief military

virtue is that they cannot be detected. There is an element of fear. Is it there or isn't it?" says Stuart Schwartzstein.

According to Gary Crocker, senior political military analyst and the State Department's spokesperson on the subject of Yellow Rain, the ambiguities of detection are precisely what make biological weapons so attractive. "Look, you use something too overt and the whole world turns around and says that's terrible. So what does the dirty little dictator want? Something that he can use to kill people, maybe make a lot of people ill. He wants something that appears to be natural."

With international treaties, the burden of proof falls on the accuser. By any standard of evidence, whether that used in a forensic laboratory, a scientific research laboratory, or a court of law, the United States has failed to make its case. "There is no convincing evidence that the Soviets violated the Biological Weapons Convention," says former ambassador James Leonard, who helped negotiate the Biological Weapons Convention in 1972. "There are no mycotoxins. The United States management of its side of the BWC is shameful. It is our responsibility *not* to make charges we can't substantiate."

It is impossible to say just how much the Yellow Rain investigation has cost the U.S. taxpayer. While Edgewood Arsenal spent $1.5 million on the chemical analysis of samples and $1 million on developing a kit to detect mycotoxins in the environment, Detrick has spent $21.6 million to research their medical effects. The CIA, the DIA, and the rest of the intelligence community spent sums that may never be known. As the government continues to press the charges, Yellow Rain will continue to cost the taxpayer. If the Dugway lab is built, aerosols of mycotoxins will be tested on defensive equipment and lab animals. If nothing else, it would be cheaper to apologize.

After all is said and done, what is Yellow Rain? "Bee feces and hysteria," says Meselson. Most critically, he believes it took on a life of its own because the Reagan administration wanted to make a political point about arms control. "The story collapsed and still had its effect," he says crisply. "It is disinformation."

"Yellow Rain is utter nonsense," says Admiral Thomas Davies. "We jump to conclusions without research. It is a hallmark of the Soviet Union that it can't admit a mistake. That's why I'm disturbed to see it in our government."

According to Richard Kenley, the army reserve chemist, "It was ego and stupidity. Trichothecenes came out of left field." The administration got locked into a position before it collected all the evidence. The issue became political, not scientific, and stayed alive for political, not scientific reasons. "They got mileage out of this. It builds programs and it builds empires."

In 1976, yellow drops fell from the sky in northern Jiangsu, China, frightening the local villagers who believed them to be poisonous. When scientists at Nanking University investigated, they discovered the yellow drops were bee feces. If Soviet-backed forces had been carrying on a military campaign against that Chinese village, one has to wonder where the investigation of the yellow spots would have led.

SIX

Mythinformation

"From the military point of view, the employment and characteristics of chemical and biological weapons have similarities that make it artificial to look only at chemicals and pretend that the biological threat does not exist; that would be to ignore what may turn out to be the most serious aspect of the problem."

> —Report of the Chemical Warfare Review Commission, 1985 (also dubbed "the forty-five day wonder" by Rep. John Porter of Illinois for the speedy delivery of its conclusion that the United States needed to build a new generation of nerve gas weapons)

Despite the fact that the scientific community discredited the government's mycotoxin charge, the Yellow Rain story has not died. On the contrary, it is alive and well within the military. For the army's Chemical Corps, the charge that the Soviets used toxins in Southeast Asia gives it one more reason for being.

The army teaches soldiers a simple message at Fort McClellan in Anniston, Alabama, a rural town on the edge of the Talledega National Forest, halfway between Birmingham and Atlanta. With a gracious, pine-tree-lined drive winding past clipped fields to an Alamo-style administration headquarters, the fort looks and feels more like a college campus than a garrison. In a sense, it is. At one edge of the fort, the U.S. Army Chemical School packs classrooms and runs outdoor exercises attracting students from all over the world ready to learn the grim truth and silent consequences of biological and chemical warfare. Every year, five thousand men and women become specialists in combating toxic threats, and a smaller number of new recruits learn the basics of protecting themselves on a poisoned battlefield.

Fort McClellan is the proud home of the Chemical Corps, an organization that has, since its inception as the Chemical Warfare Service, suffered from second-class citizenship within the military's bureaucracy. It came into being in World War I when soldiers wheeled industrial tanks of poisonous chlorine gas to the battlefield and opened the valve as the wind blew toward the enemy. World War I witnessed the use of twenty-five different types of poisonous gas, a quantum jump in scale and variety from past uses of poisons. Long accustomed to hurling metal objects at the enemy with much more precision and control, traditionalists resisted the new weapons, arguing that the weather affected the spread of the vapors, and once the enemy put on a mask, the advantage disappeared. Civilians also resisted because they suffered a much higher rate of casualties from gas than with conventional weapons.

At the end of the war, the military moved to reduce drastically the size of the Chemical Warfare Service. But the director, General Amos Fries, fought back, personally lobbying Congress and building a case that chemical weapons were the most economical, efficient, and humane weapons known to military science. In the phrase of the day, uttered by a poison gas pioneer, Fritz Haber, as he received his Nobel Prize, they were a "higher form of killing."

Although Congress backed Fries, public opposition

mounted. In 1925, the League of Nations drew up the Geneva Protocol, which banned the first use of chemical and bacteriological weapons. But the Chemical Warfare Service had such political muscle with the chemical industry that it prevented the United States from ratifying the Protocol for almost fifty years. The Chemical Warfare Service ballooned during World War II, encompassing the nascent biological weapons program. Only in 1969, when Nixon halted the production of chemical weapons and banned biologicals altogether was the Chemical Corps "disestablished." It lost its institutional identity and footing, and any other organization might have died altogether. But the Chemical Corps, like a tenacious vine, seemed to thrive on being whacked back. In 1980, when budgets throughout the military began to surge, it came back to life, and the Chemical School reopened its doors with a new vitality.

A symbol of the Chemical Corps' vitality is a new museum that displays the twentieth century's version of armor: the gas mask and overgarment used by the Soviet bloc and rumored to be a favorite black market item for fishermen; toxin-proof cages for World War I carrier pigeons; gas masks for cavalry horses and even camels. But the most unusual artifact is stored in a plastic box behind the exhibits. During World War II, the military asked Walt Disney to design a gas mask for children. Though never manufactured, the museum owns one of the few in existence. Mickey Mouse's friendly face has been scaled down to child size, and his cheery mouth equipped with a tubelike respirator: child's play twisted into a death mask.

On a sunny fall day at the U.S. Army Chemical School, new recruits stand in a semicircle on a gravel apron outside a warehouse filled with the gear needed to survive a biochemical war. Today, they are learning how to suit up in the Battledress Overgarment.

The sergeant barks: The first one finished does not have to

clean up. Ready-set-go. They run a race standing still, stepping into stiff, foam-impregnated pants, pulling them over the standard-issue khakis, then struggling into a stiff, foam-impregnated jacket. Intent on winning, one kid has laced up his black rubber overboots before the others have even yanked them on. By the time he's ready to put his mask on, he sees the missed lace, a mistake that could cost him his foot in a truly toxic environment. He goes back and still manages to put on the mask, hood, and oversize butyl rubber gloves, finishing first.

It is easy to see why war planners do not hold chemical or biological weapons in high esteem. Who wants to fight in this getup? The group looks like swamp monsters from the Paleolithic era. They look ready to take a vacation at Love Canal. With the lovely heat outside, and the fact that every inch of their bodies is covered, they look very, very uncomfortable. As a longtime Chemical Corps officer later says, you feel like a roasting marshmallow under all that gear. The sergeant's voice, which had sounded so crisp, now comes through muffled and distant, a problem on the battlefield. In one exercise, government investigators with the General Accounting Office noticed that the instructor threw stones to get the soldiers' attention. But the strangest feeling is the sense of confinement that leads some soldiers to freak out.

"We didn't appreciate the seriousness of putting on the gear until these last five years," says a desk officer at the school who develops doctrine, the basis for how-to manuals that explain what the soldier is expected to do in a biochemical conflict. "There'll be two psychological casualties for each medical or heat exhaustion–dehydration casualty. Other problems are lack of vision, confusion, insecurity. You kill a lot of your own. Four percent fratricide in conventional battlefields. Twenty percent in a chemical environment. Good guys killing good guys. You use twice as much ammunition. It takes twice as long to do anything."

The act of mobilizing an army is like taking an enormous

camping trip. If the trip's destination includes a toxic battle-field, then the soldiers carry not one but two of everything, as well as cleanup and decontamination equipment. Tents, food-handling equipment, helicopters, everything must be protected against the invisible weapons. The result is a logistical night-mare.

That logistical nightmare will only get worse. In the last couple of years, the military has changed its mind about the right way to wage a chemical war. The idea now is not simply to survive, but actually to stay and fight. Since even the military appreciates how ridiculous it would be to fight in any place but the Arctic Circle wearing the current Battledress Overgarment, army labs are busy contemplating ways to cool the soldier down, including backpack air conditioners and to-tally sealed, self-contained, astronaut-style spacesuits.

For the recruits, the next lesson covers the identification of the invisible weapon on the battlefield. This is where chemical and biological weapons go their separate ways. "We have no alarms for biological agents," says the desk officer. "The first alarm is the symptoms." For most biological and toxin weap-ons, two or more days pass before the first wave of people are stricken. By then, it is too late to do much and the attack is usually over.

In the school's classrooms, instructors say that soldiers express real interest in "bio." They know about Yellow Rain from the media's attention, and it sticks in their minds. "Yel-low Rain? I don't see how anybody could deny the evidence," says the desk officer when asked for his opinion on the contro-versy. "They have talked to dozens and dozens of refugees. People are dying in strange ways, large numbers over and over again. No doubt, they're using it as a test ground. I know that DOD [Department of Defense] has conclusive evidence." In fact, he opens a booklet, the army's "Field Manual for NBC Operations."

NBC is not the television network, but military shorthand

for the three big toxic threats—nuclear radiation, biological and chemical weapons. The desk officer flips to the page that reads:

The biological weapons threat to the U.S. is real because:
- The Soviet Union and its allies view toxins as chemicals, not biological agents.
- Soviet-backed forces have used toxins (yellow rain) in Southeast and Southwest Asia in this decade.
- Natural disease even in modern times has caused far more casualties than have weapons. The intentional use of toxins or disease-causing germs could cause even more casualties.
- Biological agents are cheap and easy to produce compared to chemical and nuclear weapons systems. Anyone with a pharmaceutical or brewing industry could produce biological agents.

Since manuals get rewritten every five years or so, this one will be read and used by recruits until 1990.

There are troubling signs that the Yellow Rain story lives on in the business community too. On the third floor of a sleek office building near Lincoln Center in Manhattan resides the magazine publishing empire of Bob Guccione and Kathy Keeton. Behind the pretty blonde receptionist, framed blow-ups of past *Penthouse* and *Omni* magazine covers decorate the walls. There are no extraterrestrial nudes, only a glowing woman wearing the headgear of an Egyptian princess, a drawing of the actor John Belushi literally cracking up, and a raunchy cartoon of Walter Mondale, his private parts covered with a fig leaf.

Evan Koslow works here on a new magazine whose covers may one day also decorate the reception office walls. In his early thirties, with a trim red beard, a nonstop energy, and a doctorate in engineering, Koslow retreats to a warren of temporarily arranged desks, blanketed with mounds of paper and winking computers. On the wall of the cramped editorial headquarters hangs a map of the United States with little flagpins piercing the fifty states, seemingly at random. "Proposed strike targets," says Koslow, then he laughs. "Just kidding." The flags pinpoint businesses that are engaged in nuclear, biological, and chemical defense.

Koslow is editor-in-chief and a prime mover behind *NBC Defense and Technology,* an international journal that made its debut in April 1986. He anticipates the first question that everyone asks.

"It is shocking," he says. "How could *Penthouse* end up backing this? Basically, I was working here, helping Guccione, who was looking at developing a technology and business magazine. I'm an old NBC man and I said, you know, what is really lacking is a magazine devoted to NBC. No one talks to anyone."

Just as the subject of sex was once taboo and unfit for polite conversation, so is the prospect of conducting and coping with a nuclear, biological, and chemical war. Even those in the weapons business veer away, finding the topic too creepy. After all, these are weapons you don't see or hear. But Koslow comes across as a modern man, a hard-boiled realist, an unflinching fact-facer, ready to leaven an otherwise grim subject with a black sense of humor.

"I developed a business plan, didn't think of this firm. Offhandedly, I went to Kathy Keeton's office, and I said, do you happen to know anyone interested in a military magazine? She said, yeah, me. We went to Bob's office. I said I had a magazine more controversial than *Penthouse.* He's a demure man. Sat in deadpan silence. Without much more conversation, they decided to go ahead."

As a business venture, the magazine is betting on the proliferation—real or imagined—of nuclear, biological, and chemical weapons; the more governments spend, the more revenue is anticipated by the magazine, since like all magazines, *NBC Defense and Technology* makes money through advertising. Few of the magazine's advertisers are household names, but most sell protection against invisible weapons, from combat wear to automatic syringes for soldiers to give themselves an antidote.

Since the Reagan administration took office, the U.S. government has dramatically increased spending on NBC protection. Over 70 percent of the chemical warfare budget goes to research, development, and procurement of equipment, most of which aims to protect against the NBC threat. In 1980, the chemical warfare budget stood at $157 *million.* In 1987, it is slated to be $1.14 *billion.*

"This is the first professional journal they've done," says Koslow. "It's not *Guns and Ammo.* It is purely for government military types and other professionals. Soup to nuts about NBC defense. Thirty-thousand subscribers initially. We expect to grow to fifty thousand. The magazine is very unusual and relates to stuff that disturbs everyone on the planet. By golly, there is a lot of curiosity about a magazine that covers that in intimate detail and with authority."

Indeed, the intimate detail disturbs the art director, who tells Koslow in passing that his paste-up people are having a hard time stomaching some of the pictures slated for the first issue. In fact, the explicit sights are sickening. War is never a pretty picture, but nuclear, biological, and chemical weapons devastate their victims in particularly gruesome ways.

When it does appear, the first issue infuses the subject of NBC war with enough fantasy to make the horror look merely spooky. Printed on glossy paper, the magazine is loaded with color photographs showing exotic snakes, burly tanks, iridescent mushroom clouds, lovable children in gas masks, and endless shots of soldiers going about their business suited up like the Three Mile Island cleanup crew. The cover shows two men in gas masks, rifles poised for action, stalking the mysterious enemy through a pale blue romantic mist. So what, if you forgot the mist is toxic?

There is a perverse thrill of novelty in these pages. The magazine puts a new face on the modern warrior, or rather covers the face of the modern warrior with a mask and a hood that resemble a medieval executioner's cowl. In a nihilistic, punk sort of way, NBC war is not only thinkable, but fashionable. You almost expect to see an advertisement for "Poison," the new perfume recently introduced by Christian Dior.

In the voyeuristic tradition of skin magazines, *NBC Defense and Technology* saves the most intimate details for the centerfold. Here spookiness momentarily ceases and graphic reality takes over. The full-page color spread looks inside a mortuary in Tehran. Three men, dead from mustard gas—which was used in World War I and is now being used in the six-year war between Iran and Iraq—their faces contorted, blackened, and pained, lie inside plastic-lined wooden coffins. At the corner of the page, two smaller photographs show close-ups of the enormous, misshapen, and fatal blisters caused by mustard, stark enough to satisfy the clinical questions of a medical student.

The authority promised by Koslow turns out to be self-serving, at least when it comes to Yellow Rain. In its second issue, the magazine reports on a Canadian study that "offers the most compelling evidence to date that 'yellow rain' is indeed a CW agent that has been used in Southeast Asia." The most crucial evidence cited is a plastic bag that the Canadian investigators received from Thai villagers who said they had been victims of a Yellow Rain attack in 1982. The plastic bag, which "may have been part of an actual chemical weapon," contained high quantities of trichothecenes and no pollen, "thus debunking the bee feces theory."

The magazine fails to mention that the origins and the circumstances surrounding the discovery of the bag were so suspect that not even the Canadian investigators came to that conclusion. The plastic bag came from the Thai village of Ban

Sa Tong near the Cambodian border. On February 19, 1982, the village health official said he saw a plane circle five or six times at 5,000 feet. Thirty minutes later, villagers told him that they found a yellow powder covering the rooftops, walls, grounds, and foliage of six homes. The Thai border patrol came to investigate, and a Bangkok TV crew that was coincidentally in the area stopped by to film.

Two weeks later, a team of Canadian investigators appeared, collecting over 200 leaf samples of the yellow powder. No trichothecenes turned up. In photomicrographs, the samples were all found to contain the pollen associated with bee excrement. Since the powder covered only six houses, an area that would be covered by bees on cleansing flights, that led most to the conclusion that a bee shower had taken place and was mistakenly associated with a plane flight overhead.

The Canadians interviewed thirty-three villagers, asking what they were doing at the time of the "attack" and how they felt upon "exposure." The "symptoms" reported most frequently were headache, dizziness, dry throat, loss of appetite, fatigue, weakness, and itching. The team concluded that the yellow substance caused the "symptoms," despite the fact that a Ban Sa Tong health officer told a BBC filmmaker that he considered the whole thing to be a case of hysteria—the association of common complaints with the presumption of a toxin warfare attack.

But two weeks after the Canadians' initial visit, a villager turned in the plastic bag to local authorities, claiming that he had seen it drop from the plane. No one knows why he did not turn it in earlier when the investigation was under way. In photographs, it resembled an ordinary kitchen sandwich bag, 6 to 12 inches on the side. The Canadians reported that they "were skeptical that it was the real container" of a weapon.

They had reason to be. No standard hardware for a biological or chemical weapon uses a plastic bag that resembles those for holding sandwiches. "It is like asking what weapon would use a seven-dollar bill," says Meselson. Even assuming that the

Soviets had taken to using plastic bags for a novel, unforeseen reason, it should have shown some distinctive clues. If the weapon had been dropped from 5,000 feet, its contents would have covered far more than six houses. Since only six houses received the shower, the weapon would have had to explode at a lower altitude. But the investigators found no timer, no release mechanism, nor evidence of powder burns on the bag. The villager who found the bag apparently heard no explosion.

Most important, there was no pollen on the bag. The absence of pollen had obvious implications. If the plastic bag was indeed a remnant of a weapon, then what came out of it? Not the yellow spots found in over 200 samples collected by the Canadians. The Canadians did find a small amount of trichothecenes on the bag. (In March 1983, 52 to 117 parts per million of HT-2 and 85 to 230 ppm of T-2 were found. When reanalyzed in May 1984, 6 ppm of HT-2 and 6.3 ppm of T-2 were found.) But the Canadians did not find the trichothecenes in or around the six homes showered with the yellow powder. If the plastic bag delivered trichothecenes, where were they? The inconsistencies were glaring, but the magazine seemed to dismiss them in favor of a conclusion that served the interest of its subscribers—the military establishment and contractors for whom a bigger Soviet threat translates into bigger budgets.

Despite the article, Koslow is well aware of the limited military utility of biological weapons and the drawbacks that led the Pentagon to renounce them in the first place. "Biological weapons . . . come on, what's the purpose? There are select terrorist or sabotage roles. But sabotage is very risky for the military planner. It must be assumed that you can do it two to three days before the attack and get safely behind enemy lines. There is a high probability of discovery. Are you going to risk retaliation? In my assessment, there are very few cases where a military can do BW."

What about small-scale, covert wars like the one currently being waged in Nicaragua?

"The Nicaraguans claim that their cotton is under attack. Cotton is the most disease-prone crop in America. Everything attacks it. Livestock is more likely. But Nicaragua is small. No way would we chance a livestock attack in a country that small. It is impossible to stop these things once they get going."

In whose interest is it to use biological weapons?

"There are countries that desire a deterrent with which they can scare the living daylights out of their neighbors. Transnational organizations that don't have a country to defend."

So why would a superpower bother with a marginal weapon, attractive only to its enemies?

"We have a lot of money so we tend to spend it."

Biological weapons come along for the ride.

The bumbling scientific investigation of Yellow Rain is seen by many as an utter failure of biological warfare intelligence. It demonstrates not only the problems faced by the intelligence community when analysis is shaped by political agendas but also the inherently difficult nature of tracking biological weapons and the overriding need for careful, thorough investigations.

Biological and chemical warfare intelligence is carried out by a relatively small group of specialists, perhaps fifty or so people based primarily at the Pentagon's Defense Intelligence Agency, the Central Intelligence Agency, the army's Armed Forces Medical Intelligence Center at Fort Detrick, Maryland, the army's Foreign Science and Technology Center in Charlottesville, Virginia, and the air force's Foreign Technology Division at Wright-Patterson Air Force Base in Ohio. Some analysts know the biological weapons business because they hail from the days when the United States had an offensive program. Some are characterized by one Washington, D.C., consultant as "less than top talent."

Whatever the skills of the individual analysts, the analysis of chemical and biological weapons rated a low priority until the 1973 Arab-Israeli war, when nerve gas antidote injectors turned up in captured Egyptian tanks. The U.S. analysts had never seen the type of antidote injector before and were so certain that the Soviets had advanced light years ahead that the army ordered a whole batch of the stuff. When the army got around to testing, it found that one ingredient triggered bad hallucinations. In 1980, the army chief of staff ordered the antidote withdrawn from use. An investigation revealed that the Russians had given atropine, the standard nerve gas antidote, to the Egyptians but the expiration date read 1969. Skeptical of Soviet assurances that the atropine still worked, the Egyptians bought insecticide antidotes, available on the commercial market from Bulgaria and Yugoslavia. It was a U.S. intelligence fiasco from beginning to end, which many regard as all too common in the CBW field.

Like intelligence analysts everywhere, the chemical and biological specialists cull leads, 80 percent by one estimate, from mundane, open sources like newspapers, radio, TV broadcasts, scientific journals, and the eleven military journals regularly published by the Soviets. They couple that reading with stories from émigrés and defectors, satellite photographs, intercepted communications, and their own knowledge of chemical and biological weapons. Still, the analysis of biological weapons, in particular, can stump even the sharpest. "You've got a confounding situation when you talk about biological weapons," says a Pentagon official who does not want to be named. "I don't like to call it confounding anymore. I think it is duplicitous."

At a distance, biological weapons programs leave a barely discernible trail, easily disguised by also doing or appearing to do legitimate work on pharmaceuticals, food processing, agriculture, or medicine. For example, an anthrax vaccine production plant looks identical to a production plant that makes the anthrax germ for a biological weapon, except that the vaccine manufacturer packages the end product in ampules, not bombs. Complications multiply when analysts try to distinguish defensive research from offensive research. Until weapons-related equipment, hardware, and devices enter the picture, the facilities look pretty much the same.

Unlike the manufacturing of a missile or a fighter plane, it does not take much sophistication to produce a biological weapon. In principle, any country that can brew beer—so the saying goes—can make a crude biological weapon. But it takes a country with the fermentation know-how plus a strong medical and military infrastructure to produce a BW arsenal like the one developed by the United States.

Not surprisingly, the United States devotes most of its attention to figuring out what the Soviets are doing. "I wish I knew what the Soviet program was," says a Department of Defense administrator who also asked for anonymity. "Most of the information we have is derived over a long period of time. A lot of it is derived from classified research. A lot is based on defector reports." In 1986 testimony to the House Intelligence Committee, Douglas Feith, then deputy assistant undersecretary of defense for negotiations policy, said, "At the very time when Soviet officials were negotiating and signing the BWC, a high-ranking Soviet defector has reported, the Politburo decided to intensify the Soviet BW program."

One of the defectors may have been Arkady Shevchenko, the Soviet undersecretary of the United Nations who wrote the 1985 best-seller, *Breaking with Moscow*. In it, he says:

> While the military strongly opposed any agreement on chemical or biological weapons, the political leadership, Gromyko, in particular, felt it necessary for propaganda purposes to respond to a proposal by Great Britain to conclude a special, separate convention to prohibit biological warfare as a first step. The military's reaction was to say go ahead and sign the convention: without international controls, who would know anyway? They

refused to consider eliminating their stockpiles and insisted upon further development of these weapons. The toothless convention regarding biological weapons was signed in 1972 but there are no international controls over the Soviet program, which continues apace.

Since 1975, the Pentagon has been skeptical about whether the Soviet Union disarmed as fully as we did. Six months after the treaty formally went into effect, the *Boston Globe* reported on satellite photographs said by administration officials to show that the Soviets were constructing and expanding biological weapons facilities in three cities. On the treaty's first anniversary, the Associated Press reported on satellite photographs that showed six plants that "may be capable of producing biological weapons."

With the advances in genetic engineering in recent years, the U.S. government has become more vocal about its suspicions of Soviet activity in biological warfare. But if you read the charges carefully, they are still filled with uncertainty. In 1984, *Soviet Military Power* reported, "Soviet research efforts in the area of genetic engineering *may* [all emphases added in this paragraph] also have a connection with their biological warfare program. . . . There is an *apparent* effort on the part of the Soviets to transfer selected aspects of genetic engineering research to their biological warfare centers." The same year, John Birkner, an analyst with the Defense Intelligence Agency, admitted that the Soviet use of genetic engineering for biological warfare was "a hypothesis for verification." In "Soviet Non-Compliance," a 1985 report on Soviet treaty violations made by the Arms Control and Disarmament Agency, the United States charged that "the Soviet Union has a prohibited offensive biological warfare *capability* which we do not have and against which we have no defense. This capability *may* include advanced biological agents about which we have little knowledge. Evidence *suggests* that the Soviets are expanding their chemical and toxin warfare capabilities in a manner that has no parallel in NATO's retaliatory or defensive program."

As time passes, the U.S. tone has become harsher. In 1986, Douglas Feith told the House Intelligence Committee that "the Soviet Union has not only violated the Biological Weapons Convention but every major prohibition in it. The scale and seriousness of the Soviet BW program are formidable. There are at least seven biological warfare centers in the USSR, all with unusually rigorous security. One such facility constitutes a veritable city with a large number of residents who work and live there full time, isolated from the rest of society. The level of effort committed to research on various natural poisons—such as snake venoms—is far in excess of what could be justified to deal with such substances for purely medical or public health purposes."

Given the story of Yellow Rain, one wonders if these public allegations about Soviet activity are built on equally questionable evidence. Are the allegations based on what analysts believe the Soviet Union is technically capable of doing? Are they based on what analysts believe to be probable by their reading of circumstantial evidence? Or are they actually confirmed by first-hand observations? There is a world of difference between what is possible and what has been confirmed.

Due to the inaccessibility of classified information, these questions are impossible to answer. Instead, consider the political purposes served by publicizing these beliefs. Julian Perry Robinson, chemical and biological weapons expert and senior research fellow at the University of Sussex in England, has noted that the decision to leak information to the press can be seen as a way to signal the administration's own worries and to invite answers, to cope with honest doubts and keep an issue alive before the court of public opinion. But in a climate of distrust, where analysts tend to assume the worst, the allegations also lend themselves to disinformation and propaganda and to a frightening image of Soviet capabilities and intentions that can easily fuel a biological arms race.

"If true, this portrayal should be of great concern in the West and elsewhere," Robinson writes. "But it should still be of concern even if it is not true, for it threatens to kill arms control and, by stirring up alarm and despondency about the sufficiency of one aspect of Western war preparedness, to promote a divisive and dangerous sense of insecurity. Moreover, if the reports are false, there is the question of how the USSR has been reacting to them: Might not the reports be presentable as a carefully orchestrated campaign of calumny aimed at, for example, loosening of the current political constraints on Western chemical weapons rearmament, even a cover for it?"

The publicity helps define the Soviet threat in the area of biological weapons. Whatever the United States does or does not do in its biological warfare program traces, on paper at least, back to the Soviet threat. In military parlance, the "Soviet threat" pops up frequently, often spoken as a single word, or shortened to "The Threat," since the country's principal adversary has not changed in thirty-five years. Once The Threat has been defined, the Pentagon designs research, training, hardware, doctrine, service, and facilities to counter it. When the Department of Defense approaches Congress for its yearly budget, The Threat is invoked. When taxpayers balk, The Threat is raised. It serves as a bureaucratic bogeyman and a rationale for the Pentagon's every move.

It makes perfect sense to design military programs to meet the enemy threat, but in practice, it rarely works that way on either side. In *The Threat: Inside the Soviet Military Machine*, author Andrew Cockburn writes:

> There is very little evidence that either the Americans or Russians have actually initiated research and development in response to a move by the opposition. Almost invariably, the development of a new weapon or expansion in production is

justified by being simply a response to some initiative on the enemy's part. But the record indicates that the desire for the new weapon, or larger production line, came first; only afterwards is the threat discovered that the weapon is supposed to meet.

Since World War II, weapons gaps between the Soviet Union and the United States have been trumpeted in public and widely disparaged in private. In the 1950s, it was the bomber gap. Based on the sighting of a new Russian bomber that looked like the U.S. long-distance strategic bomber at the annual May Day military parade in Moscow, the air force argued that the Soviets were far more advanced, far more threatening than the United States believed. It turned out that the Russian bomber looked better than it really was. It lacked the jet engine of its American counterparts and had been built in smaller numbers than initially believed. (The Russians had flown the same plane in different formations, inflating in our eyes the actual size of their fleet.) But in response to the feared bomber gap, the United States boosted the size of its own strike force.

Next, it was the missile gap. In 1956, at the height of the Cold War, Senator Stuart Symington declared that the United States was falling behind the USSR in the development of guided missiles. He had no specific evidence until a year later when the Russians launched Sputnik. A country with the sophistication and skill to make a satellite launching rocket was surely making advances with missiles. The air force pushed the idea that the Soviets had a larger than suspected ICBM force. In his election campaign, Kennedy carried on about the missile gap but his opponent, then Vice-President Richard Nixon, had seen photographs taken by spy planes and knew it did not exist. But in response to the feared gap, the United States boosted the size of its ICBM force.

According to the Reagan administration, the lesson of

Yellow Rain is that the Soviets have waged biological warfare. The United States has boosted its budget for BW research, justifying it in the name of defense. If history is a guide, one must ask: Is the threat of biological warfare being inflated by those who want the United States to get back into the business? Is this the gene gap?

SEVEN

The Gene Gap

"Call it the technological imperative. It is a shorthand way of saying that our society is poised to take advantage of almost any new technology provided someone can make money off it, or the military can find a use for it."
—Robert Sinsheimer, Chancellor, University of California, Santa Cruz, and biophysicist

The renewed U.S. efforts in biological warfare are officially justified in the name of the Soviet threat. Unofficially, they are fueled by something far more powerful, uncontrollable, and menacing: the fear that science will produce a new, improved generation of biological weapons. It has not yet happened, but, like the myriad variations on the story of the mad scientist–evil genius who brews destruction in the laboratory, it exerts a formidable grip on the imagination. In an age in which many ideas are taken from laboratory to arsenal in a seemingly inexorable, lockstep process, a strong and adamant suspicion may be enough to rekindle a biological arms race.

In 1969, on the eve of discovering simple ways to recombine DNA, the Pentagon supported the renunciation of biological weapons because they were full of headaches and uncertainties that made them only marginally useful. Since then, genetic engineering has revolutionized all biomedical research, opening a horizon of possibilities that the United States had only dimly glimpsed when it decided to get out of the weapons business. These possibilities, as they come into sharper focus, are introducing a new variable into the fragile arms control equation. "We have changed our opinion about the military utility of BW," Douglas Feith told the *Washington Post.* "What we are saying is that BW, based on the new technologies, may indeed be a great weapon."

Many disagree with the Pentagon's reassessment on the grounds that genetic engineering does not overcome the specific headaches and uncertainties that made biological weapons unattractive to the troop commander. For example, the new technologies do not make the weapons any easier to aim or guide, any less prone to backfire on one's own troops. "The rational arguments against tailor-made biological weapons are no different from those against naturally occurring ones. They make no more and no less military sense," declared the British medical journal, *The Lancet,* in an editorial.

But something irrational may be taking place in military establishments where research is conducted on biological warfare. The scientists there are not asking what makes sense, but what is possible. If policymakers fail to distinguish between the two, the answers are more likely to shape the future of biological warfare than any controversial charges about treaty violations. "Outlandish crazy things can really catch on," writes Susan Wright, historian of science at the University of Michigan. "One cannot eliminate the possibility that if the treaty was eroded, or genetic engineering discovered a novel thing, that this [BW] would not be tried."

As a rule, the Americans and the Soviets look aggressively at the military applications of science, especially when scientific research has led to such an incandescent technological breakthrough as genetic engineering. Given that rule, it was probably inevitable that military establishments would explore genetic engineering and its implications for biological warfare. But it was an inevitability that some scientists feared and hoped to forestall. Their efforts met with little success.

One could say that the revolution in molecular biology began in 1953 when James Watson and Francis Crick, working at Cambridge University, cracked the genetic code of life, deciphering the chemical alphabet and the double helix structure of DNA, the molecule universal to all forms of life. Working in the dim boundaries between chemistry and biology, the molecular biologists began to ask questions they could never have asked before about the mechanisms of life. How do genes work? Why are some diseases, like Huntington's, passed down from generation to generation? What allows viruses to invade and take over the DNA of a cell? Where do bacteria acquire resistance to penicillin and other wonder drugs?

In 1970, MIT professor Har Gobind Khorana created the first artificial gene by linking chemicals together in the test tube. But the astonishing breakthrough came one year later when Stanley Cohen at Stanford University and Herbert Boyer at the University of California at San Francisco discovered naturally occurring enzymes that gave scientists unprecedented control over manipulating the genetic code. Like surgical knives, some enzymes cut DNA in precise spots. Like surgical stitches, other enzymes neatly sew the DNA back together again. The enzymes allowed scientists to take a gene from one organism and insert it into another, to delete a gene or to add a gene, in short to scramble the genetic code.

The ability to manipulate the genetic code meant that its byproducts could also be manipulated. A gene is a segment of DNA that directs the synthesis of many different types of molecules. Genes might direct the production of an enzyme that regulates body growth, or a toxin that fends off enemies. Because the chemical sequence of the DNA determines the chemical sequence (and thus the structure and function) of the molecule to be produced, scientists say that genes "code" for particular molecules.

Genetic engineering theoretically gave scientists the ability to produce large quantities of potent molecules that had previously been available only in tiny amounts. For example, by inserting the gene that codes for the tetanus toxin inside the DNA of a bacterial cell, scientists could cause billions of bacteria to start producing billions of molecules of toxin. With the help of genetic engineering, in other words, scientists were able to turn bacteria into factories, production lines ready to make almost any molecule they wanted.

The scientists soon grasped the inherent dangers that would accompany this newfound power. For a thesis project, a Stanford graduate student named Janet Mertz planned to splice a tumor-causing monkey virus into the bacterium *E. coli,* which lives harmlessly inside the large intestine of every human being. She wanted to know if the virus would be expressed (synthesized) by the bacterial cell. But someone asked her if she wasn't worried about the *E. coli* escaping from the laboratory and wreaking havoc? Even with the safest lab bench techniques, who could say what would happen with a chimera that had never existed before? Her thesis advisor argued that a small but distinct possibility of a hazard existed, and Mertz chose another thesis project. As she would later say, "I started thinking in terms of the atomic bomb and things. I didn't want to be the person who went ahead and created a monster that killed a million people."

But the idea that genetic engineering might unleash a dangerous monster had sprung up and needed to be faced. The scientists moved cautiously, fearful of alarming the public or jeopardizing their funding and say-so over the types of research they could do. They eagerly wanted to do genetic engineering experiments, but also knew they bore a responsibility to the public to conduct them safely.

In 1973, Paul Berg, Mertz's thesis advisor and a well-respected biochemist, organized a conference at Asilomar in Pacific Grove, California, inviting one hundred prestigious molecular biologists to discuss the potential hazards of gene-splicing experiments. The most practical outcome of the conference was that the National Institutes of Health (NIH) in Washington, D.C., set up what has come to be known as the RAC, or the Recombinant DNA Advisory Committee, to develop safety guidelines for dangerous experiments conducted in NIH-funded labs. In the interim, Berg and others asked for a voluntary moratorium until the scientific community could reach a consensus about the risks of genetic engineering at a larger international meeting. Once again, the meeting would take place at Asilomar, overlooking the Pacific Ocean.

David Baltimore sat on the organizing committee for the second Asilomar conference. Intense, with piercing eyes, a trim beard, and a passion for fly fishing, Baltimore now heads the prestigious Whitehead Institute for Biomedical Research, a quasi-private organization affiliated with MIT. Baltimore won the Nobel Prize for Physiology and Medicine in 1975 for his work on tumor-causing RNA viruses.

Fresh from criticizing the military's adventurism in Vietnam and protesting its secret programs in biological warfare, Baltimore approached Asilomar with a keen sense of the scientist's social responsibility. In the late 1960s, he and others had pushed the American Society of Microbiology to adopt a resolution that its membership would not work on biological weapons. It was a provocative and unsuccessful move, since a large segment of the society's membership worked at Fort Detrick. "My own interest in biological warfare led me naturally to be concerned about biological safety," he says.

The organizing committee set the format of the meeting, creating three working groups that would prepare position papers on the hazards of different types of experiments. The committee selected Richard Novick to head the Plasmid

Working Group. Plasmids are loose strands of DNA found inside a bacterial cell that are easily exchanged between bacteria and carry genes that code for the bacteria's resistance to particular antibiotics. When it comes to shuffling DNA, plasmids make good vehicles.

Novick works in a ragtag office with a grimy view of Bellevue Hospital on Manhattan's East Side. He is director of the Public Health Research Institute of the City of New York, a private research organization where he has worked since 1965, specializing in the molecular biology of antibiotic resistance, particularly in the bacterium *Staphylococcus aureus*. Trained as a physician, Novick first heard about biological warfare in the mid-1960s when the army invited him to apply for a research grant on the bacteria that causes food poisoning. And he knew Baltimore from trying to get the American Society of Microbiology to go on record against biological warfare.

At the second Asilomar meeting, in 1975, Baltimore and Novick did not share the same agenda regarding the impact of genetic engineering on biological weapons. "In his opening remarks, Baltimore said that BW would not be discussed," says Sheldon Krimsky, Tufts University historian and author of a social history of the genetic engineering debate. After all, there was a Biological Weapons Convention; Fort Detrick had been dismantled; it seemed pointless to stir up fears when they had so expertly been lain to rest.

In fact, the Asilomar agenda was designed to sidestep any moral or ethical dilemmas and focus only on the question of safety. According to Novick, "The atmosphere at Asilomar was that the whole idea of gene manipulation, gene splicing, genetic engineering was in some jeopardy because of some of the press it had gotten, and I think there was a strong feeling among the," he pauses, "pardon the expression, power group, at Asilomar that this issue [BW] ought not to be brought into the fore because it might jeopardize the whole operation."

But Novick did bring it up. The report of the Plasmid

Working Group ran to thirty-five single-spaced typed pages and, in very clear language, spelled out the broad environmental concerns of genetically engineering bacteria. The report recommended that the experiments be classified in six groups, from those with insignificant hazards to those with hazards potentially so severe they should not be done. Toward the end, the report included this politically charged statement: "We believe that the greatest potential for biohazard involving alterations of microorganisms relates to possible military applications. We believe strongly that construction of genetically altered microorganisms for any military purpose should be expressly prohibited by international treaty and we urge that such prohibition be agreed upon as expeditiously as possible." The organizing committee, however, would not touch the issue of biological warfare, although it rested on the minds of other participants, including a team of stony-silent Russian scientists who, according to Krimsky, were skeptical about the moratorium. "They felt it was a way to keep them from developing this as a weapon."

Mindful of the physicists' role in constructing the atom bomb and their subsequent guilt and horror over the massive destruction unleashed by their discoveries, many molecular biologists wanted to prevent the use of genetic engineering for nefarious purposes. "The potential for misuse was obvious from the onset," says Richard Goldstein, professor of molecular genetics at Boston University School of Medicine. "When it was understood that you could move genes, it became a question of who would make the decisions about the uses [of genetic engineering]." But these decisions could not be easily controlled without the scientists forfeiting their academic freedom.

In the tradition of science, the discoveries of genetic engineering were widely disseminated and shared. Like Pandora's box, once the knowledge had been opened, how could it be controlled? As Columbia biochemist Erwin Chargaff said at a

1977 meeting sponsored by the National Academy of Sciences, "Science is not equipped to restrain or police the sick imagination of a few of its practitioners."

The RAC stuck to its narrowly drawn purpose of regulating laboratory safety in labs with NIH funding. In a new area of research where the risks could only be guessed, the committee initially erred on the side of caution. The guidelines prohibited a handful of experiments outright because they seemed so dangerous. At the top of the list of forbidden experiments were those that involved the deliberate creation of dangerous microbes which, if they escaped, could cause untold damage. They included the introduction of genes that code for (that is, direct the synthesis of) toxins, plant pathogens, or antibiotic resistance into normally harmless microorganisms.

But as time wore on, the scientists admitted that they had been overly cautious, and RAC relaxed its guidelines, requiring only that scientists first apply for permission to do the forbidden experiments. The relaxation of the guidelines coincided with the reawakening of government interest in biological weapons. The anthrax outbreak in Sverdlovsk and Yellow Rain in Southeast Asia put biological weapons back into the newspapers after a five-year hiatus, and put the idea into public discussion that the Soviets had sped ahead, drawing on the revolution in genetic engineering while the United States stood helplessly watching.

It also coincided with the Department of Defense's increasing sponsorship of genetic engineering work. In 1980, *Science* magazine quoted an unnamed DOD official who said, "We are not now using recombinant DNA techniques in any of these efforts, partly to keep ourselves out of trouble." By "trouble," the official explained that he meant public protest. But by the time the Reagan administration took office, the Department of Defense took the plunge. In 1983, it funded twenty-seven recombinant DNA projects, most with outside contractors. By 1985, the number had grown to sixty, with twenty-one being done in house, and at least seven on work related to biological weapons.

As the military funding for biological research increased, federal support for the life sciences decreased. Between 1980 and 1984, $50 million in funds for biological studies were transferred from the civilian to the military sector. Many researchers began to argue that the shift in funding was skewing biomedical research. "The army funds research on viruses that make people sick in North Africa, not North Roxbury," MIT geneticist Jonathan King told the *Wall Street Journal* in September 1986. Even within the military, funds shifted from research on medically important diseases to medical defense against biological warfare. At Walter Reed Army Institute of Research in Washington, D.C.—which specializes in research on diarrheal diseases, the number three killer in the world—civilian scientists in the biochemistry division faced layoffs because of budget cuts. In a memo, the director told them they could save their jobs by forming "a credible research group in biological toxin defense." They were eventually reassigned to work on BW matters.

The resurgence of interest in biological weapons was clear, particularly when the army asked the National Academy of Sciences to do a classified study on BW. The academy refused, but the request drew Novick back into action, and into conflict again with Baltimore. In 1982, Novick and Richard Goldstein, a molecular biologist then at Harvard Medical School and a member of RAC, proposed an amendment to the RAC guidelines in a letter that read: "The experience of many scientists throughout the world during the past seven or eight years has demonstrated that original fears of catastrophic laboratory accidents involving microorganisms constructed by molecular cloning were largely unfounded." But they went on to repeat their concerns about the hazards of the forbidden experiments—transferring antibiotic resistance to bacteria that cause clinically important diseases, inserting genes that control the synthesis of toxins into bacteria, and deliberately releasing genetically engineered bacteria into the environment.

"A fourth area—one that is perhaps of greatest concern, has never been adequately addressed by the RAC. This is the use of recombinant DNA technology for the development of new weapons of biological warfare. It is our position that the use of molecular cloning for the deliberate construction of biological weapons is, per se, the most serious biohazard imaginable for this technology and that it constitutes an egregious misuse of scientific knowledge." They wanted the eighteen-member RAC to add nine words to Section I-D of its regulations: "Construction of biological weapons by molecular cloning is prohibited."

Most letters to the RAC supported the proposal. But Baltimore, who also sat on the RAC, did not. When the meeting convened, packed with observers and representatives from the Department of Defense, the media, and the business community, Baltimore led the discussion. He said the proposal generated tremendous initial sympathy because the concept of biological warfare is so horrible. But he found the amendment dangerous because it suggested that something was wrong with the BWC treaty, a no-confidence vote that could only weaken it. He did not want to telegraph a message that the United States found the treaty inadequate or somehow not explicit in its failure to prohibit biological weapons made by genetic engineering. Could the wording of the amendment echo, or reinforce, the treaty? Members suggested compromise wording consistent with that of the treaty. But in the end, Baltimore and others balked, voting the amendment down 17 to 2.

"It seemed like an innocuous but reasonable proposal," says Goldstein. "But no one wanted to deal with it. It was too emotional and too sensational." Shortly thereafter, in October 1982, the RAC approved a request to clone diphtheria toxin. By 1983, the RAC guidelines dropped all restrictions on toxin cloning experiments, except for the most potent toxins on earth, those the military viewed as biological weapons candidates. In toxin parlance, these have an LD-50 ("LD" stands for "lethal dose") of less than 100 nanograms/kilo. In other words, it takes less than 100 nanograms (a nanogram is one-billionth of a gram) of these toxins for each kilo of an animal's body weight to kill 50 percent of all animals tested. For humans, that translates to a droplet smaller than the head of a pin.

In 1984, researchers at the Uniformed Services University of the Health Sciences (USUHS), the military's medical school, applied to RAC to clone the *Shiga* toxin to make a vaccine against shigellosis, a form of diarrhea that sweeps across Third World countries, claiming the lives of many babies. It is no secret that Detrick researchers have also viewed and studied the *Shiga* toxin as a biological weapon. The USUHS researchers maintained the innocence of their work but Jeremy Rifkin stepped in and, along with arms control expert Paul Warnke, demanded that the RAC table the proposal until an arms control impact statement could be written. (They are required for programs involving technology with potential military applications.) The RAC refused.

Robert Sinsheimer, chancellor of the University of California at Santa Cruz and a prominent biophysicist, wondered how the Soviets would interpret these experiments. "I think you have to look at this from a real-world point of view, which is to suppose you are in Russia and you read that NIH has approved this experiment. You are not too paranoid to read something into it. The problem is that no one at NIH is looking at this from, if you will, an arms control perspective."

At the same time, the fledgling biotechnology industry felt the impact of the military's growing budgets for biological warfare defense. In 1986, the United States biotechnology industry consisted of over two hundred companies, representing an investment of $2.5 billion and very few products. While

human insulin, growth hormone, and a few diagnostic kits—
like those used for in-home pregnancy testing kits—had
reached the market, most companies were still in the research
and development stages, many exhausting the first round of
investment capital provided for start-up. Military funding was,
by and large, welcome.

In 1984, the army awarded nine contracts to develop test
kits using monoclonal antibodies (the same concept as home
pregnancy test kits) for detecting biological warfare pathogens
on the battlefield. The pathogens included plague, Q-fever,
meningitis, VEE, coccidioisis, and Rift Valley Fever, but the
list would later grow to include a total of twenty-two diseases.
The $2.5 million went to Covalent Technology corporation,
Daryl Laboratories, Dynatech R and D Diagnostics, Electro-
Nucleonics, Enzo Biochem, Genetic Diagnostics, International
Health Sciences, Litton Bionetics, and Microbiological Associates.

It bothered some researchers to take money from the military. "We have a young staff and it is hard to convince folks we
should be talking to DOD," says a spokesperson for Dynatech.
"But this is not a classified project. What could be an endog-
enous disease in one area could be a warfare agent in another.
My mentality would be very different if I thought it was a warfare situation."

The same hesitations came up at New England Bio Labs in
Beverly, Massachusetts, a leading supply house of the enzymes
essential for genetic engineering, when it received large purchase orders from the military. (The orders came from the
navy's Biosciences Lab [NBL]. NBL was closed down in 1987
after being in the BW business for fifty-three years, longer than
any other military laboratory. It had originally been housed by
the Department of Bacteriology at the University of California
at Berkeley until 1950, when in response to internal pressure, it
moved off-campus to the Oakland Naval Supply Center. During the Vietnam War, the lab, then linked to the University's

School of Public Health, drew/picketers who called it the School of Public Death. In the early 1980s, it produced the monoclonal antibodies against the BW pathogens that would be used to make the detector kits.) "I didn't want the product of my efforts being used to clone tetanus toxin," explains biochemist Mike Nelson. Nelson knew how genetic engineering had revolutionized the economics of toxin production. When he was a Princeton graduate student in the early 1970s, Nelson said he synthesized his own ricin toxin, extracting it from castor beans because it could not be purchased from a commercial supply house. He estimates that genetic engineering has reduced the production price a thousand to a million times, depending on the toxin. It has also shortened the manufacturing time to a minimum of one year and reduced the initial investment to $50,000.

New England Bio Labs did something unusual and called a vote. Should the company sell to the military? How did the employees feel about the possible misuse of their labors? While Nelson had gathered no evidence that the United States was making biological weapons, a consoling finding, he could not guarantee, in view of the economic incentives, that the temptation was not there. If we don't sell to the military, someone said, others will. When the company voted, the majority agreed to keep selling.

The Pentagon feared that advances in commercial biotechnology would strengthen Soviet efforts in biological warfare. Indeed in just a few years, the biotech business had ressurrected and recast some of the infrastructure dismantled by the treaty. As James Larrick, chief scientist at Cetus Immune Research Laboratories in Palo Alto, California, noted in a 1983 letter to *Nature,* the British science magazine, biotechnology companies were now on the verge of manufacturing large quantities of toxins, particularly ricin and diphtheria, that would be combined with antibodies, creating magic bullets that, one hoped, would destroy cancerous cells. What was once solely produced by Fort Detrick would soon be available on the open market. "This is laudable but a potential Pandora's box is about to be opened," he wrote. "It is my fear that these toxins could be used for military purposes."

Likewise there was a resurgence of interest, among agro-chemical giants like Rohm & Haas, Ciba-Geigy, and Monsanto, in the deliberate release of microorganisms for agricultural purposes. For example, you could improve a crop's resistance to cold weather by spraying it with bacteria that prevent the formation of ice. The knowledge needed to formulate the bacteria in such a way that they survive the spraying and the adverse conditions in the environment, as well as the technology to spray the microbes, closely overlap the knowledge and technology needed for germ warfare.

It was no surprise then that under secretary of defense Fred Ikle singled out microbiology as one of the sciences and technologies that "poses the greatest risk to U.S. security." The Pentagon moved to restrict exports, first by putting biotech-nology on the Militarily Critical List of Technologies, a watch list that covers everything from robotics to semiconductors and sensors. The most recent MCLT flagged small-bore nozzles, capable of spraying aerosols 1 to 10 microns in size, tiny enough to pierce the lungs and enter the bloodstream; microencapsulation equipment that can be used to "harden" germs, protecting them from sunlight and dessication; high-ca-pacity culturing vessels and filtration equipment needed to mass-produce toxins; the equipment needed to construct and operate a maximum containment laboratory.

Alfred Hellman, technical advisor on biotechnology to the secretary of commerce and consultant to the army on its BW vaccine development program, was working to insure that the Pentagon list did not lead to unnecessarily restrictive export controls. There are people at the Pentagon, he jokes, who would not sell shoelaces to the Soviets. "We're trying to define what to control," he says. "Is it feasible to control? Is it necessary? Are these things of such a critical nature that they'd be giving our adversaries a significant advantage? Is it available through other sources?"

Any attempts to limit exports met with strong reaction from the biotechnology business community, which does not believe that restrictions will have any impact on Soviet development of biological weapons. Alan Goldhammer, director of technical affairs of the Industrial Biotechnology Association, says, "I can't think of anything manufactured in this country that is not manufactured in Sweden, Switzerland, Japan, or other countries that have liberal trade policies with Eastern-bloc countries. Is there a way to prevent the technology from being used for nefarious purposes? The answer is no. All the things are available in the open literature, so what is the point?"

In fact, the Pentagon would have been happier if the open literature was not so open. In 1984, DOD announced plans to create a new category of research contract, dubbed "classified but sensitive." The Pentagon asked for the right to review scientific papers prior to publication and delete information deemed sensitive to national security. But the proposal died in the face of overwhelming university opposition.

What would the new generation of genetically engineered biological weapons look like? First, consider what the United States says the Soviets are doing. In April 1984, *Soviet Military Power,* a slick, well-illustrated Pentagon pamphlet produced once a year, blasted the Soviets for using genetic engineering in seven top-security biological warfare centers. According to the pamphlet, "For biological warfare purposes, genetic engineering could open a large number of possibilities. . . . Normally harmless, non-disease producing organisms could be modified to become highly toxic, or produce diseases for which an opponent has no known treatment, or other agents now considered to be too unsuitable for storage or bio-

logical warfare applications could be changed sufficiently to be
an effective agent."

Shortly afterward, the *Wall Street Journal*'s editorial page
followed with an unprecedented eight-part series called "Beyond Yellow Rain—The Threat of Soviet Genetic Engineering." In the first part, editorial-page writer William
Kucewicz wrote, "The worst fears of molecular biologists may
soon be realized. A seven-month investigation by the *Wall
Street Journal* reveals that the Soviet Union is engaged in an
intensive research program focused on using the revolutionary
technique of recombinant DNA to create a new generation of
germ warfare agents." He compared the splintering of the gene
to the splitting of the atom and raised the specter of a worldwide plague that could rival nuclear war. The yardstick for
horror was changing.

Kucewicz's sources were Soviet émigrés who did not themselves work on military genetic engineering projects and had
left the Soviet Union by 1979. He coupled their stories with a
Soviet literature review that covered ricin, botulinum, snake
venom, and other lethal compounds. Based on his own as-
sumptions about the Soviets and their economy, he concluded
that the Soviets sustained an extensive biological warfare effort
dedicated to exploiting the latest advances in genetic engineering.

While the series found willing ears in Washington, the scientific community reacted with skepticism and criticism. According to Elkan Blout, a Harvard Medical School biochemist
who has collaborated for the last twelve years with Yuri Ov-
chinnikov, the man fingered by the *Journal* as the mastermind
of the Soviet BW program, the series was an unwarranted attack. "They have no real evidence that this work is in any way
related to BW," he says. A literature review of American research would reveal a great amount of attention being paid to
the same toxins—but for ostensibly peaceful purposes. Norton
Zinder, a Rockefeller University geneticist and a member of
the army's Defense Science Board, ridiculed the *Journal*'s

claim that the Soviets were trying to create a cobra venom-producing strain of the influenza virus. "The flu virus is the one virus I consider impossible to modify," he says.

Most scientists dismiss the idea that genetic engineering will allow weapons makers to create a Doomsday Bug or an Andromeda Strain, simply because scientists know too little about the mechanisms of pathogenicity or infectivity to make "improvements." "Attempting to create a worse pathogen is preposterous," says Novick. "There are pathogens out there that you will never equal in terms of deadliness." Stanley Falkow, a microbiologist at Stanford Medical School, agrees. "There is a certain arrogance about people who think they can do bacteriological warfare. We don't understand a great deal about the organisms that cause disease."

Within the Department of Defense, veteran observers of biological warfare do not believe in the Doomsday Bug either. "People think of genetic engineering as being the creation of a new organism. Not necessarily so," says one official who asked for anonymity. "My own view is that we will alter organisms so they behave the way we want them to behave. What concerns us, with the advent of biotechnology, is if you can get some organisms with a shorter incubation time, then it starts to become attractive for tactical battlefields, which has been a drawback in the past." In the past, BW was seen primarily as a strategic weapon, useful for striking the enemy's homeland but not useful for killing soldiers on a battlefield.

It is clear that genetic engineering brings down the cost of some biological weapons and lengthens the list of candidates. "Some of the new techniques have made it feasible to produce materials in large quantities which would have been unavailable ten years ago," says another Pentagon official. For example, it took Detrick scientists almost two decades to isolate over thirty grams of saxitoxin. With genetic engineering, that could be brewed in months instead of years and in huge vats instead of precious cupfuls.

It also means that, with less effort than expended in the

past, viruses and bacterial strains can be modified ever so slightly to elude wonder drugs and vaccines. "It doesn't take too much smarts to realize that the selection [of BW agents] can be much greater," says Colonel David Huxsoll, commander of the U.S. Army Medical Research Institute of Infectious Diseases at Fort Detrick.

In a May 1986 report to Congress justifying the need for the BL-4 laboratory at Dugway, the army listed possibilities that few, if any, scientists would dispute. Beneath the dry language emerges the army's view of the next generation of biological warfare agents:

—Viral pathogens could be constructed to maximize infectivity and pathogenicity. Infectious particles could be modified to increase or decrease their environmental stability, persistency and potency.

—Naturally occurring protein toxins could be made in host organisms by modifying their DNA. Plant and/or fungal toxins could be mass produced.

—Physiologically active peptides have significant potential to be developed for future biological warfare agents. They are active at very low concentrations. Their activity covers the full range of life processes, mental and physical.

—Potent toxins, which until now were available only in minute quantities and only upon isolation from immense amounts of biological materials, can now be prepared in industrial quantities after a relatively short developmental period . . . as short as 9 months from concept to full-scale production. This process consists of identifying genes, encoding for the desired molecules, and transferring the sequence to a receptive micro-organism which then becomes capable of producing the substance. The recombinant organisms may then be cultured and grown at any desired scale. They might be employed as agents themselves or used to produce toxins which can be extracted and concentrated.

—Biotechnology could be used to alter the immunological character of agents for which vaccines have already been developed, thus circumventing protective properties of the vaccines.

—It is possible to artificially produce the natural biological substances which exert potent regulatory effects on the body. These substances are normally present in the body in minute quantities and control mental states; mood and emotion; perception; organ function; growth and repair; temperature; and other body processes. These substances are not considered toxic and are indispensable for the normal functioning of the human body. But even slight imbalances can cause profound psychological effects, leading to incapacitation and death.

From the list of possibilities opened by genetic engineering, the Pentagon has taken a leap that many find frightening for its illogic. "The stunning advances over the last five to ten years in the field of biotechnology ... mean more than new foods, pharmaceuticals, and fertilizers," Douglas Feith, then deputy assistant undersecretary of defense for negotiations policy, testified to the House Intelligence Committee in 1986. "They mean new and better weapons for any country willing to violate ... the international norm against the possession of such weapons. . . . The prevailing judgment of years ago that BW is not a militarily significant weapon is now quite unsustainable. BW can be designed to be effective across the spectrum of combat, including special operations and engagements at the tactical level."

But history contradicts the Pentagon's new conclusion. In 1969, the Department of Defense decided that biological weapons were only marginally useful, in large part because their effects proved difficult to guide, predict, or control. They spread in a cloud, and thus their impact varied, depending on the wind, temperature, sun, humidity, and landscape. They could not easily be tested. Despite the advent of genetic engineering, these problems and liabilities remain unsolved, casting doubts on the Pentagon's claim that, based on the new technologies, BW may indeed be a great weapon.

What is frightening is that the Pentagon has equated novelty with military significance. The assumption that novelty always confers a military advantage and the expectation that an enemy will exploit every conceivable advantage override the more pragmatic conclusion, first reached by Nixon in 1969, that biological weapons are riddled with special problems that limit their military and political usefulness. At the very least, the claim will accelerate the exploration of genetically engineered biological weapons. At the worst, it could lead the world back into the biological weapons business. If biological weapons are so great, why don't we have them? If the treaty is a failure, why don't we have BW as a deterrent? These are natural questions for policymakers to ask.

"If the nuclear path is increasingly blocked as a plausible means, then other options become correspondingly more attractive," explains Richard Falk, Princeton University professor of international law and author (with Robert J. Lifton) of *Indefensible Weapons.* "One would predict . . . that there will be strong pressures to at least explore whether biological weapons could not be introduced into the military capabilities of a major power like the United States. You can even imagine certain rather humanitarian justifications being advanced such as the weapons could be incapacitating rather than lethal, and it would be a way to humanize warfare so that no property in the cities would be destroyed, that it would help give war back its good name again. My sense is that we are just at the early stages of grasping the full implications of potential military extensions of genetic engineering."

Ironically, arms control advocates see the advances in genetic engineering as a distraction, an obfuscation of the real reasons that the United States gave up BW. Since biological weapons are still cheap, and the superpowers need to deter their use and proliferation, now more than ever the logic of the ban remains steadfast. In this regard, it matters little if at all, they argue, what genetic engineering can create or what the Soviets may be chasing. "The idea of unilateral renunciation is predicated on the principle that one is entirely unconcerned with any possible action by a potential adversary," testified Richard Novick of the Public Health Research Institute of the City of New York at a congressional hearing in December 1985. "The advent of genetic engineering cannot alter the fact that biological weapons have no place in open warfare, and they are useless as a deterrent."

In this century, scientific and technological advances have paced the arms race. That fact is not likely to change in the future. The possibility that genetic engineering would weaken the treaty was foreseen when it was negotiated. To the Geneva Conference Committee on Disarmament, Joshua Lederberg, Nobel laureate, geneticist, and now president of Rockefeller University, made some informal remarks in 1972 that now seem prophetic. He said, "Molecular biology might be exploited for military purposes and result in a biological weapons race whose aim could well become the most efficient means of removing man from the planet."

PART II

LEGACIES

EIGHT

Inhuman Experiments

REGARDING BW TRAINING

*Class Motto—We seek something which can not be seen, smelt
   or felt*
Discovered by means which we do not have
*To be cured by something which we make from nothing, not
   later than yesterday*

Class Colors—globigii yellow and methylene blue

Class Song—(Tune-Mares Eat Oats)
Saprophytes and parasites
And little botulinus
Hyaluronidase too
Wouldn't you?
Hyaluronidase too
Wouldn't you?

Class Yell—
Brucellosis, Psittacosis
Pee! You! Bah!
Antibodies, Antitoxin
Rah! Rah! Rah!

   —1945 document found in the National Archives

In Washington, D.C., just across the street from the Capitol, the House Committee on Veterans' Affairs held a well-attended hearing on September 17, 1986. Under the glare of lights and in front of four swiveling television cameras, Montana representative Pat Williams spoke into the microphone:

"Some veterans today, veterans captured and imprisoned in World War II's Pacific Theater, have a story to tell and an agonizing chapter in their lives to resolve. . . . These men are victims of a terrible secret, born forty-four years ago deep in Manchuria in Japanese prisoner camps. Theirs perhaps has been the best-kept secret of World War II—long denied by Japan and long concealed by the United States government. Bit by bit and year by year, despite our government's public statements of ignorance, the truth has been leaking out. We know now that Mukden was more than just another Japanese POW camp for allied soldiers."

Frank James, POW #1268, recently retired as an accountant due in part to his ailments, which include emphysema, diabetes, atherosclerosis, loss of hearing, loss of feeling in his extremities, and cardiac problems. "I was one of those POWs," James told the hearing room, "captured by the Japanese armed forces after the fall of Bataan and Corregidor in the Philippines during the early part of 1942. Of the Americans captured, 1,500 were moved by ship in 1942 from the Philippines to Manchuria. This group was joined en route in Korea by some British and Australian soldiers captured in Singapore."

The American soldiers who survived the defeat in the Philippines then faced a forced march and a trip to China under the most inhuman conditions. After the starvation rations of the Bataan death march, a journey on board the infamous, excrement-filled hellships, and then overland, the prisoners who did not die found themselves in a camp just outside the walled Manchurian city of Mukden. Behind an eight-foot-high brick wall topped with electrified wire, inside three brick buildings and a hospital, the horrible odyssey taken by the prisoners of war continued.

"Upon arrival at Mukden on November 11, 1942, we were met by a team of medical personnel wearing masks," said James. "They sprayed liquid in our faces, and we were given injections. We were subjected to having a glass probe inserted in our rectums. This group left the camp and returned only two more times to my knowledge."

James did not know where the Japanese medical team went, what they did, or why they came, only that they seemed to be conducting experiments, not routine procedures, because the prisoners did not all receive the same shots or treatments. The team first returned in the spring. Some three hundred POWs had died during the winter—from what causes James did not know—but instead of being cremated, their bodies were stored above ground in an old wooden building until the ground thawed. This time, the medical team brought an autopsy table and containers to take specimens.

"The table was installed in the wooden building where the dead were stored, and two POWs were selected to work with the team. I was one of those two men. Our duties were to lift the bodies that had been selected off the table. These had been identified by a tag tied to the big toe which listed the POW's number. The Japanese then opened the bodies and took out the desired specimens, which were placed into containers, marked with the POWs' numbers and taken away by the Japanese medical group."

Why were some bodies selected and not others? Did it have to do with the earlier spraying and probing? James did not know. But when the medical team returned a second time to examine the survivors, it asked James to walk in footprints painted on the floor, to describe his ethnic background in detail, to answer extensive questions about his family's medical history, and to stand quietly while they measured his head, shoulders, arms, and legs with calipers.

Greg Rodriquez, Sr., POW #768, was also at Mukden. A smelter worker in Henryetta, Oklahoma, he did not come to the hearing, but his son, Greg, Jr., did. In fact, Greg's concern for his father's health led him to research the Manchurian prison camps for a master's thesis and later to ask his congressman, Pat Williams, for help in getting compensation. According to his son, the Japanese had waved feathers under the elder Rodriquez's nose and placed him inside a room into which something was sprayed. Today, at least four times a year, Greg Rodriquez, Sr., suffers fevers of unknown origins, spiking as high as 104° F within twelve hours. The Veterans Administration cannot explain them or tie them to any service-related trauma because it has no record of what happened to Rodriquez in Mukden.

Other Mukden survivors broke a silence that had lasted for decades with equally bizarre stories. After the war, the American POWs held by the Japanese were sent home and told not to talk about their experiences. The country wanted to build a friendship with the former enemy. More important, it did not want the world to learn that Mukden was one of many sites for deadly biological warfare experiments conducted by the Japanese or that the United States had struck a deal with the Japanese war criminals, granting them immunity from prosecution in exchange for the biological weapons data they had collected by experimenting with human beings.

At Representative Williams's request, the Veterans' Affairs Committee convened the hearing to see if it could unearth the records acquired by U.S. biological warfare researchers. After enduring the cruelties of being a Japanese POW, the few remaining, living veterans suffered from medical ailments that no one could explain. The committee assured the people in the hearing room that it did not want to dredge up a sordid chapter in American history; it just wanted to give these veterans access to any records that could suggest what diseases the Japanese had used in their experiments with them. Without the records, the veterans could not get compensation.

But the spokesman for the army, Dr. John Hatcher, chief of Army Records Management, came forward with bad news.

He told the committee: "We have been unable to locate any documentary evidence to corroborate the allegations that are the subject of this hearing." He did admit that the United States might have gotten some records during the occupation of Japan but vowed that these were all sent back in the late 1950s without any copies having been made. "The absence of such records suggests that Americans were not subjected to biological experimentation as alleged," he said.

It was a statement that strained the belief of almost everyone in the hearing room. That the United States had once had the biological weapons data collected by the Japanese in hand, no one disagreed. But did anyone believe that the United States had returned the data to Japan without making a copy, asked one incredulous congressman. The Japanese conducted biological warfare experiments on human beings, and to this day the information they derived is so unique, acquired by means so heinous and taboo, that it remains of appalling value. After all, it represents fifteen years of "pioneering" research into biological warfare that began, in one sense, as far back as 1925.

The newly formed League of Nations met in Geneva in 1925 to curb the burgeoning international trade in arms, a task that almost immediately proved intractable. Instead, the delegates turned their attention to an issue with far greater popular support—a comprehensive ban on poison gas. In the course of negotiations, the delegation from Poland suggested that the ban encompass germ weapons as well, thus creating an international sanction against invisible weapons of all kinds.

At that time, biological weapons had not taken a strong hold on the military imagination. True, the Germans had planned and launched a number of sabotage operations during World War I. They did succeed in infecting livestock in Argentina—pack animals bound for Europe—with anthrax, reportedly brought into the country on sugar cubes. And in the

United States, a Maryland-based German spy inoculated cattle with glanders and other diseases cultivated in a backyard lab. But no one had taken the idea one step further, to transform germs and poisons into an arsenal of battlefield weapons. In fact, the Americans saw very little promise in that step, questioning the effectiveness and practicability of spreading germs.

The legacy of the 1925 meeting was the Geneva Protocol, a document that tried to forestall the eventuality of biological bombs by prohibiting any and all bacteriological methods of warfare. Ironically, it had the opposite effect. The Protocol planted a demon seed in the mind of a young and ambitious Japanese army surgeon named Shiro Ishii. With simple, child-like logic, he reasoned that if germ weapons had been banned, then they must be valuable.

For a poor country, with one foot in the medieval world and one foot in the modern, germ weapons held two special advantages. They would be cheap, and they would draw on Japan's world-class expertise in biomedical research. At the turn of the century, Japanese scientists had discovered the cause of bubonic plague at the same time as French scientists, a feat then equivalent to isolating the AIDS virus. The forward thinkers in the Japanese army astutely recognized the strategic power that good medical knowledge bought, and by the simple decision to vaccinate soldiers, applied it to the battlefield. In the Russo-Japanese War, fought from 1904 to 1906, four times as many Japanese died of weapons as of disease, reversing a pattern that had prevailed for millennia.

Until this century, one rule held throughout the history of armed conflict: Natural disease took a greater toll on soldiers' lives than any man-made weapon. In the Napoleonic wars, deaths from infectious disease, especially typhus, far surpassed battle deaths. In the Crimean War, ten times as many British soldiers died of dysentery as from Russian weapons. In the Boer War, disease killed five times as many British soldiers as enemy action.

Vaccination and, later, antibiotics, the bona-fide miracles of modern medicine, tipped the balance of that equation. A decade after the Japanese, European armies began to vaccinate their soldiers as well. If it had not been for the virulent global flu epidemic of 1918 (which was rumored, without basis, to be German germ warfare), deaths from enemy action in World War I would have outpaced those from natural causes.

If soldiers could be protected from disease, then perhaps disease could be marshaled to the soldier's advantage. From his training in medicine and bacteriology, Ishii knew how easily medical advances could be twisted toward destruction. Born in 1892, Ishii had attended the Kyoto Imperial University, trained as a surgeon, served in the army, and then traveled to Europe on a two-year tour of inspection. He returned to Tokyo in 1930 to teach at the Army Medical College, eager to put the theory of biological weapons into practice.

In an organization where high status belonged to those who possessed weapons, Ishii's ideas mapped a path to power for the Surgeon General Branch. After Japan invaded China in 1932, Ishii ran a small lab at the college in Tokyo and set up another, much more secret one in Manchuria. According to an anonymous source, Ishii told his higher-ups that "research connected to offense would not be carried out on Japan's mainland. He was of the opinion that the research on BW offense should be done in a Japanese colony to keep it secret."

In 1935, Ishii's program got a boost. Japan's Kwantung Army, based in China, blamed an outbreak of disease among its own troops on spies who carried ampules of dysentery, cholera, and anthrax behind enemy lines. The commander took the threat of biological weapons seriously and enlisted Ishii's help to protect the army.

In the name of defense, Ishii built a biological weapons empire that has yet to be duplicated. He located the headquarters in a town called Pingfan, now part of Harbin, a city of three million people, sixteen hours north of Beijing by train.

The operation was called "Boeki Kyusuibu," which translates into the innocuous-sounding "Anti-Epidemic Water Supply Unit," but it was also known as Unit 731.

Staffed by villagers from Ishii's home near Tokyo and eventually by three thousand military and civilian workers, the unit had a yearly budget of $2.2 million (in 1944 dollars). It boasted an airstrip, a special fleet of planes, a hospital, enormous vaccine production facilities, vats capable of breeding 8 tons of germs a month, laboratories for breeding millions of fleas and other insects, large vegetable gardens, and its own herds of livestock. Ishii's program reached far beyond Pingfan—exactly how far no one knows—to include at least eighteen other outposts where more than five thousand people worked. It has been said that his empire stretched from Harbin to the Dutch East Indies, from Hokkaido to the Celebes.

As many others have argued, Ishii considered the best defense to be offense. In Manchuria's isolation, he directed the search for the most effective disease weapons, selecting salmonella, typhus, smallpox, botulinum toxin, brucellosis, tuberculosis, tick encephalitis, glanders, gas gangrene, and tularemia.

Human beings served as Ishii's guinea pigs. Initially, he experimented on Russian, Chinese, Korean, and Manchurian prisoners of war, bandits, spies, dissidents, petty criminals, and others he deemed somehow inferior. The experiments ranged from gruesome to horrific: Ishii's researchers injected tetanus into the heels of prisoners; left naked men outdoors in 40 degrees below zero until their limbs froze solid as rock; fed them typhus-contaminated tomatoes; placed prisoners in glass rooms and sprayed them with anthrax, cholera, typhoid, plague-infected fleas, and other diseases to calculate the minimum lethal dose; contaminated chocolate, bread, tooth powder, milk, cream, and butter with anthrax spores; tied prisoners to a stake and then exploded germ bombs overhead while soldiers wearing protective gear timed their deaths with stopwatches; infected women with syphilis, impregnated them and, after the child's birth, vivisected both; drained blood from humans and replaced it with horse and monkey blood in order to create artificial blood; dissected prisoners alive. In these hellish ways, three thousand died. But the death toll might have been three to four times higher.

As others have rationalized before and after him, Ishii justified his experiments on human subjects by his need for data and by their "inferior" status. The medical researchers at Pingfan—civilian bacteriologists, pathologists, and medical college professors recruited by Ishii—cooperated, although some felt pressured. "I felt I was forced to do it to promote my study," said one researcher. In published papers, the biological warfare researchers referred to the humans used in experiments as "monkeys." The code apparently fooled few people. The experimental use of human beings was an open secret in Japan's biomedical community.

Despite the methodical, cold-blooded way they were executed, the experiments were often too crude even to yield useful information. Searching for the cause of epidemic hemorrhagic fever, scientists collected fleas and lice, placed them on prisoners with the illness and later on symptom-free prisoners. Some of the symptom-free prisoners developed epidemic hemorrhagic fever, but the scientists never knew if the insects had transmitted it or if the prisoners acquired it by some other route. Without resorting to human experiments, Russian scientists later isolated the fever-causing virus, a discovery that eluded Ishii.

The workers themselves faced accidental death. Despite the precautions of working inside a rubber "spacesuit" equipped with a gas mask and respirator, at least twenty workers died each year, many as the result of Ishii's ignorance of infectious disease. One man died from cutting the grass after an anthrax bomb test.

The study of diseases led to the development of at least eight different types of bombs, including a ceramic insect bomb that insulated the mosquitoes and fleas from freezing or frying on their descent from the plane, and an anthrax "shrapnel" bomb, reportedly able to kill 90 percent of those it struck. Ishii's group manufactured four thousand bombs, as well as some of the first tanks for aerial spraying.

Ishii tested the bombs against the Chinese. According to the People's Republic of China, at least eleven cities were attacked, but there may have been more. His favorite seemed to have been the plague bomb. On October 4, 1940, rice, wheat, and plague-infected fleas fell on Ch'ü-hsien, a city in Chekiang province. One month later, plague broke out. On October 27, 1940, a plane dropped infected wheat grains over Ning-po, another city in Chekiang province. Two days later, plague broke out. A dispatch from the American embassy in Chungking noted: "Although it was a curious fact to find 'grains from heaven,' no one at the time seemed to appreciate the enemy's intention and no thorough examination of the grains were made."

One year later, the germ bombing drew worldwide attention. It was a misty dawn on November 4, 1941, when a plane circled over Ch'ang-te in Hunan province, dropping grains of wheat and rice, paper, and cotton wadding. Within three weeks, the plague struck. As in Ch'ü-hsien and Ning-po, the city had no history of plague and its rat population apparently harbored no germs. In addition, the plague broke out in and around the area where the bomb fell, leading Dr. Politzer, a member of the League of Nations Anti-Epidemic Commission, to conclude it was a disease weapon that had flourished in the city's crowded, poverty-stricken conditions.

When the Japanese captured the American POWs, they brought them to Mukden—just a few miles along a railroad line from Ishii's main headquarters in Pingfan. The team remembered by Frank James came, in all likelihood, from Pingfan, perhaps to test theories about the susceptibility of different ethnic groups to different diseases. According to "Unit 731—

What Did the Emperor Know?," a British documentary produced in 1985, the Americans in the POW camps were the experimental subjects and the British and Australians served as the controls.

The Allies became aware of the Japanese biological weapons progam in 1942 when Chiang Kai-shek wrote to Winston Churchill. The Americans responded by initiating a joint biological weapons program with Britain, which had been working on a small-scale project since 1934. From wartime intelligence reports, the United States knew of Major General Ishii, the existence of units trained in biological sabotage, and a bacillus bomb, but never guessed the extent of the empire that had been constructed. The United States doubted that the Japanese would actually stage a large-scale biological attack against American troops because of Japan's vulnerability to far worse forms of retaliation. Still, in January 1945, the War Department put a navy biological weapons research lab in California, the Public Health Service, and the U.S. Department of Agriculture labs on alert for any unusual disease outbreak.

There was no lack of desire on Ishii's part to drop biological bombs on U.S. troops, but his wishes were apparently never carried out. In 1944, the Japanese dispatched a ship to Saipan Island in the Pacific with biological weapons on board, but it sank before arriving. One year later, Ishii proposed using biological weapons on Iwo Jima, but officers in the surgeon general's office refused to sanction the operation. In fact, the United States came closer to a first strike with biologicals. As the war came to an end, the country shipped anticrop agents to its forward bases for attacking the Japanese rice crop.

Ishii's biological weapons program ended abruptly, one week before Japan's unilateral surrender. In August 1945, Russian troops invaded Manchuria. Before the Russians could reach Pingfan, the Japanese researchers destroyed all evidence of Unit 731, dynamiting the buildings, burning the laboratories, and slaughtering the remaining four hundred to five hundred prisoners. For two days, explosions could be heard coming from the compound. The Japanese released laboratory animals—horses, monkeys, dogs, cats, camels, and rats—which ran free across the countryside, some of them spreading plague to nearby villages. Ishii fled to Japan, but not before salvaging his laboratory specimens and data, the most tangible and valuable fruits of his fifteen years of dedication and labor. In the chaos following the dropping of the atomic bomb and the surrender, Ishii disappeared.

Precisely how Ishii masterminded the subsequent course of events is impossible to say. His hatred for the Russians, whom he believed to have an active and advanced biological weapons program, eclipsed his feelings about the Americans. While Ishii hid at his country home, he appointed Dr. Ryoichi Naito, who had conducted biological weapons research at the Army Medical College in Tokyo, to make contact with the Americans.

Actually, Naito had made contact before the war, when he approached the Rockefeller Institute in New York City, asking for a strain of yellow fever virus. The Rockefeller Institute refused because yellow fever was not endemic in the Orient and the League of Nations had prohibited its introduction there. Shortly afterward, a technician in the yellow fever laboratory was offered a $3,000 bribe to steal some of the virus, which he refused to do.

Naito discovered that Lieutenant Colonel Murray Sanders was the biological warfare specialist on the United States Scientific Intelligence Survey. He got Sanders's photo and met him when his ship docked in Yokohama between the dropping of the first and second atomic bombs. When Naito offered to be his interpreter, Sanders agreed. Many years later, Sanders said in the British documentary film that "his job was to see that I didn't learn too much."

Naito succeeded, at least initially. Armed with a list of seventy-five questions and his own experiences at the U.S. biological weapons headquarters at Camp Detrick, Sanders began to interrogate Japanese army officers about the biological weapons program. Fairly quickly, Sanders sized up Naito as someone far more knowledgeable than the shy, modest interpreter he appeared to be. When Sanders threatened to bring the Russians into the investigation, Naito sent him a twelve-page, hand-written note entitled, "Private (secret) information to Colonel Sanders." In stilted, rudimentary English, Naito wrote: "There occurred a big consternation in the circle of higher officers of Head Quarter when your inquiry about B.W. began. (about ten days ago). A long time disputation was done whether they should answer to you with the true or not." Then the letter spelled out names and the chain of command, leading to the emperor. At the end, Sanders jotted a note in his own handwriting. "I have asked Dr. Naito whether prisoners were ever used as experimental 'guinea pigs.' He vows that this has not been the case."

Little did Sanders know that he had been set up, even for this veiled confession and assurance. But he rose to the bait with a clear conscience, just as Ishii must have wanted all along. Naito's obvious knowledge led Sanders to recommend to General MacArthur that they offer the Japanese researchers immunity from war crimes prosecution in exchange for their data.

Even then, Sanders had little inkling of how the gamble would pay off. In his Scientific Intelligence Survey report, Sanders wrote that the "Japanese offensive BW was characterized by a curious mixture of foresight, energy, ingenuity and at the same time, lack of imagination with surprisingly amateurish approaches to the work." Still, any information would be an advance over what the Americans had developed.

Although rumors circulated that Ishii had died, he emerged from hiding, suffering for the rest of his life from chronic dysentery. He was interviewed from January 22 to February 25, 1946, and soft-pedaled the offensive work, stressing that weapons were created only to develop adequate defenses. But the Americans sensed that Ishii was holding back. Arvo Thompson, one of Sanders's Camp Detrick colleagues and executive assistant to George Merck, the pharmaceutical company president who ran the American BW effort, wrote that "Ishii's amazing familiarity with detailed technical data" made him skeptical of Ishii's repeated contention that all biological weapons records were destroyed.

The investigation dragged on over months while Ishii and his associates played the American investigators like fish on a line. But disturbing reports surfaced and made their way to the International Military Tribunal for the Far East, which was conducting the war crimes trials. Chinese nationalists had discovered an outpost of Ishii's operation in Nanjing, a large 1,500-person, semiautonomous organization set up in 1939 which had also performed hideous human experiments. When the Chinese pressed, the American prosecutor briefly raised the issue before the tribunal. The tribunal's president sounded surprised and interested. "This is something entirely new. We haven't heard this before," he said. But the American prosecutor never introduced any more evidence to substantiate the claims, in all likelihood because a decision to protect Ishii had already been made.'

Like a corpse that refused to sink, reports of the human experiments kept coming up. An anonymous letter-writer told the legal section of general headquarters that "I was once attached to his [Ishii's] corps so I know quite well about his work. . . . His summoning will provide evidence and data against 'A'-class war criminal suspects and even one Imperial Family member will be affected." While the letter detailed an elaborate way to contact the writer on a given date, a meeting never took place because the letter was not translated in time.

The emperor, in all likelihood, knew about Unit 731. In the documentary, Sanders says he believes the emperor must have known because the budget was very large, involved top-level people, and was formed by imperial decree. Ishii had friends in court, and the staff officer of the operations division was a Lieutenant Colonel Miyata, also known as Prince Takeda, the emperor's brother. The emperor himself went to Manchuria in 1939, and, given the size of Ishii's operation at that time, it seems that he must have been aware of its mission.

Meanwhile, the Russians, who had captured twelve Japanese biological weapons experts when they overtook Manchuria, informed the Americans in no uncertain terms that the Japanese had conducted human experiments. They demanded to interrogate Ishii. For January, February, and March of 1947, the Russians hounded the Americans with daily requests. The last thing the Americans wanted was to share Ishii's biological weapons know-how with the Russians. The harder they pressed, the more the Americans wanted Ishii to themselves. But the squeeze-play created an ethical and political dilemma.

On May 6, 1947, General MacArthur radioed the War Department with a top secret cable. "Experiments on humans were known to and described by three Japanese and tacitly confirmed by Ishii. Reluctant statements by Ishii indicated he had superiors (possibly general staff) who knew and authorized the program. Ishii states that if guaranteed immunity from 'war crimes' in documentary form for himself, supervisors and subordinates, he can describe program in detail. Ishii claims to have extensive theoretical, high-level knowledge, including strategic and tactical use of BW in defense and offense, backed by some research on best BW agents to employ by geographical areas of Far East and the use of BW in cold climates."

The War Department answered immediately: "Possibility desired information can be obtained from Ishii and associates without formal United States commitment. Information will be retained in intelligence channels and will not be employed as 'war crimes' evidence and danger commitment might later be cause of serious embarrassment to United States makes it inadvisable to make such statements."

The promise apparently satisfied Ishii, who agreed to deliver a manuscript detailing his fifteen years of experience with biological weapons. He ordered an associate to excavate eight thousand slides of human tissues, representing over two hundred prisoner autopsies, and over six hundred pages of reports on artificially disseminating disease. He had hidden them in temples and buried them in the mountains of southern Japan.

As the Americans glimpsed the horrible scope of Ishii's work, they continued to debate and justify the deal. In a report issued by the State, War, Navy Coordinating Committee for the Far East on August 1, 1947, the calculation was spelled out in pragmatic terms: "The value to the US of Japanese BW data is of such importance to national security as to far outweigh the value accruing for 'war crimes' prosecution." Although the report recognized that Ishii certainly violated the rules of land warfare, it went on to say there was not sufficient evidence to show the Japanese had experimented with American POWs.

Still, the United States was not sure that American POWs had escaped unharmed. "It should be kept in mind," the report went on to say, "that there is a remote possibility that investigation conducted by the Soviets in the Mukden area may have disclosed evidence that American prisoners of war were used for experimental purposes of a BW nature and that they lost their lives as a result of these experiments."

In the final analysis, the Japanese data appeared so valuable that the United States would overlook the way in which it had been acquired. "This Japanese information is the only known source of data from scientifically controlled experiments showing the direct effect of BW agents on man," noted the August 1 report. "In the past, it has been necessary to evaluate the effects of BW agents on man from data obtained through animal experimentation. Such evaluation is inconclusive and far less complete than results obtained from certain types of human experiments."

The deal split the Americans back in Washington, with the State Department refusing to take part because "it might be a source of serious embarrassment to the United States if assurances were given." But the State, War, Navy Coordinating Committee pushed on the grounds of national security. "The Army Department and Air Force members strongly believe that this information, particularly that which will be obtained from the Japanese with respect to the effect of BW on humans, is of such importance to the security of the country that the risk of subsequent embarrassment should be taken."

The United States made the deal, shortly after it had publicly prosecuted Nazi war criminals for equally hideous "scientific" experiments on human beings. In December 1947, two scientists from Camp Detrick, Dr. Edwin Hill and Dr. Joseph Victor, arrived in Tokyo for exhaustive interviews with Ishii and his twenty associates about their work with anthrax, aerosols, cholera, glanders, food poisoning, tetanus, TB, smallpox, brucellosis, botulism, flu, and the pufferfish toxin. They came home with eight thousand slides, experimental results, and a sense that the deal was a bargain.

"Evidence gathered in this investigation has greatly supplemented and amplified previous aspects of this field," they wrote. "It represents data which have been obtained by Japanese scientists at the expenditure of many millions of dollars and years of work. Information has accrued with respect to human susceptibility to these diseases as indicated by specific infectious doses of bacteria. Such information could not be obtained in our own laboratories because of scruples attached to human experimentation. These data were secured with a total outlay of 250,000 yen, a mere pittance by comparison with actual cost of the studies."

In December 1949, the Soviets brought twelve Japanese prisoners, biological weapons experts, to trial for waging biological warfare against China. In 1950, Moscow challenged the United States to bring Ishii to justice for his war crimes. But Washington dismissed the request as a Communist propaganda maneuver.

Ishii disappeared in 1947, although Sanders says he

thought Ishii lectured at Camp Detrick on his human experiments. But many of Ishii's colleagues survive today, including Dr. Yoshimura, professor at Kobe Women's University; Dr. Tanaka, head of the Osaka Country School of Medicine; Dr. Yagasawa, Secretary of the Japanese Penicillin Society; and Dr. Tamiya, president of the Japanese Medical Association. Dr. Naito, now dead, founded the Green Cross Corporation, a successful Japanese company specializing in artificial blood products, a lucrative spinoff from early experiments.

Murray Sanders guarded his secret until 1985 when, in poor health, he came forward. Trained as a physician, Sanders taught at the University of Miami and Florida Atlantic University, and served as the director of medical research for several companies until 1971 when he started his own foundation to look at diseases of the nervous system. Sanders said that if he had known of the human experiments from the beginning, he doubts he would have suggested a secret deal. At a press conference held in the fall of 1985, Congressman Pat Williams introduced Sanders by saying, "We not only have the smoking gun but the U.S. military officer who was there when it was fired." Sanders murmured softly and with regret, "I was the gun."

NINE

"Ten Seconds and the Dog Is Dead"

The secret deal with Ishii gave a boost to the United States's fledgling research center at what was then Camp Detrick, in Frederick, Maryland. Compared with Japan's fifteen years of experience and testing, the U.S. effort was a late bloomer. In fact, it had only been launched in 1943.

At the beginning of World War II, Frederick was a placid, country town set among the rolling hills and dairy farms of western Maryland. "Friday night was the only night the stores were open. You couldn't walk down Main Street, it was so full of people walking three abreast. The farming community came in to socialize," recalls Alice Olson, who moved to Frederick in 1943. "Now it's a large bedroom community," she says.

In her sixties, Olson is a tall, forthright woman, dressed in pants and a loose sweater vest, who welcomes questions about the changes that Frederick has seen. Even though she has lived here over forty years and taught in the local high school, she does not call herself a Fredericktonian. "You have to be born here or live here a generation to qualify," she explains. Olson's ties are to the Detrick community, the newcomers in town. From the neat brick ranch house her husband built on the hillside, she can see the fort, but, like many other denizens of this

country town, she knows very little about what has taken place
inside its chain-link, barbed-wire fence over the last forty
years.

World War II rousted Frederick out of its sleep. On the
outskirts of town, a mile and a half from City Hall, a small airstrip known as Detrick Field stretched between farm plots and
pastures. The Office of Strategic Services, the CIA's forerun-
ner, trained pilots for intelligence missions there until, in April
1943, the War Department announced to the townspeople that
Detrick Field would become Camp Detrick, an installation of
the Chemical Warfare Service.

The town hardly had enough housing for the tight-lipped
newcomers who almost overnight took over the hangars and
tar-paper shacks at the field. The strangers, who came in both
civilian dress and military uniform, were scientists, and many
drove cars whose license plates identified them as physicians, a
different class of people than Frederick had known. None
would discuss the mission of Camp Detrick, not even with
their wives.

Alice Olson moved to Frederick with her husband, Frank,
whose thesis advisor at the University of Wisconsin, Dr. Ira
Baldwin, had been chosen to head the secret project. "Frank
said, 'I can't tell you anything about it. They're starting a new
program.' He was frightened and excited at the same time. Just
as we speculated about the atom bomb project—you have
friends who are physics majors and they all go to Los
Alamos—we knew when we came here; all the wives said they
must be working on germ warfare." She pauses. "For young
couples trying to establish a life together, it didn't help in sharing."

Behind the cyclone fence at the end of Seventh Street,
Camp Detrick bustled and swelled. The postal service delivered large shipments of autoclaves, microscopes, and corn
steep liquor, a hearty medium used for growing vats of microorganisms. Smokestacks poked out of the converted and newly

constructed buildings, which included machine shops, a meteorological station, greenhouses, laboratories, animal breeding facilities, a pilot production plant, and test grids. By the end of the war, the compound ranked as the largest single employer in the town and county, employing more than four thousand people.

"The only agency that had more priority than we had, if one hadn't a uniform on and was in this country, was the Manhattan Project," said Ira Baldwin, the camp's first technical director, in a 1965 speech. Only the Manhattan Project overshadowed the urgency, scope, and budget of the work at Detrick. Propelled by fear that the Germans had raced ahead, a cadre of scientists worked with patriotic fervor to build a bomb that had never been built before.

There were rumors about what went on at Camp Detrick, including the possibility that it was an extermination center for Axis prisoners. But Fredericktonians, for the most part, made the fair assumption that Camp Detrick worked on chemical weapons, and worries clustered around what dangerous chemicals might escape. As the camp quickly grew, local health officials wondered about the adequacy of its sanitation facilities and decided to test the camp's sewage where it entered the city's system. The results must have stunned them: It proved sterile. Wary of inadvertently infecting the town or revealing its mission, Camp Detrick took the elaborate precaution of sterilizing its own sewage. The efforts paid off. The work at Detrick was one of the war's best-kept secrets.

The United States saw no reason to launch a biological warfare program before World War II. The idea of bacteriological bombs scuttled around military circles in the 1920s and 1930s, enjoying feasts of attention and then suffering famines of interest. Too many problems stymied its future. How would the army spread germs or toxins effectively when diseases spread through the water could be stopped by good sanitary practices and diseases spread by insects would infect one's own troops? That left diseases that spread through the air, a process so poorly understood at the time that it was discarded. Toxins would be easier to control and disperse, but few had been isolated in appreciable quantities. On balance, military thinkers concluded that explosives did a better job.

The War Department learned two months before Pearl Harbor that neither Germany nor Japan doubted the value of biological weapons. The Secretary of War, Henry Stimson, rounded up a committee of twelve scientists and charged them with the task of deciding how feasible biological warfare would be. The WBC Committee, as it was called, responded promptly that biological warfare was not only feasible but was an eventuality for which the United States had better prepare. "The value of biological warfare will be a debatable question until it has clearly been proven or disproven by experience. The wide assumption is that any method which appears to offer advantages to a nation at war will be vigorously employed by that nation," reported the committee.

In November 1942 the WBC Committee, along with several other invited scientists and military men, met at the National Academy of Sciences. A colonel posed the question: Would it be possible to produce living pathogenic microbes in ton quantities? Could it be done so the microbes stayed virulent? Could it be done without infecting the workers at the facility or the community at large? The medical bacteriologists with no experience in large-scale production of microorganisms shook their heads discouragingly. But Baldwin, who had worked in the fermentation industry, said, "If you can do it in a test tube, then you can do it in a ten-thousand-gallon tank." The can-do attitude helped win him the job.

To avoid alarming the public and to keep American intentions under wraps, Stimson appointed George Merck, head of the giant Merck pharmaceutical company, to oversee the preparations for offense and defense through a civilian organization called the War Research Service. At first, the surgeon general of the army was picked to oversee the development of defenses against biological weapons, but when the physicians realized the inseparability of offense and defense, the surgeon general backed out and the Chemical Warfare Service, which already had a nucleus of officers interested in biological weapons, stepped in. One of the first orders of business in 1943 was to find a site for the biological weapons program that would be close to Washington, D.C., and to the Chemical Warfare Service's headquarters in Edgewood, Maryland. Detrick Field fit the bill.

For the next three years, biological scientists thronged to Frederick. It was clear you could do sabotage with biological weapons. But it was not clear that you could infect a large number of people simultaneously. The only possibility was to unleash germs through the air. "The idea that you might infect through the respiratory tract, *with organisms other than typical respiratory diseases* [emphasis added], was a totally new idea and many people were extremely skeptical," recalled Baldwin.

The Detrick scientists worked on ways to create aerosols of infectious disease, testing paint sprayers, artists' air brushes, medicinal atomizers, and nebulizers inside cloud chambers. The key was to create a particle small enough to pierce the alveoli of the human lung, bypassing the lung's filtering mechanisms and directly entering the body's bloodstream. If scientists could transform a microbe into an aerosol between 1 and 7 microns in diameter, then any disease could, in principle, infect through the respiratory tract. Then any disease, in principle, could be used in a biological weapon.

The scientists tried to isolate the botulinum toxin, experimented with a new antibiotic that Merck's company had found called streptomycin, and fooled around with chemicals that would affect plant growth, discovering many of the defoliants and herbicides that were later used in Vietnam. They studied anticrop and antilivestock diseases and developed a vaccine for rinderpest, a disease of cattle, which would make a good antilivestock weapon. The research carried risks, and, despite extensive safety procedures, over three hundred infections occurred before the end of the war.

Of all the diseases that held promise as biological warfare agents, anthrax was the closest to being ready for use. In collaboration with the British, the Americans pushed ahead, holding small tests at Horn Island, ten miles off the Mississippi coast (until it was discovered that prevailing winds blew onshore), and at Dugway. The United States built an anthrax production plant in Vigo, Indiana, but the war ended before it actually produced any anthrax spores to fill the bombs.

Merck's friend and Harvard classmate, the novelist John Marquand, took charge of biological warfare intelligence, focusing almost exclusively on Europe. News of Germany's activities filtered back through the War Department's ALSOS Mission, which monitored the activities of key European physicists and biologists. But by and large, the intelligence was sketchy. In 1944, intelligence reports warned that the Germans might outfit their new V-1, cross-Channel rockets with anthrax or botulinum, contaminating the heart of London. When the first rockets exploded in the conventional manner, the military seemed relieved. Still, the Americans wanted to vaccinate Allied troops against botulinum before the Normandy landing, but the British seemed so skeptical of the German threat that the troops carried a general antidote with self-inoculating syringes instead.

After the war, the Americans discovered that the Germans never intended to use biological weapons and in fact had a much smaller program than anyone dared to imagine. The Germans only decided to investigate biological weapons in 1943, two years after the Americans had first begun to launch preparations. Through the Military Medical Academy in Posen, Poland, the Nazis conducted experiments on five hundred concentration camp inmates at Dachau, Buchenwald, and Natzweiler. But more work went into defense against saboteurs in the Polish underground, who successfully used poison parcels, as well as arsenic, typhoid fever lice, and typhus bacteria against the Nazis.

Still, the Americans wanted German biological warfare experts after the war ended. Just as the United States competed with the Russians for Japanese experts, so it also competed for the Germans and Austrians. "Operation Paperclip," a program run by the Office of Strategic Services, located and recruited the Nazis' top biological warfare scientists and brought them back to America.

The United States notified the world of its biological weapons program in 1946 with a press release written by George Merck. "Work in this field, born of necessity of war, can not be ignored in time of peace; it must be continued on a sufficient scale to provide adequate defense," wrote Merck. "It is important to note that unlike the development of the atomic bomb, the development of agents for biological warfare is possible in many countries, large and small, without vast expenditures of money or the construction of huge production facilities. It is clear that the development of biological warfare could readily proceed in many countries, perhaps under the guise of legitimate medical or bacteriological research."

By then, the atomic bomb had become the yardstick against which all future weapons would be measured. The newspapers, which had cooperated with the government to keep the lid on biological weapons, now gave them play. At a closed hearing of the House Appropriations Committee, the navy said, "Biological weapons, consisting of the spreading of disease, could occupy a position similar to atomic warfare." Others called them "more frightful," "even more deadly and malignant" than the atomic bomb, "capable of wiping out large cities and entire crops at a single blow." One congressional representative boasted, "We have something far more deadly than the atomic bomb. Furthermore, it is in usable shape."

The public had seen pictures of the mushroom cloud, but could only imagine the horror that the biological bomb would bring. The feverish speculation prompted Dwight Eisenhower, then Chief of Staff, to silence the military on the subject, making the mention of biological warfare taboo. Three months after Merck had made his announcement, biological weapons abruptly disappeared from the public eye.

The silence lasted three years, and it blanketed the bitter controversy that raged inside the government. "The subject was so shrouded in secrecy, it could not be discussed in an open scientific fashion," says Alexander Langmuir, the founder of the Epidemic Intelligence Service at the Centers for Disease Control and an early participant in high-level discussions about biological warfare. Informed opinions varied in the extreme about the future of biological weapons. While the atom bomb was seen as the latest in a long tradition of high explosives, the biological bomb was qualitatively different, something new under the sun. Was it a weapon of mass destruction, capable of wiping out another country's political, economic, and industrial systems? Was it an unconventional weapon, with delayed actions, producing no gaping wounds but insidious psychological terror, like chemical and radiological warfare?

Biological warfare seemed to offer a limitless variety of ways to wage war, from instant death to lingering illness to the destruction of livestock and crops. Yet at the same time, its success hinged on controlling more critical variables than any other type of warfare. It seemed like an ideal terror weapon, especially when used in conjunction with the atomic bomb, but prospects for defense looked dim. Unlike the atomic bomb, which required costly plutonium production facilities, the United States realized that it would never own the monopoly on the ways and means to produce the biological bomb.

To complicate matters further, some of the scientists who could help settle the arguments about the efficiency and usefulness of the biological bomb refused to get involved. "The atom bomb was built with consummate skill on a sound basis and understanding of physics," says Langmuir, who lobbied to declassify BW. "The Detrick program was built on a sound basis of aerobiology. The atom bomb had the total support of physicists, down to schoolteachers. The BW program never had the support of the medical community."

The upper echelons of the military finally decided that biological weapons possessed a great deal of potential that, in the face of the Soviet threat, had to be tapped. After the war, Detrick had dwindled to three hundred to four hundred people, but that number soon doubled. Budgets rose to $4 million in 1949, and preparations began to field-test anthrax, botulinum, and brucellosis, the first three biologicals slated to be turned into reliable weapons. A one-million-liter sphere, known as the Horton sphere and later dubbed "the eight-ball" because of the difficulties of working inside it, was built at Detrick as the world's largest container for testing aerosols of pathogens.

To carry out the biological warfare program, the government needed public support for, not antipathy toward, the idea of biological weapons. And so the veil of silence was lifted. On March 13, 1949, the *New York Times* carried a front-page article whose lead read, "James Forrestal, Secretary of Defense, broke an official three-year military silence today on the use or discussion of the term 'biological warfare.' In a formal statement, the Secretary characterized much of what had been written about germ weapons as 'fantastic,' 'exaggerated' and 'unduly spectacular.' "

While the military publicly disparaged the wild-eyed commentators on biological warfare, it encouraged its own advisors to speculate. Forrestal had asked a group of scientists called the Ad Hoc Committee on Biological Warfare to be "highly imaginative" in its report on the potentialities of germ weapons. In its report, the committee characterized biological weapons as in their infancy but with a potent future as weapons of mass destruction. "The committee is impressed by unconventional forms of biological attack which advances in biology may permit now, or in the future," the report noted. These included electroshock, hypnosis, drugs, glandular or hereditary changes, and "other biological chain-reactions," an allusion to nuclear chain reactions.

In the midst of arguments over the offensive potential of biological weapons, everyone agreed that civil defense merited top priority. In 1951, the Civil Defense Administration distributed films and a disarmingly frank pamphlet entitled "Here Is What You Need to Know About Biological Warfare." It spelled out the problem: "Biological attacks could be aimed at people, animals or food crops. But biological warfare is no supersecret weapon. There are defenses and you should know what they are." Unfortunately, the defenses amounted to little more than those spelled out for a nuclear attack—duck and run for cover. For biological weapons, the Civil Defense Administration also counseled washing your hands.

Through the Centers for Disease Control in Atlanta, the United States took a critical step in building a sound civil defense. Alexander Langmuir took the public health threat of biological warfare seriously, so seriously, in fact, that he estimated in one newspaper interview that he devoted 20 percent of his time to the subject during his twenty-one-year career at what was first known as the Communicable Disease Center. His lasting contribution was the Epidemic Intelligence Service, which he launched in 1950. Conceived as a biological warfare intelligence unit, it initially gave fifteen physicians and other medically trained personnel a special training course in medical detective work, put them in charge of fifteen strategic areas, and gave them the responsibility for tracking mysterious disease outbreaks back to their source.

Although the Epidemic Intelligence Service has not found any Soviet-launched biological attacks in its thirty-five-year history, it has proved a boon to public health. The higher a country's standard of public health and the stronger its monitoring of unusual patterns of disease, the better its defense against a surreptitious biological attack.

By 1950, a potent fear of the Soviet Union possessed even the soberest imaginations. According to an army intelligence report, Russia could occupy all of Europe, most of the Near East and Middle East, and a large part of China within six months. Imagine what the Soviets could accomplish with subterfuge and sabotage? In response to the Cold War, the Special Operations Division launched by the army in 1948 to gain expertise in the strange and exotic arts of secret biological warfare grew with a vengeance.

The Special Operations Division (SOD) won hands down as the most secret place at Detrick. Housed in a one-story cinderblock building, staff and visitors needed the highest security clearance—the classification of "need to know"—and a shot-card with an updated roll call of ten to twenty immunizations just to get in the door. So rigorously did SOD enforce these requirements that even generals making an inspection of the base would bypass the building. Special Operations worked for the army's Special Forces, the elite units in charge of paramilitary, covert operations. Although no one ever made an official announcement, other Detrick employees guessed by the layers of security that SOD also had ties to the CIA.

The spirit of SOD reflected that of Stanley Lovell, a consultant to the organization from its inception and a scientific whiz kid who had helped launch the Office of Strategic Services during World War II. Unlike England, which had a rich tradition of secret agents and spies, the United States started from scratch. In a short stretch of time, William "Wild Bill" Donovan built the Office of Strategic Services into the largest intelligence organization in the world, with over twelve thousand people. Donovan recruited Stanley Lovell, a Boston businessman and scientist whom he called his Professor Moriarty after Sherlock Holmes's evil archnemesis. Lovell described himself as a "saucepan chemist," and many of the things that Lovell cooked up over his tenure were half-baked. His specialty was dirty tricks—unorthodox, no-holds-barred warfare.

"We were an amateur group and utterly uninhibited," he would say in a later speech. In the search for ways to defeat the enemy, nothing seemed too underhanded, no idea too preposterous. At one time during World War II, Lovell heard that goats outnumbered people in Spanish Morocco and proposed bombing the country with simulated goat dung. The idea was to saturate the dung clods with tularemia, psittacosis, and a fly-attracting chemical to lure the flies that would later spread the germs. Lovell supplied sex hormones and, "just for variety's sake, a few poisons which we always called medications" to be injected into Hitler's "carrots, beets, or whatever went up to his larder." The plan failed, but the OSS succeeded in preventing one Nazi leader from attending a major economic conference by tainting his food with food poisoning.

Out of the many schemes Lovell hatched, he seemed to hold a special fondness for biological weapons because of the endless skein of possibilities. When he wrote his memoirs, *Of Spies and Strategems,* he sent this inscription to the British Biological Warfare liaison officer: "My deepest respect to the little band to which you contributed so much during your Washington days. You were glorious pioneers in an uncharted field of warfare."

By 1950, Lovell had retired from day-to-day operations and was working as a consultant to both the CIA and Detrick. The CIA's Technical Services Staff took over the task of furnishing the props and gadgets of tradecraft: the false papers, suicide pills, letter bombs, bugs, taps, and tiny cameras. Within that staff was the Chemical Division, led by a bright, stuttering chemist named Sidney Gottlieb and charged with bending the latest advances in biology and chemistry to covert operations. Gottlieb arranged that SOD would provide an arsenal of toxins and germs for CIA use, an agreement that CIA chief Allen Dulles formally documented on April 13, 1953, and declared "ultra-sensitive." The CIA paid SOD $3 million over the next seventeen years for the privilege of access, expertise, and information, often riding piggyback on requests made by the army's Special Forces.

In the early fifties, the CIA professionals met with their SOD counterparts twice a year to brainstorm. Frank Olson, who had worked at Detrick during the war and stayed on as an aerosol specialist, was asked to join SOD. According to Alice Olson, Frank had considered leaving the military but stayed because the salaries were higher than in universities. Alice believes the transfer to SOD pleased him. "It was much more challenging, which he liked. I believe he also found it more distressing. Nothing I can put a finger on. He had an ulcer. The only way to gauge how he felt was when that ulcer acted up," she says. While the Detrick program worked on creating weapons to kill enemy troops, SOD concentrated on unusual ways to kill individuals, a much more freewheeling mission.

On November 18, 1953, Olson, who was then chief of the Plans and Assessment Branch of SOD, met with Sidney Gottlieb and other CIA and SOD colleagues for a weekend retreat in the Maryland woods. Without the knowledge of those present, the Cointreau had been spiked with LSD, a recently discovered chemical considered promising for covert operations. Gottlieb's division had already tested LSD on people, but wondered what would happen when unsuspecting individuals took it. Twenty minutes after the drinks went down, Gottlieb, who had not drunk any Cointreau, broke the news.

Olson took the news badly. The feeling of being duped, in combination with the uncontrollable and strange effects of the LSD, seemed to shake him. Everyone at the weekend retreat described Frank as an optimistic, loyal friend, strong family man, and lover of practical jokes. Despite his ulcer, he had no history of psychiatric problems, but the LSD apparently affected something deep inside him. After the LSD had worn off, he found himself "all mixed up." The "experiment" ended ten days later when Olson, still suffering from LSD-induced paranoia and delusion, jumped out of the window of a tenth-floor hotel room.

Just weeks before Christmas, Alice Olson and her three children learned that Frank had committed suicide. Five days later, the army awarded her a generous compensation. "I knew he did not commit suicide as a willful act. My feeling was that he had had a bad dream and went through the window as an escape," Alice recalls. Beyond that, Alice had no satisfying explanation. But she trusted the military establishment, which had always taken good care of her.

In 1953, neither Alice Olson nor the world at large had heard of LSD. She never suspected that Frank's work might have caused his death. As far as she knew he studied dangerous diseases, and she believed the Detrick labs to be safe. "The men were always getting shots," she says. "I knew about one death. Frank went to the funeral. I said, what did he die of? Frank said pneumonia. I said, you liar. I knew if he hadn't died of a classified disease Frank would not have gone. But the precautions were incredible. They were so very very careful [at Detrick]. We picked up the men's attitude that everything was okay."

Although the CIA gently reprimanded Gottlieb (who never returned to Detrick's SOD offices), Olson's suicide did little to disrupt the relationship between Detrick and the CIA. The Agency had a technical agenda—it wanted a better suicide pill, one that acted faster and less painfully than hydrogen cyanide; it wanted a "knockout" drug, a substance that would render its victim temporarily unconscious or helpless; it wanted substances that would disguise assassinations and harass the enemy; and it wanted the means to carry out these deeds with unusual stealth.

The knockout problem eluded researchers, but they

chalked up a few successes in other areas. SOD relied on Detrick's Basic Sciences Division to develop better poisons. Detrick scientist Edward Schantz succeeded in isolating saxitoxin,
the potent Red Tide poison. Secreted by a tiny marine micro-
organism known as a dinoflagellate, which is then eaten by
clams, oysters, and other plankton feeders, the poison commonly contaminates shellfish during the summer months.
When Schantz heard that the Alaskan butter clam concentrated the most potent form of the toxin, he headed north to
collect infected specimens. He ground up several thousand
clams before isolating 20 grams of the pure toxin, more than
had ever been obtained, in 1954.

The toxin proved to be almost unbelievably strong when
first tried out on animals. "Ten seconds and the dog is dead" is
the way one researcher described its potency. One gram was
enough to kill five thousand people. When Francis Gary
Powers was shot down in 1960 flying a secret surveillance mission over the Soviet Union, he carried (but didn't use) the
toxin, hidden inside a drill bit which was itself hidden inside a
silver dollar.

SOD developed weapons that updated the idea of poison-
tipped arrows, long used by South American Indians. True to
the tradition of neutered military jargon, SOD dubbed its new
device a "microbioinoculator." It was a .45-caliber pistol, si-
lently powered by batteries stored in the handle, which at a
close range of 100 yards fired a poison-tipped dart as thin as a
human hair. So tiny were the darts that the victim never knew
he had been hit, and if you picked the right poison it never
showed up in the autopsy. After testing on mannequins, SOD
came up with a dart that pierced clothing. It styled a version
for walking canes, umbrellas, and fountain pens.

In addition, SOD branched off into the fabrication of a
slew of remotely controlled aerosol sprays, rigging a cigarette
lighter that sprayed when lit, a light switch that sprayed when
switched, and an engine-head bolt that shot off when the en-

gine heated, releasing a deadly vapor. The researchers compacted dried forms of dread diseases into a button that could be sewn on a shirt, allowing an agent to seed a disease in a foreign country. They also devised a drillcap that could be used for infecting a city's or building's water supply pipes. Like traveling salesmen, the SOD engineers kept prototypes of their hardware in a small suitcase which they showed off to visitors from the CIA, the FBI, and occasionally Congress.

What came out of this frenzy of effort? No one is really saying. In congressional testimony before the Church Committee in 1975, Charles Senseney, project engineer of the microbioinoculator, bemoaned the fact that the CIA people would borrow the dart gun, bring it back without darts five or six weeks later, and never tell him how well it did or didn't perform. (Apparently, Senseney never asked too directly either.) The CIA claimed it only used the guns against dogs, to tranquilize them. But, as one congressman pointed out, the dart carried a poison designed to be undetectable in an autopsy. Why bother if you are only shooting a dog?

In 1960, the CIA planned to assassinate Patrice Lumumba, the first prime minister of the Republic of Congo, with a microbe masquerading as a natural disease. Suspicious of Lumumba, who smoked marijuana and practiced witchcraft, and fearful when he accepted Soviet aid that the Congo would become another Cuba, top U.S. officials—perhaps even President Eisenhower—authorized the assassination. Sidney Gottlieb traveled to the Congo (now Zaire) with the microbe which is now thought to be brucellosis, an endemic disease, in a diplomatic pouch. Two assassins—CIA-trained professional killers—were each given a toxic biological kit, but Lumumba died before they got to him, the victim of another coup, probably engineered by a political rival.

In Eisenhower's last year in office, the CIA considered the assassination of Rafael Trujillo, the president and dictator of the Dominican Republic, and of Iraq's Colonel Abdul Kassem. But Trujillo died in an ambush sprung by his own domestic enemies using CIA-supplied guns, and Kassem died in front of a firing squad before receiving a toxin-impregnated handkerchief sent by the CIA. No one else was reported to have died after opening the package.

Fidel Castro was another target for wild ideas. They included a batch of pills containing botulinum toxin, designed to be dissolved in a glass of water; treating a box of Castro's favorite cigars with botulinum; spreading toxic powder in Castro's diving suit; dusting his shoes (if left outside a hotel room at night) with an unnamed substance that would make his beard fall out and his charisma disappear; planting an explosive seashell in a favorite diving spot; and, of course, the usual poison pens and dart guns. None of the plans worked. One of Castro's mistresses, who said she was given poison pills by the CIA, hid them in a cold cream jar, where they melted. The poison wet suit idea was scrubbed when an American official negotiating for the release of the Bay of Pigs brigade gave Castro an ordinary wet suit as a present. Wouldn't he get suspicious if the Americans gave him another one?

In 1961, the CIA launched the Cuban economic sabotage program. In the 1975 Church Committee hearings, the CIA admitted developing "methods and systems for carrying out a covert attack against crops and causing severe crop loss." As part of its harrassment campaign, the CIA seriously considered attacking Cuba with a sugar cane disease, but the plan was killed at the last minute. In 1962, a Canadian agricultural technician said he was paid $5,000 and given a container of Newcastle virus to infect Cuban turkeys with a fatal disease. But the technician said he threw away the vial before flying to Cuba. When more than eight thousand turkeys later died (for reasons believed natural), the Cubans suspected germ warfare and prepared to retaliate by spreading hoof and mouth disease in the United States.

There is compelling evidence that the CIA actually used

biological warfare against Cuba in 1971. *Newsday* reported in 1977 that an unnamed intelligence source said he was given a sealed, unmarked container at Fort Gulick, an army base and CIA training ground in Panama, and told to turn it over to members of an anti-Castro group. At Bocas del Toro, Panama, a trawler picked up the container and put it ashore near the U.S. navy base in Guantánamo Bay. Six weeks later, African swine fever, a debilitating hog disease, broke out for the first time in the Western hemisphere, killing five hundred thousand pigs on the island. Its introduction, blamed on merchant seamen and infected garbage brought in by airplanes, was never fully explained.

The Soviets cooked up equally nasty devices and used them against their own worst enemies, dissidents living abroad. In 1959, KGB agent Bogdan Stashinsky murdered a dissident with a spray gun of prussic acid, a chemical that provokes a heart attack within minutes of being inhaled. (Two years later, Stashinsky defected and described the Soviet's CBW spy arsenal to the West.) In 1978, Georgi Markov, an exiled Bulgarian writer living in London, was stabbed by a man who appeared to be merely picking up his umbrella from the pavement. Within the night, Markov died, but not before he had told his wife about the man with the umbrella. Scotland Yard found a small pellet in his thigh, coated with ricin, a poison made from castor beans.

In Paris, another Bulgarian exile, Vladmir Kostov, escaped a similar death when French doctors removed the ricin pellet in time. The pellet lodged in Kostov's fat layer, where the temperature was not high enough to melt the layer of wax surrounding the ricin. No one knows how many others died without noticing or mentioning the umbrella's deadly brush. According to Washington, D.C., defense consultants Joseph Douglass and Neil Livingstone, "Intelligence sources in the West say that a similar pellet-firing weapon has been responsible for at least six assassinations in recent years, including the leader of a Third World country whose death was attributed to natural causes." CIA-sponsored assassinations are now prohibited by U.S. law.

Alice Olson learned the truth about her husband's death in 1975. After the *New York Times* reported that the CIA had spied illegally on domestic dissidents during the Nixon and Johnson years, President Ford set up a commission to look into other illegal CIA actions. Led by Vice-President Rockefeller, the commission discovered that an unnamed army employee had committed suicide after taking an LSD-spiked drink. The *Washington Post* carried the story and a friend who guessed the connection phoned Alice Olson.

"I screamed," she says. Alice had just left the hospital where she had undergone tests and, shortly after hearing about the *Post* article, her doctor called to tell her she had cancer. "For the next six weeks, I didn't know what pain was where," she says. The army never notified her directly.

The Olson family received a $750,000 settlement and an apology from the government for Frank's death but Alice, who recovered from cancer, feels the potential for another dangerous, overly zealous experiment still exists. "I believe very strongly that the CIA must be supervised when they are allowed funds to do what is fashionable and expedient. The Reagan administration has lifted that supervision," she says, setting her coffee cup down with a pained sigh.

TEN

Plan Schoolyard

Special Operations ran as a sideshow to Detrick's prime mission, the production of biological weapons. During the Korean War, that effort hurtled forward on a crash basis. The Joint Chiefs of Staff gave BW top priority, and the army entertained bright hopes. "BW had a strong emotional appeal. It was new. It seemed to offer fabulous possibilities," according to the in-house "History of the Air Force's Participation in the Biological Warfare Program." As the army's main customer, the air force initiated procurement plans in October 1950 for five thousand biological cluster bombs.

The army had produced some workable biological bombs, but many problems remained to be ironed out. To protect the army's own soldiers from hazards, the bombs had to be monitored for leaks, and to insure their operation, they had to be stored at the proper temperature so the microbes would stay alive. Since the army owned no mobile, refrigerated storage facilities, that meant filling the bombs and flying them in, as needed, to the theatre of war. Working with biological bombs was further complicated because many had to be dropped to start an infection, but with conflicting information on fallout, persistency, and rate of infection, no one knew precisely how many would be needed to do the job. "The Air Force could be fairly accurate in predicting what a biological warfare attack would do to a city full of monkeys but what an attack would do to a city full of human beings remained the $64,000 question," noted the air force's official history.

The army has admitted that it had prepared biological bombs for the Korean War. Furthermore, the highest levels of the military approved a plan to use them covertly, according to a top-secret memo that refers to a "Cover and Deception Plan for Biological Warfare" known as Plan Schoolyard. In February and March 1952, the North Koreans and the Chinese both accused the United States of waging germ warfare. The Americans vehemently denied the charges. Did we or didn't we? To this day, the question remains unanswered.

Bill Powell and his wife, Sylvia, live and work in a quiet San Francisco neighborhood, where they own the House of Charms, a shop filled with the brass, marble, and honey-colored oak of American antiques. Upstairs, in their tall-ceilinged, sunny apartment, they do most of their business in the kitchen, where a heady cup of coffee is always warm. Bill Powell is working, as he has been for the last twenty-five years, on his own account of the germ warfare charges in Korea, and he greets inquiries cautiously. Thin, with dark-rimmed glasses, he smokes cigarette after cigarette, and one senses in him a mixture of obsession and wariness. He has never doubted that the United States did wage germ warfare and over the years has collected many documents and hired many researchers to substantiate his view. But the proof, the smoking gun, the definitive documents, if indeed they do exist, remain elusive.

Powell was born in 1919 in Shanghai, where his father owned and ran the English-language *China Weekly Review.* Raised in the United States, Powell went to journalism school at the University of Missouri and worked during World War II at the Office of War Information in Chungking, China. After the war, Powell's father's health failed, and Powell took over the magazine, which eventually became the *China Monthly Review*. He supported the Communists, a stance that got him branded by the U.S. Passport Office as "a known Red sympathizer." As he locked horns with the United States over its "adventurist policy" in Korea, the Americans would occasionally prohibit the magazine's mailing to the United States.

But the fiercest fight came in 1952 when the Chinese and North Koreans accused the Americans of waging germ warfare. When Powell heard the reports, he was not surprised. "I had some knowledge that the Japanese were doing this [BW]. I didn't come into it cold." In the *China Monthly Review,* Powell wrote, "Proceeding in a vein which surpasses the savagery of Hitler Germany and Hirohito Japan in the last war, the American invaders, by a systematic spreading of smallpox, cholera and plague germs over North Korea have shocked and horrified the entire world. Since VJ Day, Japanese war criminals turned into 'experts' have been working for the Americans in developing bacteriological warfare." He reported that the American planes dropped "special paper and cardboard containers filled with various types of flies, fleas, ticks, spiders, mosquitoes and other bacteria-carrying insects" during February and March of 1952.

In 1953, two months before the Korean War ended, Powell shut the magazine down, citing financial problems, and returned to the United States, aware of Senator Joe McCarthy's witch-hunts but with little inkling of the vehemence of anti-Communist feelings in America. When he spoke publicly in support of China's Communists, it angered the FBI's J. Edgar Hoover, who recommended that the Justice Department's Criminal Division prosecute Powell. Lacking any grounds for prosecution, the Justice Department authorized an investigation into Powell's support of the germ warfare allegations against the United States.

The Justice Department asked for evidence to refute Powell, but the army was reluctant to talk about the subject.

General Crawford Sams, named in one of Powell's articles as commander of a navy "epidemic control" ship involved in BW activities, had filed a report, but it contained "related intelligence information" that made Sams's testimony in court unlikely. When the FBI looked into Powell's allegations that Japanese biological warfare experts conducted research on American POWs during World War II, the Department of Defense conceded that the experiments had taken place, but regarded the information as highly sensitive. Powell's contention that the United States had relied on Japanese BW experts in Korea was also "highly sensitive."

Hauled before Red-baiting committees, Powell took the Fifth Amendment and refused to testify, but he continued to speak out in public, repeating the germ warfare charges and further incensing Hoover in the process. Hoover wanted Justice to act, but the Justice Department doubted that Powell could be convicted of treason. There was a possibility, however, of getting him on a charge of sedition—giving aid and comfort to the enemy.

On April 25, 1956, a San Francisco grand jury charged Bill and Sylvia Powell and their editorial assistant, Julian Schuman, with thirteen counts of sedition. Although many other journalists had reported the germ warfare charges, Powell was the only American who included his opinion that the charges were true, and in the government's view, Powell had done this deliberately to help the Chinese and the North Koreans. To defend themselves, the Powells and Schuman were put in a position in which they had to prove the truth of the articles, but the government controlled all the evidence that might support their case. When the defendants' lawyers subpoenaed the army, State Department, CIA, National Security Council, and other organizations, the Department of Defense wanted to drop the trial. But the State Department pressed on.

After many delays, the trial began in January 1959. Powell now explains, with mock horror, "It was a very different time. They were going to show that Powell accused the government of *lying*." After three days of testimony, something strange happened. The government's lawyer mistakenly referred to evidence that established "actual guilt of treason." But they were on trial for sedition, not treason. In an apparently innocent effort to clarify the remark, the judge repeated that yes, the evidence "would be *prima facie* sufficient to sustain a verdict of guilty under the treason statute." That afternoon, the headline of the *Oakland Trubune* read: "Judge Says Powells, Aide Guilty of Treason." The Powells' lawyers moved for a mistrial on the grounds of prejudicial publicity. The government's lawyers had no objections, but the judge angrily insisted that his remarks had been taken out of context and reluctantly declared a mistrial. Two years later, President Kennedy ordered all charges and investigations dropped. "The government went to extraordinary lengths to make an example of Powell for endorsing the Chinese and North Korean accusations, yet it also went to extraordinary lengths to limit any inquiry into those charges," writes Stanley Kutler in *The American Inquisition.*

The government stopped hounding Powell, but Powell did not stop hounding the government. After the Japanese media, in the mid-1970s, delved into and exposed the twisted past of Unit 731, Powell broke the story in the United States in 1980, detailing the deal cut by the Americans. That deal, which had been heatedly denied by the Americans for over forty years, cast doubt on the denials of the germ warfare charges during the Korean War. "What the Americans did in Korea is almost a carbon copy of what the Japanese did," maintains Powell. He believes that the archives in China and the United States hold the secrets of what really happened, and that they will remain secret since, in today's friendly atmosphere, neither country wants to go over past disputes. Still, some disconcerting bits of information have emerged.

In 1950, the United States had no clearly stated policy concerning the use of biological weapons, but assumed that the retaliation-only policy for chemical weapons also applied to biological weapons. The secretary of defense appointed Earl Stevenson, president of the Cambridge, Mass., consulting firm of Arthur D. Little, to head the Ad Hoc Committee on Biological Warfare and review this and other questions regarding BW. On June 21, 1950, Stevenson met with the secretary of defense for an hour in the afternoon to discuss his committee's report and recommendation that the policy on biological weapons be explicitly changed to use "when militarily advantageous." Although Stevenson's recommendation was not officially approved until 1956, he had a number of supporters during the Korean War.

Four days after Stevenson's visit to the secretary of defense, the North Koreans invaded South Korea. Although the war was conducted under the command of the United Nations, President Truman ordered General MacArthur to send American troops from Japan to help the South Koreans. The United States worried that the North Koreans might unleash BW, and stepped up its own BW preparations. Two weeks after the war began, *Science Newsletter* ran the headline, "Germ Warfare in Korea?" and noted that "germ warfare may get a trial very soon if the fighting in Korea continues." In November 1950, just as MacArthur expected the war to end, China entered, backing the North Koreans. Shortly afterward, Rear Admiral Ellis Zacharias, head of navy intelligence, testified before a congressional committee that "germ warfare combined with devastation of crops and cattle could soon reduce the Russians and their satellites to impotence."

In the spring of 1951, with the war at a stalemate and MacArthur ousted, the first hints of germ warfare surfaced. On April 13, the *New York Times* reported that the U.S. Army had set up bacteriological weapons research labs in Japan, run by World War II Japanese specialists. *Newsweek* and the Associated Press carried brief reports at about the same time of "the secret mission of a Navy epidemic control laboratory" cruising off the shore of North Korea. General Crawford Sams, the ship's commander, made a report, of which the army would only release a sanitized version for Powell's trial. In it, Sams revealed that he planned to kidnap a North Korean patient allegedly ill from plague and take him back to the ship for examination, an act that would have been a war crime.

On May 8, 1951, the North Korean minister of foreign affairs lodged a protest with the United Nations, stating that the United States had used biological weapons in Korea. The charge was smallpox, more than 3,500 cases in the provinces. Nothing more was said, and the protest attracted little attention. Peace talks started up, broke off, and the subject of biological weapons died down until December, when a newspaper dispatch from Rangoon, Burma, said that according to two U.S. officials who requested anonymity, General Ridgeway, the U.S. commander who replaced General MacArthur, had sent the Japanese BW specialists, Shiro Ishii, his second in command, Masajo Kitano, and Jiro Wakamatsu, to Korea with a freighter "carrying all the necessary equipment."

On February 22, 1952, one year after the first charges, the North Korean minister of foreign affairs accused the United States of dropping insects infected with plague, cholera, and other diseases over North Korea. On March 8, Chou En-lai, the foreign minister of the People's Republic of China, accused the United States of the same actions over China. They said that American military aircraft dropped paper packets containing insects, many never seen before in North Korea and China. In the dead of winter, while snow and ice lingered on the ground, villagers claimed that a week before an outbreak of disease, they found clumps of flies, spiders, and bugs on the ground, clustered in unusual clumps. It was not the season for insects to be breeding and hatching and besides, none of these appeared to be native. Villagers said they also found empty containers of leaflet bombs near the insects.

General Ridgeway angrily denied the charges, saying that no man under his command was responsible for any such thing. The secretary of state, Dean Acheson, echoed him, blaming the outbreaks on the "Communists' inability to care for the health of the people under their control," and calling it a ploy for diverting attention from peace talks. The *New York Times* published photographs of the alleged germ bombs and said they were really leaflet bombs and thus fakes. But the same day, General Bullene, head of the Chemical Warfare Service, told a congressional subcommittee that "the means of delivering germs to enemy territory are simple" and involved easily available equipment "such as the containers used for dropping propaganda leaflets."

In fact, one organization with both leafleting capability and knowledge of BW during the Korean War was the CIA. The CIA had a fleet of B-29s and B-50 transport planes, and an extensive capability for printing leaflets and making leaflet drops. A squadron known as the ARC Wings (for Air Resupply and Communications) had six hundred to eight hundred men and specialized in unconventional warfare (UW) activities that could easily have included germ warfare. Whether it did or not is a subject for speculation. A top secret memo, dated October 1952, mentions plans to use the ARC Wings in support of "psywar [psychological warfare] and UW activities" and "an excellent opportunity to evaluate ARC Wing concept under conditions of limited scope."

Public-opinion polls showed that only a small percentage of Americans and Europeans believed that the United States had waged germ warfare. To bolster their case, the Chinese released "confessions" made by twenty-five captured American pilots. While they clearly contain contrived propagandistic statements, the statements regarding biological warfare are, in many respects, plausible. Were the confessions based on fact, or were they elaborate lies concocted by the captors? Whatever the case, the POWs who made confessions were told when they returned that they could face charges of treason for collaborating with the enemy.

After the war, the POWs spoke only reluctantly about their

experiences, with the exception of Colonel Walker Mahurin, one of the highest-ranking officers captured. He became a sort of spokesperson for the group, actively denying that there was an iota of truth to the "confessions." But there are some interesting details in his background. An ace fighter pilot in World War II, he was thirty-two years old in 1950, executive assistant to Thomas Finletter, the secretary of the air force, a position in which he had contact with Fort Detrick and the CIA and knowledge of germ warfare. He was posted to the Far East in December 1951 for ninety days, rather than for a certain number of combat hours as was usual. For the first couple of weeks, he adapted F-86s to making low-altitude flights for attacks on transportation and communication lines. Germ warfare also demands planes capable of low-altitude flights.

In his autobiography, Mahurin mentions one episode that raises more questions than it settles. In Korea, it was unofficial policy that American fighters could follow an enemy plane in hot pursuit into the neutral territory of China. When General Frank Everest saw an F-86 on the control center radar cross the Manchurian border into China and circle the city of Mukden twice, he got mad. The plane was alone, not in hot pursuit. F-86s did not do reconnaissance. The Chinese said they saw low-flying planes spraying something three times in March. Was the F-86 on a germ warfare mission without General Everest's knowledge?

The charges attracted international attention. In Canada, James Endicott, a prominent Presbyterian minister who had worked and lived in China for decades as a missionary, decided to make a special trip to investigate. When he arrived, he was, according to a biography written by his son, York University historian Stephen Endicott, "aware of a massive public health campaign in process—the stopping of southbound trains for disinfectant spraying, the blocking off of certain areas and rapid quarantine measures, the wholesale inoculation of the population for cholera, typhoid and other diseases."

Endicott traveled to rural areas, visited hospitals and labs, questioned eyewitnesses, and examined "bomb-like containers of the type normally used by the Americans for dropping propaganda leaflets." He also saw "smaller, porcelain type bombs in which it was claimed infected insects and bacteria had been delivered," a description that is reminiscent of Ishii's work.

What Endicott saw convinced him that the charges were true, and he cabled the Canadian minister of external affairs: "Personal investigations reveal undeniable evidence large scale continuing germ warfare on Chinese mainland. Urge you protest shameful violation United Nations agreement." Endicott made a broadcast over Radio Peking, repeating his convictions. In Canada, his actions prompted angry editorials about his treasonous and seditious behavior; politicians urged revocation of citizenship. But when Endicott returned and repeated his claims at an enormous peace rally in Toronto almost as soon as he had landed, he received a standing ovation. The government, realizing how difficult it would be to get a jury to convict him, did not press charges.

The International Association of Democratic Lawyers organized a formal investigation in March. It found leaflet containers but no leaflets and, on the basis of this and other evidence, came to the conclusion that the United States had used germ weapons. Shortly thereafter, a much more extensive investigation was undertaken, under the auspices of the World Peace Council, with seven scientists from six countries. The scientists included two Italian scholars; one Brazilian scholar; the director of an animal physiology laboratory in France; the director of a medical laboratory in Sweden; Joseph Needham, Cambridge University professor and expert on Chinese history and science; and Dr. Zhukov-Verezhnikov, the Soviet medical expert who presided over the trial of twelve Japanese BW researchers captured by the Russians. Skeptics would later say that the group was predisposed to hearing China's side of the story.

Whatever its leanings, the members did have their scientific reputations to protect. The commission met in Beijing on June 23, 1952, for almost two weeks, hearing evidence from witnesses, visiting laboratories and libraries. In July, the group visited Mukden, China, and Pyongyang, North Korea, two sites of alleged attacks, where they interviewed witnesses, inspected leaflet containers, and spent a few days with captured American pilots.

In the fall, the International Scientific Commission for the Investigation of the Facts Concerning Bacterial Warfare in Korea and China delivered a seven-hundred-page report. "On account of its very nature, the use of biological weapons is an act exceptionally difficult to prove. Perfect proof might require, for example, that an airplane be forced down with its biological cargo intact and its crew prepared to admit their proceedings forthwith," the report noted. In the absence of perfect proof, the commission looked for a coherent pattern of circumstantial evidence. For example, it wrote that not only were the insects found in connection with U.S. aircraft flying overhead, but leaflet bombs were found nearby; the insects were found in the wrong habitat; in the wrong season; in tens of thousands; with other insects also not found in the same habitat; and along lines of communication.

The commission noted that its "final conviction naturally rested to some extent upon the reliability of hundreds of witnesses interviewed and interrogated. Their testimonies were too simple, too concordant and too independent to be subject to doubt." And it emphasized that the insect drops bore a striking resemblance to those made by Ishii during World War II. "Whether occupation authorities in Japan had fostered his activities and whether the American Far East Command was engaged in making use of methods essentially Japanese were questions which could hardly be absent from the minds of members of the Commission."

Commission member Joseph Needham used to say that he

was 97 percent sure that the charges were true. Today, he says, "everything that has been published in the past few years has shaken the very 3 percent of doubt which I had before and has instead abolished it. So I am now 100 percent sure."

The Korean War ended on July 27, 1953. Unlike the other POWs, who were flown back to the United States, the airmen who made germ warfare "confessions" returned home by ship. "Slow boat," says Powell. Within a few months, *Time* reported that the confessions had been extorted and our boys had been brainwashed (a new term at the time). Germ warfare was propaganda, a Commie plot. According to the air force, it "demonstrated the intention to condition the Russian people psychologically for biological warfare."

What really happened? You can believe that there are natural explanations for the evidence reported by the Commision; that the Koreans and the Chinese concocted the evidence or that the United States waged biological warfare with or without the knowledge and/or authority of higher command. You can believe one of these three possibilities or a mixture of them. It seems unlikely that two countries could orchestrate events, fabricate data, and coach hundreds of witnesses without some suspicion being raised, some hedging, some voice of skepticism, particularly from the International Scientific Commission. While some incidents might easily be explained by poor public health measures, the descriptions of strange insect clusters in the middle of winter, next to leaflet containers dropped by enemy aircraft, cast doubt on the natural occurrence of the diseases. And the stories of American involvement with the Japanese are very suggestive. But until evidence surfaces that would directly implicate the United States, the case of germ warfare in Korea remains a mystery without a solution, a riddle without a satisfactory answer.

ELEVEN

This Is a Test

In the aftermath of the Korean War, the leaders of the biological weapons program retrenched and scaled back their optimism and efforts. Biological weapons were dubbed "an unwarranted luxury." No one in the air force viewed them as a profitable career path. The emphasis shifted to a long-term research and development program that encompassed not only lethal but incapacitating diseases. The research on antilivestock diseases was phased out of Frederick for fear of unintentionally sabotaging the local agricultural industry. As BW budgets hovered around $5 million a year, Camp Detrick was renamed Fort Detrick.

Testing became the backbone of the research and development program, the only real means of resolving the uncertainty that dogged the future of biological weapons. At the University of Maryland, prisoners from Maryland's state penitentiary became the first human volunteers to be deliberately infected with diseases as a means of testing vaccines. In 1956, the army recruited Seventh-Day Adventists (a Christian fundamentalist sect whose strict beliefs in the Ten Commandments made them conscientious objectors, unwilling to participate in combat), with the full backing of church leaders, for Operation White

Coat. The classified program developed vaccines for anthrax, Q-fever, tularemia, psittacosis, and Venezuelan equine encephalitis, as well as information about the symptoms of the diseases and infections and the lethal nature of the strains that cause them. From the Seventh-Day Adventists the army learned, for example, that it took only ten to twenty-five microbes of tularemia to infect someone with the disease, and that if people inhaled 100 to 250 microbes, the disease struck in two to three days instead of five days.

Research on individuals gave useful data on the progress of infectious diseases, but did not begin to answer the army's questions about the effects of wind and weather on the viability of germ bombs. The solution to that problem was to test the weapons themselves. From 1950 to 1969, for almost twenty years, the army tested live organisms outdoors. The tests involved both simulants—supposedly harmless microbes—and the real, pathogenic, disease-causing organisms. They were conducted under such secrecy that the public knew nothing about the scope or the risks of the open-air testing program until Ed Nevin came along.

Edward J. Nevin III looks as though he is enjoying the prime of his life. With wide-spaced eyes and receding gray hair, he moves vigorously through his one-man law office in San Francisco's financial district, handling his business with something between a cajole and a hector. In the transient West, he is a native San Franciscan, the hard-working, successful grandson of an Irish immigrant for whom, in all of its glory and its failings, the American Dream came true.

When Nevin remembers the day in 1976, he sounds as though he is unconsciously taking the witness stand. "I live in Berkeley, and I bought a paper at the BART Rockridge station, left the escalator, and was waiting on the platform when I opened the paper and began to read an interesting story that the army admitted doing a bacteriological warfare experiment in San Francisco. There was a slight headline—very small part of the story on the front page and the bulk of the story on the back page. I have a kind of cynical attitude from my work. I'm not surprised to see the government involved in that sort of thing, so I read it with a little bit of a snicker." He pauses. "Then I turned over to read on the back page that the only known victim was Edward J. Nevin, a retired P G and E [Pacific Gas and Electric] pipefitter. It was a shock."

The article, originally written by John Cummings and Drew Fetherston and run in Long Island's *Newsday,* led off with the headline: "Invisible War Game That Killed. The Army believed the bacterium was harmless when it released it. Then a man died." It detailed an experiment conducted by the army in 1950 to test San Francisco's vulnerability to germ warfare attack. Within a week after the mock attack, eleven patients in a San Francisco hospital developed an infection so rare and so unusual that three medical researchers felt compelled to write the event up in a prominent medical journal. One month later, one of the eleven patients had died. It was Edward Nevin, the grandfather of Edward Nevin III.

The *Newsday* reporters had gotten their lead from Matthew Meselson, who had indirectly heard about the Nevin case in the mid-1960s from a postdoctoral student in his lab. An acquaintance at the navy's Biosciences Lab in Oakland told the student about an army test that had led to the death of a man. Meselson spoke to McGeorge Bundy, President Johnson's national security advisor, urging that secret, open-air BW testing be stopped. Meselson believed the tests had been stopped until the Church Committee hearings in 1975 revealed that the tests had continued until 1969.

According to his grandson, Ed Nevin was born in Ireland on St. Valentine's Day in 1875, immigrated to the United States at the turn of the century, and settled in San Francisco, where at first he took care of horses for a drayage company. Later, Nevin went to work for Pacific Gas and Electric, carving out the trenches and then laying pipe for the wires and gas that would bring the city into the modern age. He framed his citizenship papers and kept the faith, assisting the priests each day at St. Mary's morning mass. Of his seven children, he named the youngest, and the only boy, Edward J. Nevin, Jr. Ed Nevin, Jr., grew up to become a policeman with the San Francisco police department. He also had seven children. He also named his first born son Edward J. Nevin.

In 1950 when Ed Nevin III turned nine, his grandfather got sick and went to Stanford University Hospital, then located in San Francisco's Pacific Heights. (It has since moved to the university's Palo Alto campus.) "My folks had a 1939 Chevy," says Nevin. "I remember sitting in the back seat, parked alongside the park, which was very near the old Stanford hospital. I remember being parked there on that slightly downsloped street, waiting for my parents. They would not let children in the large ward where my grandfather was. I did not have a lot of information about his disease, but I did know my parents were concerned and spent a lot of time there."

His grandfather had an infected prostate, nothing unusual for a man seventy-five years old. The doctors operated on September 7, and, after recuperating, Nevin went to stay with one of his daughters. But the grandfather's chills and fevers sent him back to the hospital a few days later. The doctors dosed him with antibiotics, but he failed to improve. On the first of November, Ed Nevin died. The attending physician listed the cause as "bacterial endocarditis, secondary to *Serratia marcescens*," that is, the bacterium, *Serratia marcescens,* had managed to infect the lining of his heart.

At the same time the hospital diagnosed the *Serratia* infection in Nevin, it diagnosed the bacterium in ten other patients in the hospital. When technician Anne Zuckerman told Dr. Lowell Rantz and Dr. Richard Wheat about the coincidence, they were baffled. *Serratia* infections were rare and neither doctor had seen one at this particular hospital. "Lord knows how many others we didn't get," Dr. Wheat told the *New York*

Times in 1977. In October 1951, Wheat, Zuckerman, and Rantz published their unusual observations in a scientific journal.

His grandfather's was the first death that Ed Nevin III remembers. The rest of Nevin's childhood memories carry a boisterous, confident quality. He describes his family's house in the Sunset district as "a vibrant household with a strong sense of partnership" that included kitchen debates about the dangers of Joe McCarthy's witch-hunt. With his family's faith, Nevin's decision to attend the seminary after graduation from high school surprised no one. But four years later, in 1963, Nevin changed his mind and enrolled at Hastings, the University of California's law school in San Francisco. After a brief stint in Washington, D.C., Nevin returned to San Francisco, practicing first with the city attorney's office, then in partnership with others, and finally on his own.

Along the way, Nevin discovered that he loved the courtroom more than the backroom. "There is a challenge to place an issue before the tryer of fact in a persuasive and compelling manner, to win, to accomplish your own view of a just cause," he says. "You get involved in so many specialties. I've become a jack of all trades and a master of none." That is not entirely true. In fact, he became well known and respected in the city for medical malpractice cases. By the time Nevin read about his grandfather's death, he could not have been in a better position to respond if the hand of fate had been guiding his actions along the way.

Nevin knew nothing about germ weapons. "Absolutely nothing," he says, shaking his head. "I had no idea we had a division of the government in charge of it, or that Nixon had stopped offensive production. I knew nothing at all." In the thick of media calls that followed the story's publication, Nevin met with his father and aunts, in part because the press kept asking, what are you going to do? "We decided that we were going to do something but we didn't know exactly what.

As can only happen in trusting families, someone said why don't we get Belli?" Nevin chuckles at this mention of Melvin Belli, the San Francisco medical malpractice attorney notorious for the enormous settlements he has won his clients. "I suggested that maybe I should humbly try and do it myself."

Immediately after New Year's, just in time for President Carter's inauguration, Nevin flew to Washington and spoke to California congressmen Pete McCloskey and Pete Stark, but it was Senator Richard Schweiker from Pennsylvania who proved most helpful. Some of the germ weapons tests reported by the *Newsday* team took place in Pennsylvania, but more importantly, a strange, perplexing disease had struck a convention of American Legionnaires in Philadelphia that summer, and rumors traveled that it had been a biological weapon.

Nevin looked into the possibility that legislation could be passed, compensating his family for the government's mistake. But such legislation was allowed only if the courts held no recourse. That decided it. The Nevin family would sue the government for negligence. "It is one of those ironies," sighs Nevin across the table in his office. "My grandfather instilled in us a tremendous love and respect for the whole system. We were about to take on that system."

Nevin knew that the odds ran against his family because the grounds for an individual suing the government for negligence are as shaky as the San Andreas Fault. "There is a tradition from British law consistent with the monarchy that you can't sue the king. If the king rolls over you with his carriage and you break your ankle, too bad. Immunity for the king became immunity for our new form of government," explains Nevin. However, that immunity is not absolute. In certain cases, the government does allow a suit, but it decides when and where. Would the government allow this case? Even if the government would not, Nevin wanted a chance to prove that the government's germ test caused his grandfather's death. He wanted his day in court.

A tort case against the government is not tried in front of a jury but before a judge, in this case Sam Conti, a man with a conservative reputation. In March 1981, Nevin and John Kern, the government's lawyer, spent two weeks examining and cross-examining, hearing testimony from scientists and generals, most long retired, many with ailing memories.

What emerged was a picture of the American biological weapons program that no one outside it had ever glimpsed before. The genesis of the army's "vulnerability testing," as the army dubbed the San Francisco test, was a report written in the aftermath of World War II. In 1948, a group of scientists known as the Committee on Biological Warfare told the secretary of defense, James Forrestal, that because biological agents made good subversive weapons, we stood susceptible to covert attack, and the biological weapons program begun at Camp Detrick during the war had its hands tied as far as preparing a defense was conceived. They wanted authorization to "engage in research and development in the field of special biological warfare operations." Special operations was then, as now, a euphemism for clandestine, dirty-tricks warfare. Forrestal okayed the creation of the Special Operations Division, the top-secret organization closely linked with the CIA.

A year later, the same scientists recommended conducting large-scale field tests to "quantify" the havoc that could be wreaked by the conscious and secret decision to spread disease. Test the ventilating systems, the water supply systems, the subways, they said. In the dead heat of August, the army placed a little over a pint of *Serratia marcescens* in only one air-conditioning unit of the recently constructed Pentagon. The bacteria, thought to be harmless, easily infiltrated one of the world's largest office buildings. In April 1950, the army turned to the coast, spraying ships anchored off Norfolk, Virginia, with *Serratia* and additionally with another apparently harmless bacterium called *Bacillus globigii*. Again, the germs contaminated the ships, and more easily and effectively than imagined possible.

Another committee of scientists reported in June 1950 on these limited but what they believed to be impressive field trials as the Cold War chilled American views of Russia. An overt or covert operation against the United States would be so easy that "with the Soviet proclivity for undercover operations and the relative ease with which biological warfare agents can be clandestinely produced and disseminated, the Soviets are not likely to overlook the sabotage potentials of biological warfare," they wrote.

But the committee also reached the equally important conclusion that neither should *we* overlook the potential of biological warfare. They recommended an "increased effort to prepare the United States offensively for biological warfare. Large-scale field tests on the biological warfare agents and munitions should be carried out as soon as possible." If buildings and ships proved such a snap, what about a city? How would the traffic, the jagged buildings, the crowds, and the heat twist a cloud of germs? Why not stage the mock attack on San Francisco? The port city squarely faced the enemy, and, besides, a navy biological warfare laboratory in Oakland would cooperate. Just two weeks later, General Anthony McAuliffe (better known as "Nuts" McAuliffe because that was the sum total of what he said when the Germans asked him to surrender in World War II) gave his blessing by secret letter.

At the end of September, Camp Detrick scientists flew to Oakland, and in coordination with the navy's lab, loaded the germs to be tested on a navy minesweeper docked at Treasure Island in San Francisco Bay. On September 20, the US ACM-13 steamed under the Golden Gate Bridge and went offshore several miles. For the next six days, the scientists on board supervised the spraying of the city.

On the seventh and last day of the tests, the ACM-13 left harbor, headed offshore 2 miles and cruised along the coast. Between 5:00 and 5:30 in the evening, just before sunset, they released *Serratia*. It was warm, nearly 70° F, and an invisible cloud, five miles long and 200 feet thick, rose above the ship, creeping across the water to San Francisco and from there across the bay into Berkeley, Alameda, Richmond, Oakland, and San Leandro. The wind blew gently, 4 to 5 miles per hour, and a temperature inversion pressed the mock-deadly cloud low over the city.

Just how far the germs spread, the army scientists tried vainly to calculate. A Detrick microbiologist flew in a helicopter halfway between ship and shore, holding a Petri plate out of the window at 50-foot intervals up to an altitude of 600 feet, and found the germs concentrated between 350 and 450 feet. But the people at the ground-based sampling stations around the Bay Area found none of the distinctive red colonies that the *Serratia* formed. Did they die before reaching the bay? As with any germ test, the scientists expected that only a small fraction of the bacteria, 5 percent in some cases, would manage to spread as a vapor. Did sunlight and salt air destroy those traveling on the wind before they drifted over land?

Scientists labeled the seventh test inconclusive because "exposure to the elements caused it [*Serratia*] to lose its ability to pigment to its usual color." Only the six earlier tests with hardier microbes allowed the scientists to conclude that you could blanket San Francisco and up to 20 miles inland with germs if you knew which way the wind was blowing. The residents of San Francisco each inhaled five thousand or more particles. If the agent had been pneumonic plague, 75 percent of those people would have gotten the disease.

The disputes at the Nevin trial turned on the origin of the *Serratia* infection that killed Nevin's grandfather. Both sides made clear how slippery it is to try a bacterium for murder, especially thirty-one years after the facts have all but disappeared in memory. In the 1950s, scientists considered *Serratia* to be a benign, innocuous, garden-variety bacterium, a perfect tracer for experiments. Before the San Francisco vulnerability test, Detrick scientists had tested it on themselves. "We used *Serratia marcescens* in such unbelievable numbers that you would have to see the kind of experiments that were done and none of us thought there was any problem. Nobody got sick, as a matter of fact," said George Connell, one of the Detrick researchers and, in 1976, assistant director of the Centers for Disease Control.

But over time, particularly as more and more doctors prescribed antibiotics, physicians realized that *Serratia* could turn deadly. Virulent, antibiotic-resistant strains flourished in hospitals, causing disease in the healthy and serious disease in the sick. Today, the disease is well recognized but not widespread. At San Francisco General Hospital, there were, in 1977, about five cases where *Serratia* infected the heart, usually among heroin addicts.

In 1952, after reading the journal article authored by Wheat, Rantz, and Zuckerman, the army convened a panel of scientists to review the safety of *Serratia,* but without directly examining the evidence cited in the paper. "Our conclusion was that it was a coincidence," says Alexander Langmuir, former head of the Epidemic Intelligence Service at the Centers for Disease Control and one of those consulted by the army. "At the time, *Serratia* was not recognized as a pathogen." In the secret meeting, the scientists recommended that one of the authors of the article—Dr. Rantz—be granted a security clearance so a more thorough investigation could be done, but somehow he never received it.

At the trial, General William Creasy, head of the army's Chemical Corps, said that Rantz died before his clearance came through. When Nevin found that he had died a decade later and showed Creasy to be wrong in court, the elderly man challenged the much younger Nevin to a fistfight. For whatever reasons, the army had never followed through.

In 1977, Dr. Wheat said that if he had known about the *Serratia* tests, "We and other bacteriologists in the area would've gone out looking to see what effects the tests really had on the population. They [the army] were not studying the potential for illness. This was an unreported ailment so that if people were ill, I don't know how they would have shown it. No one checked with our hospital to see if there was an influx of illness. We might not have published our report and if we did [know], it would have been in quite a different vein—about the potential for airborne infection."

When and where did grandfather Nevin pick up the *Serratia* that killed him? The army argued he got it in the hospital. All eleven patients with the *Serratia* infection had catheters, which could have served as routes for the infection, which the doctors and nurses could have passed along as they treated the patients. Although dates are disputed, the army said Nevin contracted the *Serratia* infection on September 7, just after surgery and two weeks before the tests began.

The scientists testifying for the Nevin family did not dispute these possibilities, but found the coincidence of the *Serratia* infection so unusual that they concluded the army's tests caused his death. Stephen Weitzman, physician and former professor of microbiology at the State University of New York at Stony Brook, testified at the trial that the coincidence of time and place was overwhelming, and there was a good probability that the organisms used by the army were the source of Nevin's infection. Matthew Meselson, professor of biochemistry and molecular biology at Harvard, said, "You have one report [of *Serratia* infection] in the right place at the right time. It would be remarkable if there was not a connection."

But according to Judge Conti, there was no connection. He believed none of the plaintiff's arguments and ruled against the Nevin family on every count. He held the government immune from prosecution because the decision and approval for the tests came from the highest levels of the government, which had what is known in legal circles as "discretionary function immunity." The army was not negligent in using *Serratia marcescens*. The army's *Serratia* did not kill Nevin. In fact, the *Serratia* sprayed by the army died before it hit the city, and

Nevin had already contracted a *Serratia* infection in the hospital. As Ed Nevin III says, the only point on which everyone agreed was that his grandfather had died. Ed Nevin III appealed all the way to the Supreme Court, which denied his motions in 1984.

Today Nevin sounds philosophical about his loss. "I was pleased because the trial brought out the story of what can happen in a free society." Even with Nevin's exposure as an attorney to the seamier sides of life, the view of the U.S. biological warfare program left him dubious of its values. The biological warfare scientists, he says, "were defending a lifetime of service and sacrifice. They gave it all up to develop weapons for the army. And I, in effect, was laughing at them, saying they were the only known people in the history of the U.S. to attack an American city other than during the Civil War. No matter how sincerely I presented my case, I was ridiculing them. And I do ridicule them. I think it was naive, a superficial, unsophisticated scientific level of pursuit. The real scientists do snicker at them because it was bad science. Who would think you can gain anything of real value by spraying bugs into the air?"

"Open-air testing was foolish. The country is not better off. No action was taken as a result of those tests," says Meselson. "Nothing was proven because the results were kept secret." Although justified as defense, the secret tests served a more significant purpose. The researchers at Fort Detrick were convinced that biological weapons had a role in the military's future, but others were not so sure. "The line officers of the navy, army and air force would not consider using such weapons without proof," says Alexander Langmuir. "These demonstrations were part of a feasibility test to show what would happen."

What bothered Nevin the most was the testimony of Dr. Charles Phillips, who as the director of physical defense at Fort Detrick had overseen the tests. When Nevin asked Phillips if he would approve the tests if he were in a position of authority and responsibility today, Phillips said yes. "A certain aspect of the trial was that this was an unfair review of an earlier time, a historical event, an activity no longer pursued, so why beat a dead horse?" says Nevin. "I felt we were validated when Phillips made it most contemporary and said he would. And we see that they are spending more and more money in each budget for bacteriological warfare."

Nevin pauses. "The current administration is backing away from the commitment of 1969. There are pretty significant increases of expenditures in that portion of the defense budget. You begin to wonder if they should not be called to question about the distinctions and definitions of offensive versus defensive. That seems to me the area of danger—they can assert and allege a defensive goal where it is really offensive. And we've promised that we would not do any more offensive work."

Documents released by the government at Nevin's trial showed that the San Francisco vulnerability, or feasibility, tests led to many more. They record that between 1950 and 1969, over three hundred took place, more than one per month. Most involved what were believed to be harmless simulants. From coast to coast the army sprayed the country with the microorganisms *Serratia, Bacillus globigii,* and *Aspergillus fumigatus;* with the chemicals zinc cadmium sulfide and sulfur dioxide; and with odds and ends like ground cork, talc, lipstick, glass beads, dye, and soap bubbles.

The army targeted every ecological niche and demographic profile: Santa Barbara and central Alaska; the Mojave Desert and Minnesota's Chippewa National Forest; the Pennsylvania Turnpike and State Highway 16; Washington, D.C., and eastern Washington state; New York City and Redwood City; San Clemente and San Diego; Saint Louis and Corpus Christi; Key West and South Carolina's Wambaw Swamp.

They put military bases to the biological test as well, dropping simulated germ weapons on forts, schools, air force bases, camps, and test stations in Maine, Virginia, Ohio, California, North Carolina, Arizona, Maryland, and Florida. Since the United States had an informal cooperative agreement with Canada on biological weapons research, the army also went north, testing over the great plains of Alberta and the eastern maritime provinces.

The local health officials knew nothing of the tests and so did nothing to monitor their potentially dangerous health effects. As a result, it is impossible to say what damage, if any, the testing did. *Newsday* reported that cases of pneumonia increased in Key West and Panama City, Florida, after germ testing there in the early 1950s, suggesting a cause and effect relationship. But Florida health officials denied it.

If local people knew about a test, they never knew its true aim. In the summer of 1953, for example, the citizens of Winnipeg believed that their city had been selected for an experiment in creating an artificial fog that would spoil attacks by Russian bombers. The test's organizers recruited sixty-two people, some to spray aerosol cans of luminescent yellow powder into the air and others to hold glass plates that would record the particles' drift. They sprayed over a one-square-mile area downtown, then over one square mile of wheat fields, grazing land, and swamp outside the city, without realizing, until many years later, that they had simulated a germ warfare attack.

The Winnipeggers had sprayed and had been sprayed with zinc cadmium sulfide, a fine powder mixture of zinc sulfide and cadmium sulfide that fluoresces different colors under ultraviolet light. Long used as a tracer in air flow and air pollution studies, its safety has been questioned. Dr. L. Arthur Spomer, a former U.S. Army scientist who now teaches at the University of Illinois, noted that cadmium is a highly toxic element and the mixture is "a potential human health hazard." But a 1980 study done by the Canadian government concluded that the concentration of zinc cadmium sulfide over Winnipeg came within acceptable health levels.

With more circumspection but no less diligence, the army tested the real diseases, exploding germ bombs on the test grids at Dugway Proving Ground in Utah. Initially, it tested psittacosis, brucellosis, tularemia, plague, and Q-fever. By 1954, the army added anthrax, San Joaquin Valley Fever (a hardy spore-forming fungus found in California's San Joaquin Valley), and Venezuelan equine encephalitis.

"The basic principle of the BW program at Dugway was that they could experiment with whatever was indigenous," says Telford Work, a physician and professor at UCLA's School of Public Health who was involved in monitoring the army's testing program. In 1953, a special oversight committee of scientists urged testing only those germs already present and relatively widespread in the country's animal populations, a recommendation that left plenty of room to maneuver since that included tularemia, brucellosis, plague, anthrax, and psittacosis. When the army wanted to test the first anthrax weapons outdoors, the committee uged caution, well aware of the British government's experience in World War II, in which an anthrax test permanently contaminated the small Scottish island of Gruinard. They wanted vaccines handy, only a minimum number of spores released, and the test conducted when the wind would not carry the germs outside the test area. Finally, the committee suggested that a public health official should keep watch in case the Dugway diseases escaped into the population.

Problems may have developed or experience proved how difficult it was to control the aerosols, because a subsequent oversight committee urged greater restraint. It suggested that new diseases be studied for at least a year in the laboratory before releasing them outdoors. It also wanted Dugway scientists to study the way aerosols drifted from Dugway's test grid to

Highway 40, thirty-five miles to the north. Apparently the committee balked at the army's plans only once, refusing to sanction its proposal to drop bombs of infection-laden mosquitoes.

In the early 1950s, Dugway hired scientists from the University of Utah to study the local animal populations and monitor the animals for the diseases that Dugway was testing. If anything leaked off the test ground, the army would know, and if not, the army would increase its fundamental understanding of the diseases. That knowledge might prove useful for offense. For example, if tick bites spread tularemia from infected animals to man, one might consider infecting the wild animal population as an act of sabotage.

The university scientists studied coyotes, foxes, mice, and jackrabbits, as well as fleas, ticks, and mites out at Dugway, and raised animals in captivity at the university campus in Salt Lake City. During the late 1960s, a fire broke out in the university's research area and fire marshals were told to let the building burn rather than enter, a comment that first alerted the university community to the existence of the classified project. At the height of the Vietnam War, the discovery of the secret research and its link to Dugway's biological weapons testing drew campuswide protest.

The army also experimented, although less avidly, with germs targeted against livestock and plants, exploding feather bombs infected with hog cholera over pigpens at Eglin Air Force Base in Florida, and dropping Newcastle disease over a chicken farm owned by the University of Washington. By 1954, the army had phased out its efforts against animals, in part because its antipersonnel weapons also affected livestock. The army turned over its research facility on Plum Island off the coast of New York's Long Island to the Department of Agriculture, whose aim was essentially biological defense, preventing foreign animal diseases from entering the country. But the idea of attacking livestock surfaced again in the 1960s, when the army tested the vulnerability of stockyards in Fort Worth, Kansas City, St. Paul, Sioux Falls, Sioux City, and Omaha. For a simulant, they chose, appropriate enough, a deodorant.

With more gusto, the army tested crop-killing diseases, spraying fields in towns in Minnesota like LeSueur, Morris, Waseca, Crookston, Duluth, and Rosemount with simulants. Other crop tests took place over Yeehaw Junction, Florida; Hays, Kansas; Langdon, North Dakota; and Beaumont, Texas. The army also tested the real thing, spores of wheat stem rust, on fields of wheat expressly planted at Dugway for that purpose, and spores of rice blast, spraying rice fields at a Florida bombing range.

In the early 1960s, the army was ready to expand beyond Dugway. There was Fort Greely in Alaska, where the army tested how biological weapons spread in cold climates like the Soviet Union's. But it was not satisfied and wanted a remote, isolated, tropical island test site too. In 1962, the Smithsonian Institution signed a partially classified contract with Fort Detrick to study the migratory routes of birds in the Pacific Basin. From the Pribolof Islands in Alaska to the atolls in the deep Pacific, ornithologists banded over two million birds, including boobies, frigates, and cormorants, collected specimens, and took blood samples which they sent back to Detrick for analysis. They tracked the birds visually and with radar and eventually found Baker Island, 1,700 miles southwest of Hawaii with an abandoned World War II airstrip and no bird life. When the army conducted field tests with pathogenic organisms, much of it was done in the Pacific. Tests with insects and probably Q-fever and Venezuelan equine encephalitis took place on Baker Island, while tests of other BW agents were also conducted over Johnson Island and Eniwetok Atoll.

In 1970 the Pacific Ocean Bird Project ended after the Pentagon had spent $3 million. Did the Department of Defense buy more than a tropical test site for its germs? In all likelihood, the answer is yes. Sidney Galler, one of the Smithsonian scientists and former researcher at the Office of Naval Research, was quoted by the *Washington Post* in 1985, saying, "I was not interested in germs. I was interested in the animals and their behavior that could be utilized by an enemy to carry the germ."

The idea was not too farfetched. In the 1950s, Detrick scientists had experimented with "bird bombs." When birds were dusted with cereal rust spores and released over a field of seedling oats, a heavy rust infection set in. Homing pigeons dusted with spores, after flying 100 miles retained enough on their feathers for almost three weeks to start an infection. The CIA had also funded research on using a wide variety of animals to carry disease. Birds migrate long distances and, as the military strategists say, reach their targets with high accuracy, which make them attractive as fine feathered intercontinental germ missiles.

From the testing years, the covert attacks seemed the easiest to carry out and the most successful. At Washington's National Airport in the early 1960s, the army tested ways to spread smallpox covertly, using several agents who roamed the main concourse, the north terminal, and the shuttle area. In a predesignated spot, one agent left his briefcase, which hid a minigenerator that spewed harmless bacteria into the air for thirty minutes. Carrying air samplers hidden in their briefcases, the other agents picked and followed a passenger at random, taking air sample readings. The study, still partially censored today, concluded in chillingly spare prose that smallpox made a fine biological weapon. Highly infectious, spread from person to person, it had a long enough incubation time to allow the agents responsible for the attack to flee out of the country long before doctors had diagnosed the first case. Besides, doctors who have never seen a case of smallpox would not recognize it at first, and the demand for vaccines would be enormous. Not only airports, but passenger terminals, national conventions, and major sporting events made good covert targets.

The Church Committee's investigation of governmental intelligence operations disclosed what is perhaps the most notorious biological weapons test. It took place inside New York City's subway system from June 7 to 10, 1966. Agents who carried letters that identified them as representatives of an industrial research organization cracked lightbulbs, filled with the harmless microbe *Bacillus subtilis,* over ventilator grills on the sidewalk above the 7th and 8th Avenue lines. Charles Senseney, the engineer who developed the "microbioinoculator," participated in the test. When the cloud of bacteria engulfed the subway riders, they looked up and reportedly kept on walking. Agents also dropped the bulbs on the subway tracks in front of oncoming trains. Dispatched to the ends of the lines, other agents recorded the levels of bacteria in the air. The upshot of all this might have been predicted: A large portion of New York City would be sick if key subway lines were hit with a biological weapon at rush hour. If 30 percent of the city was sick enough to seek medical help at the hospitals, so the report indicated, the city's health care system would be totally incapacitated.

TWELVE

Army Field Manual 3-10

At the time the army was combing the Pacific for a remote island test site, the U.S. chemical and biological weapons program prospered. When President Kennedy took office, he ordered a far-ranging review of the Defense Department. As part of that review, the Joint Chiefs of Staff asked the Chemical Corps to give an update on progress in CBW, a move akin to asking the wolf to size up the chicken coop. Not surprisingly, the Chemical Corps found CBW preparations to be desperately weak and requested $4 billion in the new budget. They got it.

The Vietnam War offered a test ground for Detrick's products. The military apparently toyed with the idea of using germ weapons. Why not drop rice blast, a crippling disease, on the Vietnamese rice paddies? It could have been done, but since the Vietnamese planted many different strains of rice, which matured at many different times, and the blast could only infect during a critical period of the plant's life, blast bombing would have been a logistical nightmare. VEE, or Venezuelan equine encephalitis, looked like a promising candidate to use against the Viet Cong, but who could insure that it would not backfire and infect our own troops? It was hard enough dodging friendly fire in the jungle, let alone a virus you could not see. In planning for a 1965 invasion of North Vietnam, BW experts apparently wanted to use tularemia to "soften up" the enemy, but this plan and other BW ideas reportedly did not receive serious attention.

Of all the weapons researched and developed almost entirely at Fort Detrick, only herbicides commanded serious attention and saw extensive use. The air force liked their predictable and apparently benign effects, as well as the ease of operation. In 1961, the Kennedy administration okayed the secret use of Agents Orange, White, Blue, and Purple in Operation Hades (later renamed Operation Ranch Hand) to defoliate the jungle and destroy crops in Vietnam. Four years later, the American public learned about the decision.

Over ten years, the United States sprayed a hundred million pounds of the herbicides, covering almost six million acres, or one-seventh of the entire country. The main idea was to make the leaves fall off the trees, deny the enemy cover, and thus prevent ambush attacks. When used along lines of communication, it drove the Viet Cong deeper into the jungle, where they continued ambushing, increasing the number of their attacks, and using stronger forms of artillery. The other idea was to destroy crops in the northern and western parts of South Vietnam to starve the enemy out. But the first people to starve were usually not soldiers but civilians. Even before the discovery of the possible dangerous long-term health effects (cancer, birth defects) on American soldiers, many believed that herbicides—the one notable "success" of Fort Detrick's years of effort—failed as weapons of war.

In the summer of 1963, Harvard biochemist Matthew Meselson entered the strange world of biological weapons. Paul Doty, another Harvard biochemist who served on President Kennedy's science advisory team, asked if Meselson would like a summer consulting job at the Arms Control and

Disarmament Agency in Washington. "I wanted to see what the world looked like from inside the government," said Meselson. After a week of analyzing ways to curb nuclear weapons, Meselson requested reassignment to a subject he knew something about. He was given biological and chemical weapons.

Meselson has the self-confident air of one who found his niche early in life. An only child of a middle-class Jewish family in Los Angeles, he grew up with a laboratory in the family's two-car garage, where he isolated rare earth metals. He sold the metals to a Scotsman in New York City who offered to make him a partner, the closest Meselson says he has ever come to making a business deal. At sixteen, he entered the University of Chicago without a high school diploma (he never fulfilled the physical-education requirements). He graduated with a degree in liberal arts after taking a year at the California Institute of Technology and a year in Paris.

It was at Cal Tech that Meselson met Peter Pauling, the son of Linus Pauling. One day when the boys were swimming in the family pool, the father asked Meselson about his plans for the future. Meselson said that he wanted to do work in mathematical biophysics at the University of California after he graduated. Pauling asked why Meselson shouldn't become his graduate student instead.

In the public mind, Linus Pauling is now associated with the idea, right or wrong, that Vitamin C thwarts the common cold. But in the 1950s, the international scientific community celebrated Pauling as a virtuoso, the great American chemist. Exuberant, brilliant, and intuitive, Pauling's studies on the nature of the chemical bond laid the foundations for molecular biology and won him the Nobel Prize in Chemistry in 1954. Pauling had been a contender in the race to decipher the structure of DNA, but James Watson and Francis Crick had beaten him to the punch. Later, both acknowledged they owed a formidable debt to Pauling's pioneering discoveries, particularly those on the helical structure of the fibrous proteins in hair, muscles, and feathers.

Pauling, who also won the Nobel Peace Prize in 1963 in recognition for his work on the nuclear test ban, knew the perils of mixing science and politics, and quietly communicated these to his student. In 1957, Meselson found himself working late in the lab. He had spent much of the term organizing a conference on the biological effects of nuclear radiation instead of working on his thesis. Pauling characteristically lowered his glasses to the tip of his nose and told him two simple and short stories. In the first, Socrates was asked what was the right activity for an old man. Socrates said politics. Then he was asked what is the right activity for a young man. Socrates said science. In the second story, the mathematician Carl Gauss was asked why he was such a great mathematician. Gauss said it was because he never did anything else. Then Pauling put his glasses back.

After that, Meselson concentrated on his scientific studies. In 1957, he received his doctorate from Cal Tech and began to collaborate with biologist Frank Stahl, whom he had met in 1955 while doing research at Woods Hole in Massachusetts. With Stahl, Meselson performed an experiment that has been called the most beautiful experiment in molecular biology.

The question was: When a cell divides, the DNA is copied, but how is it done so that each daughter cell winds up with the same genetic information as the mother? There were three possibilities: Each daughter DNA double helix could get one chain of the original DNA, and one of the copy; one daughter molecule could get both original chains and one could get the copies; or the original and copy could be dispersed at random in the daughter molecules. Meselson and Stahl grew *E. coli* in a solution containing the heavy isotope of nitrogen, and at each stage of the bacteria's growth extracted and isolated the DNA. By tracking the "heavy" DNA over successive generations, they found that half of the original DNA molecule went to each of the two daughter molecules. In other words, in replication, the double helix of DNA unwinds or "unzips" and a complementary copy forms along each side of the original. The pattern of inheritance — each new generation getting one-half of the original — matched the pattern originally demonstrated by Mendel.

In 1963, Meselson was thirty-three years old, a professor at Harvard with a top-notch scientific reputation and enough accomplishment to risk entering the political arena. At the Arms Control and Disarmament Agency, he received top security clearance and devoured all the documents he could find on the subject of biological weapons. (Since he was only there for the summer, he decided to concentrate on biological weapons.) He visited Fort Detrick and the CIA. What bothered him most was Army Field Manual 3–10, "The Employment of Chemical and Biological Weapons," an unclassified document written for the soldier that described in simple prose and with a series of graphs how to deliver biological bomblets.

Princeton physicist Freeman Dyson shared the office with Meselson that summer, an experience Dyson describes in his memoirs.

Field Manual 3–10 said that the U.S. was equipped and prepared for biological warfare, that this was the way a modern army should be trained, that every country which wanted to keep up with the Joneses should have its own biological agents and bomblets too. After he read Field Manual 3–10, Meselson vowed that he would fight against this nonsense and not rest until he got rid of it. He worked indefatigably, in private and in public, to expose the idiocy of American policies concerning biological warfare. His arguments rested on three main points. First, biological weapons are uniquely dangerous in providing opportunities for a small and poor country, or even for a group of terrorists, to do widespread damage to a large country such as the United States. Second, the chief factors increasing the risk that other countries might acquire and use biological weapons are our own development of agents and our own propaganda as typified by Field Manual 3–10. Third, biological weapons are uniquely unreliable and therefore inappropriate to any rational military mission for which the United States might intend to use them, even including the mission of retaliation in kind for a biological attack on our own people. Meselson found that it was not difficult to persuade military and political leaders to agree with his first two points.

Persuasion on the third point came later, but as Meselson acknowledged in 1986, at a meeting of the American Association for the Advancement of Science in Philadelphia, it ranked as the least important of the three. "It was not the low military utility of biological weapons that led us to renounce them. The reason was their disutility," he said, emphasizing "dis" with professorial clarity. "It is in the interests of the United States for war to be very very expensive. It would be in the interest of the United States for war to be so expensive that only the United States could do it. It was to limit the number of players in the game. That is the essential argument. It was not lack of utility. It was disutility and that will last indefinitely."

Meselson wrote a paper at the end of the summer urging a ban on germ weapons, but it was classified, and he wonders now how many people saw it. Clearly, it would take more than a summer to ban the weapons. As Meselson continued to consult for other government agencies, he lobbied, wrote reports, letters, and memos, and learned the ropes in Washington. The subject of chemical and biological weapons came into the public eye as the United States escalated its use of herbicides and tear gas in Vietnam. In 1967, Meselson and John Edsall, another Harvard biochemistry professor, organized a petition, signed by five thousand scientists, urging President Johnson to halt the production and use of chemical and biological weapons.

Then in 1968, without any warning, six thousand sheep keeled over in Skull Valley, Utah, victims of a secret and botched nerve gas test. The deaths and subsequent denials by the army alerted the country to the dangers of secret chemical and biological weapons testing in America. NBC-TV broadcast an exposé on the subject which caught the eye of Richard McCarthy, a New York congressman who started an investigation of the CBW program. He revealed a dubious plan conceived by the army to dump old and leaking nerve gas weapons in the ocean. Dubbed "Operation Chase" (for Cut Holes and Sink 'Em), the army planned to ship the leaking weapons from the Rocky Mountain Arsenal in Denver to New Jersey, load them on ships, encase them in concrete, and sink the ships. But a study by the National Academy of Sciences revealed that the army had not properly evaluated the possibility that the operation would set off large-scale sympathetic explosions as the ships sank, endangering the entire East Coast of the United States. The plan was struck down.

Both domestic and international opposition mounted to the use of herbicides and tear gas by the United States in Vietnam. U Thant, then head of the United Nations, sought a ban on both weapons, arguing that the Geneva Protocol prohibited their use. (Only two other nations supported the U.S. position.) Formidable pressure built for the United States to ratify the Geneva Protocol, an action that had been successfully blocked by the Chemical Corps for over fifty years.

In Geneva, the twenty-five nation Conference on Disarmament was looking into ways to further curb biological and chemical weapons by international treaty. In what was a very unpopular move at the time, the British wanted to split chemical and biological weapons and deal with them in separate treaties. "Grab what you can and worry about the rest later," is the way James Leonard, later U.S. representative to the Geneva committee, described the move.

In 1969, Richard Nixon became president and brought

Henry Kissinger to Washington as his national security advis-
or. As a Harvard professor, Kissinger had worked in a building
across the street from Meselson's lab, and since it had the best
lunch room in the area, the two came to know each other. Kissinger had heard Meselson's arguments about biological weapons, and when Meselson offered to prepare a position paper on
the Geneva Protocol, Kissinger agreed.

At the same time, the Chemical Corps asked to have its
missions clarified. Between the ferment in the United Nations
and the uncertainty within the Chemical Corps, President
Nixon decided that the subject of chemical and biological
weapons needed a full-blown review. Enlisting the National
Security Council, along with the Department of State, Department of Defense, Arms Control and Disarmament Agency,
Office of Science and Technology Policy, and the intelligence
organizations, he asked each agency to answer two questions:
What should the United States do with the Geneva Protocol?
What should the United States do with biological weapons?
Each organization would explain the pros and cons of what it
believed to be the best policy and the pros and cons of alterna-
tive policies.

In the fall of 1969, Nixon was presented with a wide range
of policy choices and made his own decision. On November
25, 1969, over a week after Congress had banned open-air testing of chemical and biological weapons, Nixon announced that
he would submit the Geneva Protocol to the Senate for ratifi-
cation, and the United States would unilaterally renounce all
biological weapons. In light of the treaty proposed by the British, it was a shocking announcement, and one that ran contrary
to all the accepted rules of negotiation. Nixon had given
everything away before he even sat down at the table with the
Soviets.

To the public, Nixon explained the decision this way: "Biological warfare, which is commonly called germ warfare, has
massive, unpredictable, and potentially uncontrollable conse-

quences. It may produce global epidemics and profoundly affect the health of future generations. Therefore, I have decided that the United States of America will renounce the use of any form of deadly biological weapons that either kill or incapacitate. I have ordered the Defense Department to make recommendations about the disposal of the existing stocks of bacteriological weapons." At the same time that Nixon was announcing his plans for the "Vietnamization" of the war, he made it sound as if he had renounced the weapons for moral reasons.

The basic objective of U.S. policy, reflected in the decision, was to prevent the proliferation of BW, to deter the use of the weapons, and to limit the damage that other nations would be able to inflict. In his statements, Nixon accomplished these objectives by striking a high moral tone, depicting biological weapons as too horrible for the United States to sanction. By equating biological warfare with an act of primitive savagery, by making the weapons taboo, the United States had drawn a line beyond which it would not go. It had created a powerful psychological firebreak, and any nation that wanted to cross it would have to risk the world's moral outrage and condemnation.

Nixon renounced biological weapons but said nothing about toxin weapons. A *Washington Post* editorial disparaged the limits of the announcement, wondering how we could give up plague only to embrace botulinum. As a result, the president ordered a review of the toxin question. Meselson submitted a paper, said to be influential on Nixon's decision, in which he argued that a toxin ban would preserve the president's credibility. Since toxins did not surpass nerve gas, the United States could renounce them without any loss of national security. Nixon considered three courses of action with toxins: keep the option to produce them, keep the option if methods were discovered to make them without bacteria, and renounce them.

On Valentine's Day 1970, Nixon declared that the United

States would renounce toxins as well. "There had to be a supplement to Nixon's declaration to satisfy the scientists in this country," says Ivan Bennett, who at the time was director of the New York University Medical Center and a member of Nixon's Scientific Advisory Committee. "The water was very muddy." The declaration was carefully worded to include toxins made by genetic engineering, a possibility that scientists had only recently glimpsed.

The agencies consulted supported the renunciation, including the Department of Defense. In fact, Secretary of Defense Melvin Laird lobbied to get rid of the weapons. "The truth of the matter was that our military did not feel they were giving up anything effective. If you read Nixon's declaration, it sounds as though BW was given up because the idea of its use was so horrifying," explains Bennett. To the military, biological weapons were marginal and problematic. It didn't really matter what the Soviets did or did not do with biological weapons. The United States had chemical and nuclear weapons that worked better.

Although Nixon's move was not based on the existence of an international treaty, he invited the Russians to join the Americans in making the ban on biological weapons multilateral. "It took two years for the United States to persuade the Soviets to join the treaty," says Leonard. "The Soviets felt it was important to keep chemical and biological together. Most of our allies supported the idea of keeping chemical and biological together. Only the British wanted to separate them. In two years of nattering away, we persuaded the Soviets to join. It happened for two reasons: The Soviets wanted detente; they were also impressed by American arguments. Once they turned, it moved rapidly." In the summer of 1972, Brezhnev agreed to the Biological Weapons Convention and between 1972 and 1975, when the treaty was signed, ratified, and put into effect, over seventy other countries had joined the superpowers.

The early 1970s witnessed the high tide mark of detente. Although the United States had signed other treaties with the Soviets, the Biological Weapons Convention represented something truly unique and hopeful. It was the first treaty to limit the use of a class of weapons, to make their production and stockpiling taboo. From the outset, the United States and the Soviet Union recognized that compliance with the treaty could never be completely verified because of the nature of biological weapons. The treaty's chief weakness had nothing to do with the issue of verification, but with the wording about what research would be allowed, or considered as defensive, and the complaint procedure that the Swedes in particular disliked. In the event that any party believed that another had broken the treaty, it could lodge a complaint with the United Nations, which could then authorize an investigation. But the investigation could easily be vetoed by any member of the Security Council.

Of all the countries in the world, only the United States admitted to having a biological weapons program, and only the United States publicly destroyed its stockpile. Planning for the process began in 1972 and ended in 1975, under the media's spotlight. "A lot of it was burned and a good deal was neutralized chemically," says Bennett. "It turned out to be very expensive." The program cost upward of $14 million.

Questions about treaty violations came up sooner than anyone imagined. At the eleventh hour, on the eve of the death of the Americans' biological weapons stockpile, the public learned that the CIA had tried to salvage its stockpile. The effort had begun in 1969, just two days after Nixon's Valentine's Day announcement about toxins, when the CIA's deputy director of plans sent a memo to the CIA director explaining how Nixon's decision would affect the CIA's Detrick stockpile. For storing anthrax, tularemia, San Joaquin Valley Fever, VEE, brucellosis, TB, food poisoning (chlorine-resistant food poisoning), smallpox, botulinum, snake venom, and shellfish poison, the CIA paid Detrick $75,000 a year. Since destruction was imminent, the memo writer proposed an alternative: "If the Director wishes to continue this special capability, it is recommended that ... the existing agency stockpile at SOD be transferred to the Huntington Research Center, Becton-Dickinson Co., Baltimore, Maryland."

In 1975, the Church Committee learned that some of the CIA's stockpile also ended up in a CIA-owned warehouse in downtown Washington, D.C., sharing freezer space with incapacitants and mind-altering drugs. Nathan Gordon, the CIA chemist who worked with SOD at the time, explained the action this way to the Church Committee: "I was not a Department of Defense employee. I did not feel under the obligation to be responsible for the DOD directive indicating the destruction of bacteriological agents or bacteriological toxins." He also said, directly contradicting Nixon's memo, that "We felt — myself, my project officer, and technical consultant — that we were indeed considering a chemical substance, not a biological agent, not a biological toxin."

While the army saved only one to one and a half grams of shellfish toxin for the research still allowed by the Biological Weapons Convention, the CIA salvaged eleven grams, one-third of all the shellfish toxin ever isolated in the United States. The CIA destroyed its toxin cache just before the Biological Weapons Convention came into force in 1975. As a congressman observed in the Church Committee hearings, "Ambiguity plagues the CIA." Does it still? When asked what quantities of toxins the CIA maintained for research purposes, the public information officer answered simply, "No comment."

PART III

BIOLOGICAL WEAPONS IN THE GENE AGE

THIRTEEN

Mission: Defense

If you live in Washington, D.C., or Baltimore and you want to ride bicycles through the farmland, or hunt for antiques, or just take an hour's drive to get out of the city, Frederick, Maryland (pop. 27,557) makes a pretty good destination. Founded in 1732 by German and English immigrants, the town was the first to challenge the Stamp Act laid down by the British, a rebellious move that helped pave the way for the American Revolution. The recently spruced-up brick buildings in the downtown historic district preserve the flavor of Frederick's past without embalming it in quaintness. With dairy farms at its edge and a peaceful view of the Appalachian mountains, the town takes more pride in the pastoral wealth and beauty of Frederick County than in any government-sponsored enterprise.

You could read the local newspaper, hang around the library, and stroll down Main Street without realizing that Fort Detrick makes its home in Frederick, employing more people than any other organization in town. The fort keeps such a low, unassuming profile, and the town pays it so little attention, that the casual visitor is not likely to know that it remains the center for U.S. biological warfare research. Like a husband

and wife who long ago reached a tacit accommodation in their marriage, the fort and the town carry on two separate lives in close proximity, maintaining a polite but cool air between them.

Fort Detrick is still at the outskirts of town, although now the town has edged so close that malls and housing developments effectively merge into the fort. Only a chain-link fence, topped with barbed wire, draws the boundary. Backyards, many filled with the debris of children's toys, butt up against fallow fields, once planted with crops to be destroyed with experimental defoliants. Defending against the threat of biological warfare—the mission of Fort Detrick—seems wildly far-fetched, out of sync with these gentle surroundings.

Although Fort Detrick's sprawling 120 acres are quiet and almost uninhabited, there is something vaguely sinister about the compound's animal pens, loading ramps, paddocks, and lean, barracks-style buildings. Like a nest of snakes, convoluted ventilation systems wrap around the outside of these buildings. Strange-looking pipes, ducts, filters, stacks, and vents are the only hint that something is not quite normal, that in fact dangerous work goes on.

Like excitement, danger has a way of numbing those who regularly taste it. After a while, danger becomes simply a risk, and those dangers that are unavoidable, or that one chooses to live with, become acceptable risks. Since World War II, Frederick has accepted the presence of Fort Detrick and its hazardous research as an unalterable fact of life, like the torpid summer heat. By and large, the fort has been a good neighbor, providing steady employment and never alarming Frederick's residents with any catastrophe.

Although Detrick pioneered laboratory safety techniques for handling highly infectious diseases, accidents inevitably happen. For example, when Larry Ware was the safety officer in the early days of the offensive program, he was working with a new technician who held a Petri plate. "He says, what do you think about this? I looked at it and said yes, that's plague. And woof! This thing went up in the air and landed on the floor." They covered the plate to prevent bacteria from being kicked up into the air, pushed the emergency button, and showered. Just to be safe, they were ordered to spend twelve days in hospital isolation, but they never came down with plague. Others were not so lucky.

Between 1943 and 1969, Detrick workers suffered 423 cases of accidental infection, falling sick with a host of the diseases investigated as biological weapons, particularly tularemia and Q-fever. Of these, three people died, two from anthrax and one from Bolivian hemorrhagic fever. Since 1969, the infection and casualty rate has dropped, a reflection of the added safety features of BL-4 labs, or "hot suites," as they came to be known. According to a Detrick spokesperson, two people have come down with tularemia and two with Rocky Mountain Spotted Fever. No one has actually gotten sick as a result of accidents in the hot suites, although there have been nine cases in which people had to be isolated as a result of exposure to the infectious organism.

Detrick has not been completely forthcoming about its accidents. In 1964, a technician named Howard Dinterman wheeled monkeys that had just been sprayed with an aerosol form of food poisoning—Staphylococcus enterotoxin B—from one lab to another. The monkeys wore no protective clothing and their fur shed the toxin, exposing the unknowing technician and fifteen others. Nine had to be hospitalized, including Dinterman. The doctors told his wife, Lena, that Howard would not survive but he did, although he never entirely recovered and took a disability retirement in 1970. The Dintermans did not learn what Howard had inhaled until over a decade later when they enlisted the help of their congressman to pry the information loose.

In the fall of 1986, Neil Levitt filed a lawsuit, along with the ubiquitous Jeremy Rifkin, charging that the army had failed to explain adequately another type of lab accident. According to Dr. Levitt, a microbiologist who worked at Detrick from 1969 to 1986 and now owns a restaurant in Frederick, the accident took place in 1981 while he and others worked to produce a vaccine against a tropical fever called chikungunya. Long mistaken for dengue fever, another tropical fever that strikes abruptly with high fever, headaches, rash, and debilitating joint pain, chikungunya is endemic in parts of Africa and Southeast Asia, where it afflicted servicemen during the Vietnam War. It has also been viewed as a biological weapons candidate.

To produce the vaccine, the researchers grew the virus in cells from the lungs of a Rhesus monkey fetus. As is common practice in the production of vaccines, the goal was to culture a weakened or attenuated strain that would give immunity but not the disease. In 1980, the scientists thought they had found the strain and subjected it and the cell line to a preliminary safety test to insure that the cell line in which the virus grew was not contaminated by another microbe that would inadvertently slip into the vaccine. But according to Levitt, it failed the test.

In September 1981, 2.3 liters, or about two quarts, of the virus disappeared from the lab in which Levitt was working. Levitt notified his superiors but claims that nothing was done, no investigation pursued. He also charges that the army did not report his findings that the cell line failed safety tests in the 1981 and 1982 official reports to Congress, and that the army "fabricated positive test results for the civil vaccine experiments."

When he quit Detrick five years later, Levitt enlisted his senator, Charles Mathias, to look into the matter. The inspector general of the army answered Senator Mathias's request for information with a letter saying that no formal investigation was conducted because the vaccine would not have threatened public health and safety, if indeed it was lost. It was an attenuated virus, "not biologically hazardous." According to an army spokesman, since there was no evidence that the virus was either stolen or missing, it must have been destroyed by a lab technician.

Today security is looser at Fort Detrick than in the days of the Vietnam War when Quakers led vigils, protesting biological weapons at the gates to Fort Detrick, and picketers lined up to protest the fort's silver anniversary with placards reading "Fort Detrick is not a respectable scientific institution," or "Want to get sick? Consult your local physician at Fort Detrick." Today, Seventh Street leads directly into the fort, and the city bus hurtles through the gates, no questions asked of the riders on board. "Detrick is part of the city now," says Ron Young, Frederick's three-term mayor, a former schoolteacher, and native Fredericktonian. "I've often thought that it would be fine to take the fence down."

Formal visitors do not hurtle through the gates but follow a protocol that involves waiting in a long line, checking in with the military police, producing a photo ID, and receiving an official pass to place on their car's windshield. Where the entire fort was once dedicated to biological weapons work, now those studies are mainly confined to two buildings on a grassy rise beyond the archery range and the helipad, not far from the main gate.

The U.S. Army Medical Research Institute of Infectious Disease, or USAMRIID, (pronounced Use-Am-Rid) occupies a new building, sturdy as a bunker, three stories tall, made of sand-colored concrete. From the roof bursts a thicket of smokestacks and pipes, guyed in place, a dead giveaway to the institute's hazardous aerosol research. The few windows on the ground floor are only slivers. In the event of a castastrophe, the building's concrete shell is designed to contain all dangers, to protect against the biological equivalent of a nuclear meltdown.

Unlike many other Department of Defense facilities, Detrick strives to accommodate journalists. A visit's approval takes weeks, not months, and can seem as simple as making an airplane reservation. For a military installation, Detrick exudes good will, eager to show that it has nothing to hide. Still, the first thing one notices is that the PR escort, Chuck Dasey, carries his own tape recorder. Detrick may have nothing to hide, but the people here are very careful about what they do and do not say.

In the hallway near the commander's office there is a bulletin board posted with an article from one of the supermarket tabloids, dated January 1986. The headline screams something about AIDS being a biological weapon. The idea has been kicking around at least since October 1985, when followers of political extremist Lyndon LaRouche ran an article in one of the LaRouche publications on "The Soviet Role in Covering Up the Deadly Threat of AIDS." Shortly thereafter, the Soviet Union accused the CIA of developing AIDS as a biological weapon, testing it on the dregs of society. Dasey shakes his head, a can-you-believe-what-a-colossal-joke gesture. Indeed, Detrick researchers know viruses and toxins that would be better by a long shot. No military commander in his right mind would pick as a biological weapon a virus that lacks a vaccine or cure.

Colonel David Huxsoll occupies the commander's nicely appointed corner office. In his mid-fifties, a veterinarian by training, his smile is as crisp as his uniform. Since 1983, he has presided over the command of the institute and has seen a prosperous renaissance in its work. Detrick received 95 percent of the total $71.2 million budgeted in 1987 for biological warfare. (The remainder went to Walter Reed and navy research institutes.) Since the Reagan administration took office in 1981, the budget for biological warfare efforts has risen from $15 million to $71.2 million, an increase, after inflation, of 375 percent.

Roughly two-thirds of Detrick's budget is contracted out to

universities, private companies, and research foundations. For example, researchers at Utah State University in Logan, Utah, are studying compounds that inhibit the tropical Punta Toro virus. At Brigham Young University, researchers are cloning anthrax bacteria. SRI International in Menlo Park, California, has four contracts, totaling almost $2 million over the next three years, to synthesize agents that immunize against staphylococcal enterotoxins; to synthesize and test tetrodotoxin and batrachotoxin antagonists; to link antiviral compounds with monoclonal antibodies; to study conotoxins.

The army's institute spends the remaining third of the research budget in house on three programs—Basic Research in the Life Sciences, Basic Research in Medical Defense Against Biological Warfare, and various steps in the development of defensive systems. It employs five hundred people—sixty-six M.D.s and PhD.s—compared with one hundred thirty-four in 1969 during the height of the offensive program. The only other scientific research organization in the country to study the rare, deadly diseases and toxins feared as biological weapons is the National Centers for Disease Control in Atlanta, which with eighteen permanent staff members and a yearly budget of $1 million committed to these particular diseases, is not even a match for USAMRIID.

Huxsoll is well practiced in soothing the fears of the uninitiated. At least once a month, he represents the U.S. Army Medical Research Institute of Infectious Disease to the public, whether it is talking to journalists or to farmers worried about the effects of a biological attack on their crops. And the questions often boil down to the same one. Just what kind of research does Fort Detrick carry out and with what intentions? After all, since the early 1970s, the guidelines for Detrick's program have been concerned less with the end product of the research and more with the motive behind it.

"USAMRIID has the responsibility for developing medical defense against biological warfare agents," says Huxsoll to not one but two tape recorders. "The primary objective is the development of a system of prophylactic and therapeutic agents, drugs, vaccines, and other types of protective strategies that deal primarily with medical management of infectious disease. And of course, we are producing a variety of these things, covering the spectrum of agents that include viruses, rickettsia, bacterial agents, and a number of toxin agents." He pauses. "We work here primarily with high hazard agents, those agents that are of potential biological warfare concern."

Like every professional in the CBW business, Huxsoll refers to "agents." Likewise, in the chemical business, the military talks about nerve agents, not nerve gas. Until recently, it was an enormous faux pas, leading to a conversational dead end, to ask anyone in the U.S. military questions about biological weapons. (You got the answer that biological weapons are banned by treaty.) But ask about biological agents or threats, and the answers come more readily. The dictionary defines the word "agent" as a force or a substance that causes some change. It is a technically correct but value-free, neutral word that diminishes the fear-laden aura of biological weapons and allows the military some psychic room to move.

What agents does the United States perceive as a threat?

"We don't respond with a program without some evidence of a threat, and uh, in the case of a potential biological warfare agent. . . . Let me first go back a bit," says Huxsoll, perhaps wary of answering too hastily. "I'm sure you're well aware that at one time there was a program developing an offensive capability, and that was renounced by President Nixon in 1969 and that whole program was disestablished and all of the agents and everything were destroyed. . . . We know from that work what agents would make good agents, so to speak. That makes up a block of agents that we feel we must be concerned with."

But in the fifteen years since the treaty was signed, how has that list changed?

Huxsoll would rather talk about the vaccines developed by

the army, but he comes round to saying, cryptically, that new-comers have been added, like diseases that weren't discovered in 1969, and which he does not specify by name. He touches on the advent of genetic engineering, the broad umbrella of bio-technology whose advances "enhance not only the number of agents but the availability and ease of production. With that, we're looking at the potential that these kinds of techniques can be adopted by an adversary to make agents available that had heretofore been unavailable."

Later, Dasey reluctantly explains that the list of agents identified by the army as threats is classified. No one at De-trick, least of all Huxsoll, likes the word "classified." In fact, Detrick advertises the fact that the BW defense program is un-classified, but with the strained logic of large bureaucracies, that does not mean that all of the information about the pro-gram is unclassified. "A small percentage of the total workload of the Medical R and D Command is classified," explains Dasey. "For example, if a new tank or helicopter employs classified technology systems, the health-effects research con-ducted on its crew or operators might be classified." That deci-sion is made by several people, including Huxsoll's boss, the head of the army's Medical Research and Development Com-mand, of which Detrick is part.

Huxsoll works hard to counter the legacy of Detrick's in-volvement in making weapons and the inherent ambiguities in a military biomedical research and development program. His concern is for the public at large and for the people who work at USAMRIID. Like the manager of any large scientific re-search organization, Huxsoll must keep the five hundred peo-ple who work under him happy. Detrick's repugnant image, as the headquarters for biological weapons work, still crops up and gnaws away at morale, leaving the scientists isolated from colleagues elsewhere in the field who look askance at the mili-tary connection.

Times have changed somewhat since 1968, when Detrick

held a twenty-fifth silver anniversary celebration and many scientists boycotted the event, including one who declined his invitation by saying, "It seems at best a little like commemorating the creation of the electric chair and at worst, like celebrating the establishment of Dachau." Huxsoll stresses the institute's humanitarian accomplishments. "A lot of people don't appreciate the enormous benefit that a program like this has for the health and welfare of people around the world," he says. "And an awful lot of people don't really believe the United States ever got out, fully got out, of the offensive program. We did."

To the Detrick insiders, the line between offense and defense is as sharp as the line between shadow and light. What happened in the 1960s was offense, what happens today is defense. The difference can be ticked off in the changes that have come to Detrick since the treaty: the jobs lost, the buildings shut down, the fact that germs are no longer produced in vat-size lots and loaded into weapons hardware.

Critics do not dispute the changes, but rather point out that at the scale of research and development allowed by treaty and practiced at Detrick, the activities of a defensive program and the activities of an offensive program are virtually indistinguishable. Consider the way that the work is described in various annual reports to Congress. The goals are "to assess aerosols of microbial organisms, or their toxins, to determine their potential as BW agents"; "to define the unique pathogenic patterns of illness produced by aerosolized organisms"; to study "the penetration, retention, clearance and replication of certain organisms throughout the respiratory tract."

The fact is that USAMRIID takes orders rather than makes them, carrying out a mission defined at higher levels. (It is common for lab-bench scientists not to know what the long-range mission of the command really is.) The unproven accusations about Yellow Rain, the administration's loss of confidence in the Biological Weapons Convention, the sizable increase in funding for biological warfare work, and the Pentagon's claim that genetic engineering may make BW a great weapon cast a new light on what USAMRIID does. What *are* the motives behind its research program?

Individual Detrick researchers argue, convincingly, that their motives are solely and purely aimed at improving defense. "With a shallow depth of field, they are right," says Jennifer Leaning, director of emergency services at the Harvard Community Health Plan in Boston and an activist with the group Physicians for Social Responsibility. "The problem is that they are doing it in a context driven by the military. The application of what they do is beyond their control." It will not be the individual scientists but the Washington policymakers who decide how the information will be used. As Jonathan King, professor of biology at MIT, explains, "The military is not in the business to alleviate suffering."

FOURTEEN

Vicious Viruses and Venoms

"Men go into this branch of work from a number of motives, the last of which is the self-conscious desire to do good. The point is that it remains one of the few sporting propositions left for individuals who feel the need for a certain kind of excitement. Infectious disease is one of the few genuine adventures left in the world. The dragons are dead and the lance grows rusty in the chimney corner."
—Hans Zinsser
Rats, Lice and History (1934)

The transition from Huxsoll's office to the research area of USAMRIID comes abruptly. Powered by electric eyes, double doors swing open onto an orange-painted cinderblock and concrete corridor, swarming with white-coated technicians pushing carts of glassware that clink and echo. Rich, acrid smells of nutrient broth and caged animals fill the gloomy, prisonlike hallway. (Indeed, in this day and age of animal rights activists, Detrick does not advertise how many experimental animals it uses. In 1984, USAMRIID's experiments required 69,106 mice, 5,830 guinea pigs, 3,545 hamsters, 3,013 rats, and about 1,000 sheep, goats, rabbits, chickens, and pri-

214

mates. These numbers suggest the occupational limits that have plagued BW research since the United States made its deal to acquire Ishii's human data. Detrick collects plenty of information on how viruses and toxins destroy lab animals, but never enough on what the bugs do to people.) Another set of electric doors swings open onto a long, battleship-grey corridor that runs the length of the whole massive USAMRIID building and is broken up by windows and doors that look inside the labs where the work with infectious viruses is taking place. Above one door, sealed ceiling to floor with duct tape, reads a sign, "Infectious Area—Crash Door—No Entrance," and then "Virology Suite #4." Next to the door is a window with a sign above warning, "No Photographs." A camera flash once startled a worker in the suite so badly that he bumbled and stuck himself with a needle harboring a deadly disease. Although hot suite workers only use blunt needles just to stay on the safe side, even these can pierce gloves, puncture the skin, and infect.

This is the scientific equivalent of the Fort Leavenworth Penitentiary where the viruses are inmates and the scientists always on guard. This is also the largest collection of hot suites (BL-4 labs) in the country. Designed and developed as a result of the 1970s debates over the safety of genetic engineering, these labs have allowed the list of biological warfare candidates to expand radically. In the offensive days, biological warriors avoided viruses because they could not grow them safely. Now, the old nasties—like anthrax and Q-fever—have been joined by exotic hemorrhagic fevers and debilitating tropical viral diseases, some of which have only recently been discovered.

An experiment is in progress. Dressed in a one-piece, flexible, urethane suit, wearing a clear plastic eyeshield, black rubber boots, and surgical gloves, the technician moves slowly, like an underwater deep-sea diver. The suit is inflated from an orange, spring-coiled tube that hangs from the ceiling, a tether and oxygen lifeline at once. She works under a hood that exhausts the hazardous aerosol particles away, filtering them out before discharging the cleaned air from the building. With an automatic pipette, she sucks liquid out of a beaker, never touching anything, letting nothing touch her. Nonetheless, she appears bothered, perhaps because visitors block her peripheral vision or stare at her like an animal in a zoo cage. Being in the suit is a small taste of what it would be like to face an attack with biological weapons.

She is working with one of the many viruses stored deep in the freezers at Fort Detrick. Their names (viruses are usually named after geographical locations while bacteria are named after people) conjure faraway places instead of the poorly understood ravages of their disease: Lassa, Ebola-Marburg, Junín, Machupo, Congo-Crimean Hemorrhagic Fever, Hantaan, Chikungunya, O'nyong-nyong, Mayaro, Ross River, Rift Valley, Sindbis, West Nile encephalitis, and Oropouche Fever. Some are exceedingly rare and some are widespread. Some kill in a few days and some are as discomforting as a mean flu. They share two key characteristics: They strike suddenly, with almost indistinguishable symptoms of malaise, fever, and muscle pain, and they can be spread by aerosol.

In the BL-4 suites, scientists work with the most dangerous, least understood viruses—those that cause hemorrhagic fevers.

Lassa: Lassa first appeared in 1969 when an American missionary nurse stationed in Lassa, a small township in Nigeria, got sick. After being evacuated to the capital, she died. When her two attending nurses got sick, medical authorities knew they had stumbled onto a powerful new disease. One died and the other was flown to New York City, where she received the best possible care and recovered. From this fortunate woman, doctors isolated the Lassa virus. By checking blood banks, doctors estimated that a mild form of the virus infected two hundred thousand to five hundred thousand people in Central and West Africa each year.

In its deadlier form, Lassa lasts for one to four weeks, with a high, long-lasting fever, chills, vomiting, diarrhea, and complete prostration. Some of the cases turn into a fatal hemorrhagic fever with shock, coma, and cardiac arrest. Of those who reach the hemorrhagic stage, half die. The virus spreads through the urine and blood of infected rats, present in African dwellings due to poor sanitary conditions. There is no cure.

Ebola: Like Lassa, Ebola came to the attention of the West suddenly, as a result of two severe outbreaks that occurred between July and November of 1976 in the Sudan and Zaire. Scientists isolated the virus, named after the Ebola River in Zaire, after 284 people came down with the disease in the Sudan and 151 died, and 318 got sick in Zaire and 280 died. A second outbreak took place in the same area in 1979, but otherwise the Western world has seen little of the virus. With a 71 percent case fatality, Ebola is extraordinarily lethal, triggering hemorrhage on the fifth day and death by the tenth day. But like the AIDS virus, it seems to spread through direct contact with infected blood, which occurs in poor hospitals when needles are reused without adequate sterilization. The virus will not grow easily in the lab, so little is known about it or possible cures.

Marburg: The Marburg virus, which appears to be genetically related to Ebola, first emerged in 1967 in Marburg and Frankfurt, Germany, and in Belgrade, Yugoslavia. After performing autopsies on Ugandan green monkeys, twenty-five laboratory technicians became very sick. Within two weeks, seven had died. The rest recovered after a long convalescence. "If you give the best supportive therapy in the world and a third of the patients die, then you've got a virus that wreaks havoc," says Michael Kiley, a virologist at the Centers for Disease Control. Only two other cases have been seen: a young Australian hitchhiker who died of Marburg in a South African hospital in 1975 and a fifty-eight year old man admitted to a Nairobi hospital in 1978. There is no cure.

Junín: The Junín virus is named after a small town in the province of Buenos Aires. It causes 100 to 3,500 cases of Argentine Hemorrhagic Fever each year in Argentina. Rats harbor the virus and, during the maize harvest from March to June, mechanical harvesters churn across the humid pampas, chopping everything in their path, including field rats. The machines throw up tiny aerosols of infected blood into the air, which the corn pickers unknowingly breathe. Discovered in 1958, Junín has a case fatality rate of 15 to 30 percent. The **Machupo** virus, discovered in 1959, causes a similiar but much rarer disease in Bolivia. The army is preparing a vaccine for both.

Congo-Crimean Hemorrhagic Fever: This virus, first reported among Russian troops in the Crimea in 1944, was later found to be identical to that which caused a fever in the Belgian Congo. It occurs in the USSR, Africa, Bulgaria, Pakistan, Central Asia, and recently in Iran. It is transmitted by ticks and strikes in rural settings near large-scale agricultural projects. Mortality ranges from 10 to 50 percent.

Hantaan: The Hantaan virus causes what used to be known as Korean Hemorrhagic Fever, one of the diseases studied by Ishii as a biological weapon. Now called Hemorrhagic Fever with renal syndrome, it is found in both Europe and Asia, where it is spread through contact with infected mouse excreta. The disease can range from benign to severe, with symptoms of high fever, vomiting, kidney complications, and, in less than 10 percent of the cases, death. A vaccine is under development.

The other viruses, studied without the protective suit but still under stringent safety precautions, are incapacitating but not as deadly. Many are arboviruses, carried by arthropods like ticks, mosquitoes, fleas, and flies. The arthropods act as flying hypodermic needles, transferring the virus from animals to people. Supported primarily by a grant from Fort Detrick, the

Yale Arbovirus Research Unit at the Yale School of Medicine catalogs the world's arboviruses, which now number over five hundred. Less than seventy cause human disease.

Chikungunya: Long confused with dengue (or breakbone) fever, *Chikungunya* is Swahili for "that which bends up," a reference to the severe pain the virus causes as it replicates in the skeletal muscle. It is carried by mosquito, striking quickly with a high fever and excruciating joint pain that may persist for weeks. Epidemics have taken place in India, Nigeria, Thailand, and Vietnam. It is related to **O'nyong-nyong,** a virus that caused one of the largest epidemics in history, afflicting two million people in Uganda, Tanzania, Kenya, and the Sudan in the late 1950s. *O'nyong-nyong* is the Acholi tribe's word for joint-breaker. It is also related to **Mayaro,** a common infection in the Amazon region also found in Bolivia, Trinidad, Panama, and Surinam, and to **Ross River,** a milder viral disease that crops up every year in Australia. Vaccines are in early stages of development.

Rift Valley Fever: This fever was named after the Great Rift Valley, which stretches from Kenya to Ethiopia, where it was first seen in sheep fifty years ago. When diseased sheep are slaughtered by slitting the throat, aerosols of the virus are unleashed into the air. It is also spread by mosquito. After three days of incubation, the virus triggers fever, muscle pain, joint pain, and headache, which subside after three to four days. In 1977, Rift struck eighteen thousand people in Egypt, killing six hundred. The stability of the organism and its infectiousness as an aerosol make it a good BW candidate. A vaccine is being produced.

Sindbis: Sindbis was named after a sanitary district in Egypt where it was first discovered in 1952. It has the widest distribution of any arbovirus. It is found in Australia, Central Africa,

India, and the Philippines, where it is transmited by mosquito and produces a relatively mild disease and no fatalities.

West Nile Encephalitis: Harbored by birds, transmitted by mosquitoes, this mild disease is widely distributed in Africa, the Middle East, the Soviet Union, and tropical Asia. Its fever, headache, and vomiting may last for a few days. In the elderly, it can produce a fatal encephalitis.

Oropouche Fever: This fever was isolated in Trinidad in 1955. It has caused several epidemics in the Amazon region. It lasts for two to seven days, during which patients feel extremely ill and may require hospitalization, but no fatalities have been reported.

Joel Dalrymple, chief of the Department of Viral Biology at USAMRIID, is one of Detrick's resident virus experts. With blue eyes and longish hair, dressed in boots and a flannel shirt, he looks like a cowboy. His body, too big for the low-ceilinged room, looms above the desk. On the wall behind him, a sports magazine photograph shows two people skiing down a glistening slope in Alta, Utah, etching perfect sine waves into the mountainside. Dalrymple confesses that he flopped belly down just moments after the picture was snapped.

One senses from Dalrymple an attitude that drives many of the individuals involved in Detrick's biological defense program. His motive for studying a complex of vicious maladies is not related to biological warfare so much as to the intellectual adventure of being on the frontiers of infectious disease research. The rewards come, in part, from being able to face, to understand, and to conquer the risks.

Dalrymple sounds like a race car driver or airplane pilot in his solemn respect for working in the hot suites. "I don't want anyone to prep my suit," he says. "It is like packing your own parachute." Indeed, it is no picnic to do experiments weighted down with all that gear and paraphernalia. The air hisses so loudly you have to crimp the air supply to talk to your lab partner. The plastic eyeshield reflects the lightbulbs in the ceiling, creating distracting shadows. Heat builds up. Fatigue sets in. You can't scratch or go to the bathroom. And all the time, there is the danger that you will slip and puncture your suit and infect yourself.

After working in the hot suite, everyone showers and checks the suit, just to make sure that no tiny punctures turn up. "It's just instinct," says Dalrymple. "You come out, pull off your glove, blow it up and hold it. You've been working with needles all day. It is refreshing to see a glove that remains inflated."

If all this sounds like overkill, remember that the margin of safety is unimaginably small. There are no vaccines, no wonder drugs, no cures for some of these diseases. Once, a veterinarian came out of the hot suite with blood on his finger after performing an autopsy on a lab animal infected with Argentine Hemorrhagic Fever. Although he found no puncture in the glove, there are no chances to take with an infectious, incurable disease, so the doctors sent him directly to the Slammer, a one-of-a-kind, ultimate quarantine suite set up in USAMRIID's clinic. Doctors and nurses work in suits, never touching the patients directly, even in surgical operations. The Slammer has seen nineteen cases since it opened in 1977—nineteen people exposed to highly infectious diseases, for whom the only hope is to receive transfusions of plasma from someone who was exposed and lucky enough to survive.

But the adventure of working with some of the least understood viruses in the world takes another kind of toll. On top of the isolation that comes from working in the suits, there is another kind of psychological isolation. Outside of the Detrick community, there are only a handful of scientists, some at the Centers for Disease Control, some in Europe, some in the Soviet Union, many tied to biological warfare establishments, who study these viruses. The exotic nature of the work puts Detrick scientists outside the mainstream.

"You go to some of these scientific meetings and somebody says, oh boy, aren't you lucky, the only people working on Lassa in the world. You've got the virus to yourself. That's one attitude," explains Dalrymple. "At the same time, no one is interested in your science. They want to hear about this deadly virus that isn't as deadly as people would like it to be, and you're a freak in many ways. You work for the military. You run around in a crazy suit, locked up in these horrible halls. No wonder people think we're doing evil. For God's sake, it looks like it to me and I work here. But it's not true."

Upstairs from the hot suites, along a tight, windowless corridor, the international sign for "No Bullshit" is taped onto a door that opens into a cramped cubicle of an office. John Middlebrook, whose beard is sun-bleached from a recent skiing trip, is wearing comfortable pants, a vest, and gold neck chain, all of which make him look like an aging graduate student. The bookshelves around him strain with texts on toxins. His desk top is clear except for a translucent, dried snakeskin, shed by a moulting snake that may or may not be on the premises.

With a background in pharmacology and biochemistry, Middlebrook came to Detrick in 1975, when the program focused almost exclusively on infectious diseases. He worked with the classic biological warfare toxins, like botulinum, until the army began to think seriously about the impact of genetic engineering on the future of biological warfare. "There was an increasing recognition by nontechnical people in the army that this [genetic engineering] could be used in nasty ways," he says.

If biological weapons enter future combat, toxins are, by all accounts, the most likely candidates. They act faster than viruses or bacteria (microbes often infect via a toxin) and are hundreds of times more deadly than chemical weapons, which means that fewer munitions would be needed. As the biotechnology industry matures and petroleum prices rise again, they could be cheaper to mass produce than nerve gas.

Today, 50 percent of the USAMRIID's research program focuses not on infectious disease, as its name would suggest, but on toxins. For research purposes, the program is divided into the low-molecular-weight toxins and the high-molecular-weight toxins, a distinction based on modern preparation techniques. Low-molecular-weight toxins are peptides, or protein fragments, which can be chemically synthesized, and those of biological warfare interest include two with particularly strange histories:

Batrachotoxin: Take from *batrachos,* the Greek word for frogs, batrachotoxin is secreted by a bold, brightly colored species of frog that lives along a remote river in western Colombia. The primitive Choco Indians learned long ago that the frogs are too poisonous even to touch and instead used their poisons to coat blowgun darts. Captain Charles Stuart, a British explorer, first described the process in 1823: "Those who use [their] poison catch the frogs in the woods, and confine them in a hollow cave where they regularly feed them until they want the poison, when they take one of the unfortunate reptiles and pass a pointed piece of wood down his throat and out one of his legs. This torture makes the poor frog perspire very much, especially on the back which becomes covered with white froth: this is the most powerful poison that he yields and in this they dip or roll the points of their arrows, which will preserve their destructive power for a year. Afterwards, below this white substance appears a yellow oil which is carefully scraped off, and retains its deadly influence for four to six months, according to the goodness (as they say) of the frog. By this means, from one frog, sufficient poison is obtained for about fifty arrows."

While present-day Choco Indians forsake the frog-poisoned blow darts for more conventional armaments, the U.S. researchers believe the toxin, which was isolated in the early 1970s, would make a good weapon. It seems to work by increasing the permeability of the nerve cell membranes, allowing sodium ions to flood in, leaving muscles in a permanent state of contraction, and ultimately causing the heart to fail.

Tetrodotoxin: Tetrodotoxin comes from the puffer or blowfish, an ugly-looking tropical fish that protects itself by gulping such large amounts of water that its predators can't swallow it. Should that scheme fail, the fish also stores in its skin, liver, ovaries, and intestines one of the most potent neurotoxins known. Experience with the deadly Red Sea pufferfish probably led to the Book of Deuteronomy's warning against eating scaleless fish. But curiously enough, some people derive tremendous pleasure from tempting fate. In sixteenth-century China, cooks learned how to prepare the puffer safely and the fish became a delicacy. In Japan today, the puffer is an item at the best restaurants, prepared by chefs who are specially licensed and schooled in techniques that reduce the concentration of the toxin to a sublethal dose.

In 1986, anthropologist Wade Davis suggested an even more bizarre use for tetrodotoxin when he investigated the story of a Haitian man named Clairvius Narcisse, who claimed to be a Zombi. According to hospital records, a doctor had certified Narcisse's death, and according to eyewitness accounts, the man had been buried. But somehow, Narcisse came back to life many years later, with a scar on his face to show where the coffin nail had passed. When Davis looked into the Zombi rituals, he found that the practitioners used a potion that, he argues, contained tetrodotoxin, presumably in amounts that caused clinical signs of death but not death itself. Several hours after the burial, the Zombi would be revived with an antidote and enslaved to his master.

As a poison, tetrodotoxin acts in minute amounts. Initially, it causes tingling, then numbing, vomiting, muscle twitching, and finally complete paralysis. Although the body is comatose, the person's mind stays clear until the end.

Other low-molecular-weight toxins include **Microcystin, Anatoxin, Saxitoxin, Gonyautoxin, Ciguatoxin,** all produced by microscopic algae; **Palytoxin,** an extremely potent toxin produced by a soft red Hawaiian coral.

The more ominous threats are the high-molecular-weight toxins, which are proteins. A single gene, which is but one segment of the very long strand of DNA in all cells, directs, controls, or oversees the production of a single protein. In the parlance of scientists, the gene "codes" for one protein because the chemical sequence of the gene's DNA affects the subsequent configurations of the protein. Genetic engineering allows scientists to snip a gene out of one cell and insert it into another. The gene that codes for a high-molecular-weight toxin in a scorpion sting, for example, can in theory be inserted into a benign baterium, whose clones will secrete the toxin in far greater amounts than the scorpion ever did.

Middlebrook works with the clonables, but like Huxsoll hesitates to name names. "We do balk at giving out the list," he says, looking to the PR guy, who is shaking his head. But Middlebrook, who apparently likes to be helpful, says, "There are two ways to drive the program. One is to ask what are the nastiest things out there, and the other is to rely on intelligence." The former is the course of action historically taken at Detrick and the cautious approach preferred by the Department of Defense, especially when intelligence is as difficult to come by as in the field of biological weapons.

Ricin?

Made from castor beans, ricin ranks as one of the oldest poisons in use and one of the most potent plant toxins known. When a tourist returned from Mexico and unknowingly sucked on the hard black beads of her necklace, she died from ricin poisoning. Once it enters a cell, it takes only one chain of the ricin molecule to kill the cell. Since it leaves no easily discernible trace in the body, it was used in the 1978 umbrella stabbing of Bulgarian BBC correspondent Georgi Markov.

Black Widow toxin?

"Contemplated but not much work."

Scorpion toxin?

"We have a postdoc coming from France to clone scorpion toxin."

Snake toxin?

"When you hit snake toxin, you cover a multitude of sins. There are eight to fifteen there."

Of the 2,500 species of snakes slithering around the world, less than 200 have a venomous bite dangerous to humans: cobras, copperheads, pit vipers, puff adders, death adders, rattlesnakes, tiger snakes, sea snakes, mambas, kraits, taipans, fer-de-lances, and water moccasins. It used to be that the only way for anyone to make weapons out of snake venom was to milk a huge number of snakes. You would begin by holding a snake firmly behind the head, opening its mouth with a hook and slipping a container under its fangs. When you press on the venom glands, tiny drops of venom fill the container. Tedious.

Genetic engineering improved on that process as radically as airplanes improved on rail travel. In theory, it is possible to isolate the strand of DNA that codes for the most powerful toxins in the snake's venom and insert that into the common intestinal bacterium *E.coli*. If theory translates into practice, the *E.coli* will produce the toxin. In the fall of 1984, Middlebrook applied to the Office of Recombinant DNA Activities, the RAC, for permission to engineer the genes for cobra snake neurotoxin and cardiotoxin into a bacterium. He wrote that "the goal of this research is to produce *relatively large amounts* [emphasis added] of the cobra snake neurotoxin and cardiotoxin by the use of recombinant DNA technology."

Although the stated aim of the research is to produce large

amounts of the snake toxins, Middlebrook bristles at the suggestion that the military's motive is to stockpile the stuff. "I've encountered people who think I'm really working on making weapons. My colleagues are free to phone me. What I'm doing is developing vaccines, and my personal hope is that they'll find their way to Third World countries where snakebites are a problem."

But the vaccine against the two toxins in the venom of the *Naja Naja Atra* cobra snake will not protect against the venom in other snakes. Worldwide, forty thousand people die of snakebite each year, 70 percent in Asia, where this particular cobra is not found. In the United States, the number may be closer to twelve, although a hundred get bitten—either pet owners, wilderness trekkers, or members of snake-handling cults, and again none by cobras. In fact, despite the incredible potency of the toxins in the cobra's venom, the snake's hiss may be worse than its actual bite, in part because the animal's fangs are at the back of its mouth. "Contrary to popular opinion, however, and comforting to know, the majority of bites from the dreaded cobra are not particularly harmful," states a medical textbook on poisoning. "A significant percentage have severe local reactions with necrosis but very few develop systemic neurotoxic effects and only about one in twenty die."

At present, the only effective treatment for a cobra bite is to take an antivenin, or antibodies to the venom, which is made by giving healthy horses sublethal doses of the venom, collecting their blood, and isolating antibodies to the snake venom. But depending on how the antivenin is prepared, as many as 40 percent of all snakebite victims face the danger of anaphylactic shock from taking the horse's antivenin. A vaccine would undoubtedly be safer.

Despite Middlebrook's intentions, the army is not funding him in the interest of public health. If Detrick is fulfilling its defensive obligations, then somewhere, for some reason, somebody in military circles believes that an enemy might actually attack with cobra toxins. The *Wall Street Journal*'s series on Soviet genetic engineering claimed, without proof, that the Soviets are working on inserting a snake toxin–producing gene into the influenza virus. Many United States scientists regard that effort as not only improbable but impossible.

But for the current program in biological defense, it seems to matter less what is probable than what is imaginable. Middlebrook points to immunotoxins as another example of the terrifying future for toxin warfare. Heralded as magic bullets for combating cancer, these are toxin molecules linked to antibodies, which in theory destroy only diseased cells and leave others unscathed. But what if the magic bullet was fired at healthy cells?

What if? The prospects are grim and chilling to contemplate. Toxin warfare taps a deep-seated, ancient fear of all biting, stinging, spitting creatures and the poisons they unleash. In marrying the techniques of genetic engineering to the ancient, clandestine art of poisoning, scientists have come in a full, eerie, and perverse circle, updating the form but not changing the agent of that fear.

What is that snakeskin on Middlebrook's desk?

"A prairie rattlesnake."

Do you raise them here?

Oh no, says Middlebrook. He explains that snakes scare him, pardon the expression, shitless.

FIFTEEN

The Fallacy

The bulwark of the military's defense against biological weapons is vaccines. In fact, the largest contract administered through Detrick's biological defense program, a five-year, $27.2 million contract to develop vaccines, goes to the Salk Institute, the La Jolla, California–based research institute named in honor of the vaccine pioneer Jonas Salk. But the Salk carries out this work at the Government Services Division, a manufacturing facility located in a tiny village in the heart of the rolling Pocono Mountains of Pennsylvania.

Billboards, restaurants, shops, motels, and the commerce of vacationland plaster the main drag through the Poconos. Past the Stardust Motel, Leisure Lake Souvenirs, and the Pocono Fudge Factory is the village of Swiftwater, no more than a forgettable intersection. If you weren't looking for the Salk Institute's building, which is set back from the road on a small rise, you could easily miss it. Behind a green chain-link fence with a guardhouse and rickety wheeled gate stretches a glimmering lawn and a one-story structure that looks like a warehouse.

For as long as anyone at the facility can remember, the building now owned by the Salk has been used to produce experimental vaccines against exotic diseases for the military's biological warfare defense. But the Salk does not promote its work in roadside billboards, nor to the scores of vacationers seeking a bucolic retreat. If the locals know about the diseases cultivated inside the unimposing building for vaccines in the event of a biological war, they ignore it. But chances are good that few, if any, people outside the circle of those who work here know.

In contrast to Fort Detrick, this facility has no sinister aura. On the contrary, there is something wonderfully noble about the development of vaccines. Of all the landmarks of twentieth-century technology, vaccines rate as the simplest, most elegant, and least appreciated. Vaccines conquered the fear of infectious disease, solving health problems that have plagued mankind since the beginning of time. They helped eradicate smallpox from the face of the earth in 1980, a technical feat on a par with placing a man on the moon, and by defeating the classic childhood scourges—measles, mumps, rubella, diphtheria, tetanus, and polio—fostered a standard of public health unknown and unsuspected by our grandparents and great-grandparents.

First practiced as early as the eleventh century by Arab folk doctors, vaccination became common in nineteenth-century England when someone noticed that milkmaids who caught a benign disease called cowpox never fell ill with the more life-threatening smallpox. Long before anyone had glimpsed the virus that causes smallpox underneath a microscope, the idea took hold that a person exposed to a gentle form of a disease is immune to the more virulent form.

Such serendipitous discoveries did not follow for all other diseases, and the science of vaccination lurched along by trial and error, building on the medical community's deepening knowledge of the agents, mechanisms, and natural history of disease. Scientists found it easier to make vaccines against viral, rather than bacterial, diseases, except that viruses, unlike bacteria, usually proved too finicky to grow in the laboratory. A breakthrough came in World War II when scientists found reliable ways to culture viruses in cells or tissue that grow in glass Petri dishes.

By the 1950s, when the United States mounted a national campaign to immunize the country against polio, two principles, two different approaches to vaccination emerged: One made use of the live virus vaccine, which takes advantage of the fact that viruses tend to mutate, becoming less savage after being repeatedly cultured in the lab; the other employed the killed virus vaccine, which is simply an inactivated live virus. Jonas Salk, a physician who had grown up in an East Harlem tenement, challenged the orthodoxy of using an attenuated live virus by insisting on the safety of using a killed virus—the basis for his polio vaccine. Four years later, Salk's vaccine was replaced with an oral form of a live virus vaccine, still used today, developed by Polish immigrant Albert Sabin. While Sabin's produced a stronger immunity than the killed vaccine, it has the unfortunate result that the virus can, in a small number of cases, revert to its virulent form. Today, about forty people each year get polio from the vaccine.

The vaccines at Swiftwater are made very carefully, either with a live, avirulent virus or by killing the infectious agent. For example, for a batch of Q-fever vaccine, work began at 5:00 A.M. one morning in a thick-walled room, so airtight that even the electrical plugs had been capped. Several days earlier, technicians had injected the Q-fever organism—technically called a rickettsia, a microbe intermediate between a virus and bacteria—into two thousand duck eggs, certified contaminant-free and specially sold for vaccine production. The Q-fever rickettsia flourished and multiplied. At the peak of their multiplication, a few days later, technicians harvested the yolk sacs. Later, the sacs will be blended together in a centrifuge and run through a density gradient to isolate the Q-fever microbes in pure form. For the vaccine, they will then be freeze-dried into a pure white cake of powder no bigger than a fifty-cent piece and later packaged into rubber-capped ampules.

In a day and age when vaccine manufacturers are getting out of the business for fear of lawsuits (and seeing little profit in a business that is essentially a one-shot deal for the dwindling toddler population), the army's BW vaccine development program looks unusually ambitious. The army has ten vaccines in various stages of development: Venezuelan equine encephalitis, Western equine encephalitis, Eastern equine encephalitis, Junín, chikungunya, anthrax, botulinum, tularemia, Rift Valley Fever, and Q-fever. Others are in early stages of development: Hantaan, O'nyong-nyong, Sindbis, and Mayaro.

While the public associates vaccines with an almost inexplicable and slightly magical protection against disease, it does not see those that fail to progress beyond the experimental stage. In fact, the vaccines produced by the military are experimental and do not always work very well. Many currently under development are expected to succeed where older versions produced unintended side effects or limited immunity: the current Q-fever and chikungunya vaccines will replace older, less effective ones.

The first group of people to test experimental vaccines is those scientists who are directly responsible for developing them. If they pass certain safety tests, they are then given to workers at risk, like those technicians handling the vaccines at the Salk's Government Services Division. If they pass further safety tests, they will be tried on military volunteers—medics in training at Fort Sam Houston in Texas—and civilian volunteers, recruited through Fort Detrick.

George French, a microbiologist who used to work at Fort Detrick and who now manages the Salk vaccine facility, has tested his share of experimental vaccines. And Alexis Shelikoff, a virologist who taught for many years at Johns Hopkins and now directs research at the Salk facility, knows the ups and downs of experimental vaccine development. In appearance, the two are a study in contrast. Dressed in a dapper suit, Shelikoff is short, with the voluble manner of a Spanish conquistador, while French is tall, dressed for a Saturday morning putter, and speaks tersely with an occasional stutter.

Why these vaccines?

"These are selected not by us but by DOD committees," says Shelikoff.

"These agents, in general, are ones that have been demonstrated in years past probably to be logical . . ." says French.

" . . . candidates," says Shelikoff.

"Candidates for a weapon. Or perhaps, they have even got some intelligence information that someone has made a weapon out of it," says French.

"It might be useful to say what is a desirable weapon," says Shelikoff. "A desirable weapon is one that affects, say, livestock, and may affect people but not kill them. Rift [Rift Valley Fever] used to be considered of very low virulence, very low pathogenicity. It has a very high virulence for a number of animals, so presumably if you used it as a biological weapon, what would happen is you would wipe out sheep, cows, horses, and cattle, all kinds of animals, and give humans a flulike illness maybe. Anytime you want a strategic victory, you may very effectively immobilize the troops, creating very little havoc for [your own] people and [your own] troops. Of course, that brings up the next question: Are we doing biological warfare? We have absolutely no part in the biological warfare effort. It is only anti."

Reassuring. Until you think about it. The idea that vaccines offer a good defense is an illusion. In the event of a biological attack, the vaccines prepared by the Salk would, in all likelihood, be useless. If a biological attack comes without warning—and no commander would plan to announce one—soldiers would receive the vaccine after the germs had been spread. Since no vaccine gives immediate immunity, at least two to four weeks would pass before the vaccine took effect. By then, it would be too late.

Furthermore, the attack would almost certainly come in

aerosol form and in concentrations far greater than anything encountered naturally. Since the Salk vaccines are meant to be injected, they will give little if any protection against aerosol infections, especially against the overwhelming doses likely to be spread as a weapon. There is also a frightening chance that injectable vaccines might even put soldiers at a greater risk when later infected by aerosol germs. In the late 1970s, army researchers found that when exposed to aerosols of Venezuelan equine encephalitis and Rift Valley Fever, test animals vaccinated by the usual injections died faster than they would have if they had not been vaccinated in the first place.

Even if military intelligence anticipated the attack weeks in advance, and even if the vaccines could be formulated to protect against aerosols, the army does not have, with few exceptions, enough doses to defend the military, let alone the civilian population. In 1983, the United States had stockpiled enough vaccine to protect 600 people against anthrax, 2,880 against Q-fever, 150,000 against Rift Valley Fever, 350,000 against tularemia, 400,000 against botulinum, and forty-three million against VEE.

The maintenance of a vaccine stockpile is expensive, since vaccines, unlike bullets, have a shelf life and must be replaced periodically. Furthermore, it is impractical to support the infrastructure needed to manufacture vaccines on an emergency basis. Generally speaking, a country's vaccine manufacturing facilities are geared to the newborn population, which in the United States makes up about 2 percent of the total.

Even if stockpiles of adequate vaccines existed, none of those currently available are licensed for use. They remain experimental vaccines with unknown, long-term side effects and, under the current law, can only be administered by a specially trained physician who first obtains the person's informed consent and then follows the medical history of that individual over time. Imagine obtaining informed consent on a battlefield. Worse, imagine taking a vaccine that did not work or that had a fluky side effect for a certain part of the population.

But most critically, a vaccine defense in the age of genetic engineering is easily circumvented. With the techniques of recombinant DNA, scientists can hand-tailor new variants and new strains of a disease by altering the genes that code for the virulence-determining proteins on the virus surface. For example, naturally occurring mutations in only two genes of the influenza virus generate the new and slightly different strains that appear each year. It does not matter if you have resistance to the old strain. The new strain can wipe you out. Likewise, immunization against one strain of Q-fever, say, would bring no protection against other strains that could be engineered in the lab. To mount a credible defense, the defender would need to know the exact genetic changes made by the attacker, an unlikely event.

In short, a vaccine defense is a one-on-one proposition, in which the enemy can easily stay one step ahead, particularly now that genetic engineering makes the list of biological weapons candidates virtually limitless. "You can't make any rational defense against biological weapons because there is such a plethora of possibilities," says Richard Goldstein, a professor of molecular biology at Boston University's Medical School. "You can't make vaccines against everything, against all the possible combinations people could make out of mutants and rearranging genes. It is just impossible."

The army is well aware of the obvious shortcomings of its vaccine program, as the authors of a 1983 study called "Vaccine and Antitoxin Availabilty for Defense Against Biological Warfare Threat Agents" wrote:

> As a nation, and as a military force, our vulnerability to biological weapons is clear. The Soviets have the technological capability and production facilities to mass produce biological warfare agents. There is also an enormous intelligence vacuum as to their intent and an even greater mystery as to which agent or agents they might employ. This creates an enormous dilemma for our medical research and development community.

They must determine which putative biological warfare agents for which to prepare vaccines and develop priorities for such development. This process is further complicated by the high cost and extended time, up to ten years, required to develop and mass produce a single vaccine. In addition, genetic engineering has opened the way for production of a wide variety of artificial pathogens. Even if we knew which agents were to be used against us, we cannot know, in the absence of adequate intelligence, whether our present vaccines would be protective.

Faced with this frank and dispiriting assessment, why pursue vaccine development under the biological defense program at all, much less make it the centerpiece? One past argument was that the army's activities narrowed the enemy's options, but this now carries little weight since genetic engineering has effectively opened a limitless universe of biological weapons. Another rationale is that the army performs a public health service. But this falters too. When the National Academy of Sciences' Institute of Medicine recently considered forty internationally occurring diseases as future candidates for vaccine development, taking into account which ones caused the most devastation and which ones scientists understood well enough to make a successful vaccine within ten years, only five diseases studied as biological weapons threats turned up: Rift Valley Fever, Q-fever, Epidemic Hemorrhagic Fever, West Nile, and Russian spring-summer encephalitis. The other diseases are just too exotic, poorly understood, or afflict too few people to merit the resources.

Although the United States did distribute its experimental Rift Valley Fever vaccine to Egypt during the 1977 epidemic, those people threatened by the diseases feared as biological weapons are not much safer for the work done by the United States biological warfare defense program.

"Who are you going to sell the VEE vaccine to?" asks Shelikoff.

To the people in Venezuela and Central America who get the disease.

"Number one, they can't afford it. To expect people in Nicaragua, Panama, El Salvador to pay what it cost the United States government to produce the vaccine is not reasonable. Animal use is something else. You see, there may be a market for animals but not for humans."

Why not for humans?

"Would you take the VEE vaccine?" Shelikoff asks. "No physician would recommend that you subject yourself to a live virus vaccine. Now, the government has to have these vaccines because of strategic and Defense Department needs."

Once again, the justification is Yellow Rain. Convinced that the Soviets have broken the Biological Weapons Convention, the Department of Defense feels compelled to gear up its operations, tit for tat. "It seems clear that our not-so-friendly friends are producing weapons," says French. "The evidence is there. Are we wasting our efforts because of the sophisticated and simple procedures available to modify the agents and invalidate the vaccines we've spent five years developing? That certainly is a risk."

What the army fails to say is that the vaccine program is essential for morale, for reassuring soldiers that there is a defense, when in fact, there really isn't.

Critics label the notion of defense against biological weapons a risky fallacy that, as funding increases and confidence around the treaty erodes, provokes more suspicion than reassurance. A number of prominent scientists argue that the defensive program is too ambiguous and too open to interpretation. Just as the United States tends to assume the worse when confronted with ambiguous information about Soviet activities, the Soviet Union may well do the same when it looks at American activities. In an atmosphere of international distrust and unresolved accusations, Detrick's program, they argue, fuels a new spiral in a pointless and terrifying arms race.

If vaccines do not offer a good defense, what do they offer? Not surprisingly, they offer a good offense. If a country wanted to strike first with biological weapons, it would develop vaccines to protect its own troops, vaccinating them well before the planned attack so they would be protected if the weapon happened to drift their way. Indeed, the advent of genetic engineering makes it easier to develop safer vaccines.

Furthermore, aerosol vaccines, in which Detrick has showed a small but renewed interest, offer even more advantages to the attacker. If a country wanted to launch a surreptitious attack, aerosol vaccines could be used to vaccinate masses of people, both military and civilian, quickly, quietly, and perhaps even without their knowledge. In the offensive days of the Detrick program, American scientists worked on aerosol vaccines against tetanus, Q-fever, and VEE, but encountered adverse health effects; the vaccine may scar the lungs and trigger asthma in hyperallergic people. It is still not clear how safely vaccines delivered in an aerosol form will work, but Albert Sabin is currently working on an aerosol vaccine for measles as an efficient way to break the rapid chain of transmission.

As a whole, the vaccine development program, particularly the contracts within the civilian sector, also serve to build up the personnel, the knowledge base, and an infrastructure capable of safely producing large quantities of biological weapons agents—in other words, the foundation for a military-industrial complex in the field of biotechnology research. According to MIT biology professor Jonathan King, these relationships begin innocently enough. "The initial contracts are not weapons contracts," he says. For example, the army lets a contract to develop a vaccine. In order to make a vaccine, large quantities of the virus must be grown. If the vaccine is really going to be useful against the enemy's suspected biological weapons, variant viruses must be grown.

The company that has the contract to develop the vaccine

in the first place is the logical choice to develop the variant viruses and the vaccine against them. "The contractor sees that civilian budgets for biomedical research are falling, while military budgets are rising," says King. "Now, a substantial arm of the business is dependent on DOD for funding. That is how you mobilize people, that is how you change priorities in scientific research. You make the money available. Boom — the army has its BW program, but nobody is working on BW."

Illustrative of this paradox, the army has contracted out the work on the Rift Valley Fever virus to Molecular Genetics, a Minnetonka, Minnesota, biotechnology firm. Although the firm does not grow the virus—it is grown at Fort Detrick—it has a $1.7 million, three-year contract to study the proteins on the virus surface and their role in producing immunity. The company hopes to make a genetically engineered vaccine to protect livestock in Africa against Rift Valley Fever. While the research is funded by the army's biological warfare defense program, a spokesman was quick to say that the company's contract had nothing to do with biological warfare.

The fallacy of defense is not limited to vaccines. Detrick supports research on antiviral drugs, a new class of compounds analogous to antibiotics but which kill viruses instead of bacteria. While few antiviral drugs have yet been found—drugs that kill viruses may also kill the cell in which the virus resides—antivirals can be circumvented. Just as bacteria can be designed that are resistant to certain antibiotics, so can viruses be tailored that are not susceptible to certain drugs. Biosensors, devices that use monoclonal antibodies to sense the presence of BW pathogens in the environment, can also be thwarted with genetic engineering. Again, the BW pathogen can be altered so that it does not react with the monoclonal antibody, and thus eludes the sensor.

In the context of the current political climate, critics say they would rest easier if responsibilities for biological warfare defense were shifted away from the military to an organization with a public health function. Robert Sinsheimer, a prominent biophysicist and chancellor of the University of California at Santa Cruz, asks, "Why should the DOD do it? Within their own organization and technological mindset, that kind of technological expertise can then be used without too much change for offensive purposes. I don't understand why it just as well can't be done at NIH or CDC."

Above the reception desk in the Swiftwater vaccine plant, twin side-by-side wall clocks show the time in Pennsylvania and the time at the La Jolla headquarters of the Salk Institute. In the field of pure biological research, few institutions match the prestige of the Salk. When you work there, you have arrived as a biological scientist. Set on a spellbinding site above the white cliffs of La Jolla, overlooking the Pacific Ocean, its 160 scientists work inside a stark, modern sculpture of a building designed by Louis Kahn. When it was launched in the mid-1960s "for the advancement and dissemination of knowledge relevant to the health and well-being of man," its founders envisioned a think tank/playground for the greatest minds in the biological sciences.

Frederic de Hoffman has served as the president of the Salk Institute since 1972. Born in Vienna in 1924, educated at Harvard as a physicist, he worked on the Manhattan Project and then, after the war, joined General Dynamics, becoming president of the General Atomic Division in San Diego in 1959 and holding that position until 1969. General Atomic is a defense contractor specializing in nuclear devices. De Hoffman, reportedly a wealthy man, avoids the public eye and lives in a house overlooking the Pacific just down the road from the Salk.

De Hoffman does not usually talk to journalists, but in 1985 he called the *San Diego Union* when he learned that the newspaper planned to report that the Salk's Swiftwater facility was the largest single contractor for the nation's biological warfare defense program. De Hoffman expressed concern that the Salk's image would be linked with biological warfare and denied knowing that a link existed. "I never thought about its military applications," the paper quoted de Hoffman. "I'm surprised that it's classified under biological warfare."

As a responsible president with over twenty years of experience with the Pentagon as a defense contractor, it strained the imagination to believe that de Hoffman had not known about the ties to the biological warfare program. In fact, according to one source who worked with him, he knew but feared publicity. The Salk Institute acquired the vaccine facility in 1978 when Richardson-Merrell, Inc., a pharmaceutical house which had the BW contract, wanted to get out of the vaccine business after suffering losses with the swine-flu vaccine fiasco. Richardson-Merrell sold the commercial side of the business to Connaught Laboratories and donated the other building to the nonprofit Salk. Richardson-Merrell got a tax break, and the Salk inherited the army BW vaccine contract.

Since the government contract operates on a cost-plus-fixed-fee basis, the deal made good financial sense for the Salk, coming at a time when the civilian budgets for life sciences research shrank while military budgets were growing. For a research institute operating without a large endowment, government grants provide the financial mainstay. Swiftwater represented 14 percent of the Salk's $32.5 million budget in 1985. According to Delbart Glanz, vice-president of operations, it "solidifies our base." In public, the Salk Institute downplays such fiscal wisdom and highlights Swiftwater's benefits to public health. "It seemed like a natural extension of what we do, improve the health of mankind," says Glanz. "We saw this as an opportunity to do R and D work for those diseases where there is a real need to help mankind. The army just happened to be the funding agency."

At seventy-three, Jonas Salk is a board member of the Salk Institute but no longer participates in day-to-day decisions. He is much more interested in his research on the fundamental principles of immunity, for which advances in not only genetic engineering but the molecular biology of immunity have made it possible to build an entirely new generation of vaccines. Rather than growing attenuated viruses or inactivating viruses, there is a third approach, the chemical construction from scratch of a vaccine, building it up amino acid by amino acid, creating not an organism but a shape, a crucial shape that mimics the disease. In theory, the shape alone will trick the immune system into believing it has encountered the real thing. If the approach works, synthetic vaccines will usher in a new era of safe preventive medicine.

Behind every medical triumph lurks a new potential for abuse. When asked about the Swiftwater facility, Salk said he was not aware that it made vaccines primarily against biological warfare threats. When asked if he thought that improvements in vaccine technology would make biological warfare more likely, he answered with emotion drained from his voice. "That leaves me cold. I don't know why we should even be thinking about it. It makes no sense whatsoever."

SIXTEEN

Is It or Isn't It?

"Nothing increases one's conscience like being carefully watched."
—Samuel Johnson

Biological weapons steal up, striking with a whimper not a bang, producing a lingering illness, not a firestorm explosion. Seismographs register the quaking of the earth when nuclear weapons explode, but only the convulsions of laboratory rats record the passage of biological weapons. They can not be seen by satellite eyes in the sky. Even if better detectors and sensors are developed, the detection, and thus deterrence, of biological weapons rests finally on a body of medical knowledge that allows scientists to distinguish the natural from the unnatural, rogue microbes from those deliberately planted.

If biological weapons return to the world's arsenals, they will, in all likelihood, be used covertly, not against armies but against civilians. According to the Swedes, who have an extensive program geared to defense against biological weapons, "The probability of overt biological warfare is very low [but] . . . there is a high probability that covert attacks with biological agents can be carried out successfully." For the Swedes, the

243

best defense is surveillance, vigilance, and a strong public health network.

But surveillance is not foolproof. If the attack involves large numbers of people over a long period of time in a central location near state-of-the-art laboratories, it is much more likely to be discovered than if it is carried out on a small, anonymous scale, in a remote location, against crops or livestock. As global conflicts drift toward small limited wars, conducted by proxies, surrogates, or state-sponsored terrorists, it is the very surreptitious nature of biological weapons that make them most attractive and most dangerous.

"It has been hoped that the risk of exposure would help deter BW use, for such exposure might trigger special, undesirable consequences which, depending on circumstances, could range from the international community's condemnation and possibly sanctions to nuclear retaliation," testified Douglas Feith, deputy assistant undersecretary of defense for negotiations policy, to the House Intelligence Committee in August 1986. "New technology, however, makes it easier to develop BW agents that would defy identification after use. Their effects can be symptoms of endemic diseases. If it cannot be clearly demonstrated that BW has been used—if, for example, the effects of an attack are attributable to natural causes—the risks of BW use diminish."

Feith stressed that his concern was not hypothetical, once again citing as proof the use of mycotoxins in Southeast Asia by Soviet-backed forces. "One must suppose that the Soviets have drawn appropriate lessons from the heated controversy in the West about the natural occurrence theory of Yellow Rain. They can hardly have failed to observe that, at least in part because of that controversy, the costs of BW use have proven altogether manageable, indeed virtually nonexistent."

Everyone would agree with Feith that an attacking group is more likely to use a biological weapon if it believes it will not be discovered. But to base the argument on the Yellow Rain investigation is as fair as a three-card monte game in Times Square. A more apt conclusion is that if the United States conducts all future investigations of biological warfare allegations without adequate controls, cross-checks, or attempts to account for contradictory data, then indeed it telegraphs a frightening message to the world—that the risk of using a biological weapon is small.

Rumors about biological warfare, ranging from the possible to the preposterous, crop up regularly, usually when a deadly new disease appears or a war of insurgency is under way. Is AIDS really a biological weapon? Was the CIA planning to use BW in Angola? Has it been used against the cotton crop in Nicaragua? Occasionally, a government official will make the suspicions into formal allegations. In 1985, the Nicaraguan minister of health told a newspaper that she suspected the United States was behind a recent outbreak of dengue fever in her country. In 1982, the Soviets alleged that American efforts to control malaria by releasing sterilized male mosquitoes in Pakistan was really germ warfare. In 1981, Fidel Castro made the same claim about an outbreak of hemorrhagic dengue fever in his country.

Most of these rumors have been ignored because the evidence is too flimsy or too easily contested. But consider three domestic incidents rumored to be covert biological warfare and what the subsequent detective work revealed. In one, investigators found proof that the outbreak was not deliberate, but the result of a newly discovered microbe. In the second, investigators believed it was a natural outbreak until the culprits confessed. In the third, investigators found no proof one way or the other. To both the attacker and the defender, the lesson is that talk is cheap while proof is essential, expensive, and sometimes elusive.

The first case took place at the American Legion convention held in Philadelphia in July 1976. A strange disease struck 179 people, most of them Legionnaires, all staying at Philadelphia's Bellevue-Stratford Hotel. The victims ran fevers as high as 106° F and suffered lung damage, suggesting that they had inhaled something nasty. Twenty-nine died.

The symbolism escaped no one. "It was the two hundredth anniversary of our country; Philadelpha is the birthplace of liberty; Legionnaires represent the military, the old guard, America's dominance. You could see why somebody with a twisted mind might say let's go after them," explains Mike Gregg, editor of the Centers for Disease Control's Morbidity and Mortality Weekly Report. Suspecting biological warfare, Fort Detrick and Edgewood Arsenal sent representatives to help solve the mystery.

According to Dave Fraser, then head of the investigation at CDC and now president of Swarthmore College, "The possibility that Legionnaires was the result of deliberate action was a possibility that we considered beginning in the first few days of the investigation." Did someone fill the hotel's air ducts with an aerosol of ricin? Did a madman mix nickel carbonyl with dry ice, spreading the deadly mixture through the ventilation system?

But as the investigation unfolded, it seemed clear that the attack was not directed solely at Legionnaires, because other people in the hotel lobby got sick. Eventually, after working around the clock, the scientists isolated the culprit, a previously unknown species of bacteria growing in the evaporator-condenser of the hotel's air-conditioning system. *Legionella pneumophyla,* as it was later named, infected the air and thus the lungs of those who breathed it.

Once identified, the CDC investigators looked over its backlog of unexplained epidemics and its bank of stored blood sera and implicated *Legionella* in a number of respiratory deaths at Washington, D.C.'s St. Elizabeth's hospital in 1965, in a Pontiac, Michigan, health department building in 1968, and an unexplained outbreak of pneumonia at the same Bellevue-Stratford Hotel in 1974. While the findings calmed those who had feared a biological attack, Detrick researchers recognized that the qualities that allowed *Legionella* to escape detection for so long also made it a good weapons candidate, and they began to study it shortly thereafter.

The second case took place in The Dalles, a small city of ten thousand people on the Columbia River in north-central Oregon's high desert. As Wasco County's seat, The Dalles draws the local cattlemen and wheat farmers with its yearly rodeo. Between September 10 and October 7, 1984, the city experienced two waves of salmonella food poisoning in ten of the city's restaurants. A total of 750 people fell ill, and 45 had to be hospitalized.

No one died, but the poisoning was far from a harmless nuisance. Two days after eating the bad food, a pregnant woman gave birth to a child who suffered from so much dehydration and septic shock that the doctor gave it a 5 percent chance for survival. The child recovered only when transferred to a larger hospital, where it received around-the-clock emergency care. The poisoning put a middle-aged man into the hospital for five months, where he underwent internal reconstructive surgery to repair damage done by the bacteria. And a couple who ran a restaurant nearly faced financial ruin, since by law they could not return to working with food until the *Salmonella* bacteria disappeared from their systems. That took three months for the wife and six months for the husband.

When the Oregon State Health Division investigated, it traced the source of the salmonella contamination to salad bars. "This outbreak resulted from contamination of raw foods by infected food handlers," said the Oregon Health Division in a preliminary report. "No common source of infection for the ill food handlers could be identified." The CDC reached the same conclusion when it was brought in to investigate. The FBI closed its investigation because it had no evidence to suggest it was a deliberate criminal act.

It was not until almost a year later that a trail of evidence

led to the citizens of Rajneeshpuram, a commune-city located
about eighty miles away, built and inhabited by the followers
of the controversial Indian guru Bhagwan Shree Rajneesh.
The Rajneeshis and the county officials in The Dalles regularly
fought over building permits and zoning matters. The story
came out when David Knapp, a one-time mayor of the commune and follower of the Bhagwan, quit Rajneeshpuram and
confessed to the FBI.

Knapp told how Ma Anand Sheela, at the time the personal secretary to the Bhagwan and effectively the commune's
leader, called a meeting in July 1984 to brainstorm ways to
upset the upcoming Wasco County elections. She and others
wanted to unseat the county officials who had blocked the
commune's building plans. Could they spread oil over the
county's roads so voters could not drive to the polls? Cause an
electrical blackout so alarm clocks would not work? What
about poisoning the voters, making them so sick they could not
vote?

So the idea began. Ma Anand Puja, who ran the medical
clinic, suggested salmonella, which the commune purchased
from a Seattle firm and grew in a clinic incubator. Since they
wanted a test before Election Day, one woman went to The
Dalles with the salmonella but got cold feet and flushed the
poison down a toilet. Then Knapp tried, squirting an eyedrop-
per filled with the noxious liquid on food in the salad bar of a
restaurant in The Dalles. But no one seemed to get sick. A
month later, Knapp accompanied Sheela and Puja to The
Dalles, stopping this time at a local grocery store.

"Puja, let's have some fun," Knapp remembers Sheela
saying.

Knapp watched them pour liquid on heads of lettuce in the
produce section.

"We'll make everyone sick," said Sheela.

Once again, no one seemed to get sick, a puzzling failure
that apparently angered Sheela. Another ex-follower of the

Bhagwan's, Ava Avalos, told the FBI that at the end of September, she drove to The Dalles, wearing a wig and blue clothes, not the commune's customary red, and squirted plastic vials filled with brown liquid into coffee creamers and salad dressings at three restaurants. This time, the poisoning took.

Sheela eventually fled Rajneeshpuram for other reasons, but the FBI caught up to her and the full story of her role, not only in the salmonella poisoning but other stranger illegal activities, came out. On July 22, 1986, Ma Anand Sheela, AKA Sheela Patel, and Ma Anand Puja, AKA Dianne Orang, pled guilty to numerous federal charges. Sheela began serving a four-and-a-half-year prison sentence in October 1986. The Rajneeshi Corporation has offered to compensate the poisoning victims with a sum that could go as high as $4.15 million.

The third case took place in a Florida orange grove. For orange growers, few diseases ignite the fear that citrus canker does. Caused by the bacterium *Xanthomones campestri,* it spreads by means of infected nursery stock, windstorms, and direct contact with people, animals, and equipment, devastating the leaves, twigs, and fruit of all citrus trees. Once it starts, the only way to eradicate the disease is to burn the infected plants.

The U.S. citrus belt was canker-free until September 1984, when a production manager at Ward's Nursery in Polk County, Florida, noticed a suspicious leaf-spot problem on one tree and called the Florida Division of Plant Industry. Two weeks later, the division confirmed the bad news: citrus canker. The U.S. Department of Agriculture snapped into action and announced a canker emergency, placing a quarantine on all Florida fruit. The canker turned up in twenty other nurseries, but fortunately none in the citrus groves. To this day, no one knows how the canker got there.

"There have been suspicions that it was intentionally started but we can't prove that it was," says Harvey Ford, deputy administrator of plant protection and quarantine at the

Department of Agriculture in Washington, D.C. "If you're going to start an outbreak, a nursery would seem like a good place to do it. Prior to finding the citrus canker, a woman overheard an individual at a motel making the statement that the industry was going to be in for a big shock. The Office of the Inspector General investigated but never found the woman. They were never able to establish what it meant."

If the canker outbreak was deliberate, one could speculate that the motive was economic competition since the United States blocks the importation of oranges and grapefruit from any country with citrus canker. If the United States had citrus canker, it could not, for example, block citrus imports from Brazil, a major orange producer. By 1986, the government had paid nursery owners $20 million in indemnity, but seemed to be winning the citrus canker war.

Leonid Rvachev works at the Laboratory of Epidemiological Cybernetics at the Gamalaya Institute of Epidemiology and Microbiology in Moscow. A specialist in the mathematical modeling of epidemics, Rvachev has been attempting to crack a problem that has long baffled scientists: how to predict the spread of a pandemic. The most familiar disease to infect regularly every corner of the world is the flu. Every year, the influenza virus makes its way through the northern hemisphere between October and April, and the southern hemisphere between April and October. As the virus circumnavigates the planet, strains change and mutate with ferocious speed and potentially devastating results. In 1917, a particularly savage form of influenza emerged, circled the globe, and within two years killed thirty million people, more than had died during the entire course of World War I.

In 1983, Rvachev contacted four prominent epidemiologists in the West: Paul Fine at the London School of Hygiene and Tropical Medicine, Michael Gregg at the Centers for Disease Control, J. Donovan at the Department of Human Health in Canberra, Australia, and Philip Selby at the Sandoz Institute in Geneva, Switzerland. He asked for information on international flights, numbers of passengers, traffic at major international airports, and types of aircraft. Later, he listed the scientists as co-authors, although none had actually participated, on a ninety-six-page document that described a technique for predicting the global spread of influenza.

Little attention would have been paid to the thick document if Rvachev had not also written an extremely troubling cover letter. In his awkward English, Rvachev raised the alarm of biological warfare, the fear that those in power would use his model to launch an infectious weapon. He called for the oversight of an international organization to insure that the opposite took place, that the model would be used to prevent a madman from seeding a global pandemic.

In the West, the co-authors registered surprise. They knew little to nothing about Rvachev and even less about his model. Few understood whether it worked at all. And how to interpret his alarm over biological weapons? Was he acting on his own, running a personal risk by revealing these fears? Or was this a deliberate leak, a way for the Soviets to signal their concern over the danger of biological weapons? Mike Gregg, for one, did not want to get involved. "I just don't want to be mucking around with genetic manipulation," he said, "and the implication of biological warfare between the two superpowers."

But Rvachev's claims caught the attention of Emory University biostatistician Ira Longini. "Most epidemiologists could not make it through his work because it was too mathematical and most mathematicians did not know enough epidemiology to get excited," Longini explains. But Longini knew enough of both to sense promise. An expanded version of a model developed twenty years ago, Rvachev's current model consists of a transportation matrix that takes into account the numbers of people who travel from city to city within a twenty-four hour period, the numbers infected with a given disease, the numbers susceptible, and the rate at which they intermingle. All you need to know is where the disease first appears to predict its spread. Indeed, Longini and Rvachev have shown that the model accurately predicted the spread of a past Hong Kong flu epidemic. Whether it is reliable enough to predict future epidemics remains to be seen.

After his initial outburst, Rvachev has grown quiet about biological warfare, but Longini, who met him in Moscow in September 1986, believes his fears have not subsided. "Terrorist use is a major concern of Rvachev's," says Longini. "He feels it is not a matter of *if* but *when.*"

The buildup of military interest in biological weapons and genetic engineering runs the risk of signaling the advantages of covert biological warfare to the terrorist. "People are concerned about state-sponsored terrorism," says Tom Thompkins, terrorism expert at the RAND Coporation in Santa Monica, California. "If the sponsoring nation has biologicals, then the potential for that group to have biologicals has to be considered."

With its origin in the Latin word *terrere,* to tremble, terrorism can be described as the act of making political powers tremble, of influencing them through intimidation of innocent people. Broadly speaking, terrorists include a number of fringe groups operating outside the law, from state-sponsored foreign agents to religious zealots, disgruntled employees bent on revenge, and advocates of political causes. For all of them, biological weapons offer a panoply of hideous ways to inflict damage.

Since the intimidating powers of biological weapons are so uncomfortably clear, bioterrorism is a sensitive subject that few want to discuss or face. "Because it is so insidious and so distasteful, no one wants to talk about it. But CBW is the poor man's atom bomb," says Joseph Douglass, defense consultant with Falcon Associates in McLean, Virginia.

Douglass and his colleague Neil Livingstone wrote a

frighteningly vivid (some would say overly sensationalistic) booklet entitled "CBW—The Poor Man's Atomic Bomb," in which they spell out scenarios for biochemical disaster—terrorists taking over the waterworks of a city in Kansas and infecting the water supply with botulinum toxin; the KGB killing Soviet experts and scholars living in America with poisons undetectable in an autopsy and methods that would never lead to a suspicion of foul play; cultists making canisters of anthrax in a basement laboratory.

Douglass and Livingstone argue that if the United States is concerned about nuclear terrorists—and indeed it is—the country would be wise to worry first about biochemical terrorists since the construction of a biochemical weapon in the basement is much easier, cheaper, and more likely to occur than the construction of a nuclear bomb. Compared to the problems of obtaining weapons-grade plutonium, it is a snap to acquire the germs and poisons needed for a biological weapon. With a little know-how, they can be isolated from nature. With no more than a purchase order, university stationery, a business letterhead, or a requisition form from a research facility, they can be ordered from a commercial supply house.

For example, from the American Type Culture Collection in Maryland, anthrax spores cost $35. To order the Junín virus, you need a permit from the U.S. Department of Agriculture (USDA) and Public Health Service (PHS). While ATCC and USDA/PHS have procedures to check the authenticity of requests, suspicions arise only if you use a bogus name or order larger quantities than those typically used in research. "The alarming fact is that marijuana is more closely regulated in the United States than access to and distribution of the most deadly biological cultures," write Livingstone and Douglass. (Some scientists believe that infectious organisms should be regulated and monitored the way that laboratory use of radioactive materials is.)

But terrorists have so far been reluctant to use biochemical sabotage in the United States, and experts can only guess what the future will bring. Dr. Glenn McWright, former chief of scientific research at the FBI, described letters received by police departments with threats to use BW as coming from "the nut fringe," people without the technical expertise. But in 1984, the FBI found that a "terrorist" group in Springfield, Massachusetts, had a cache of ricin, and the Buffalo office helped prosecute two Canadians posing as scientific researchers who ordered cultures of the bacteria that produce botulinum and tetanus toxins from the ATCC. Their motive was never clearly established.

In Europe, the incidents have been equally few but frightening. A cell of the Baader-Meinhof Gang in Paris was found to have manufactured botulinum. In 1978, Palestinian terrorists injected no more than a few dozen pieces of Israeli citrus—lemons, grapefruit, oranges—with mercury. A group identifying itself as the Arab Revolutionary Army Palestinian Commandos wrote a letter to the Dutch government saying it was their goal to "sabotage the Israeli economy." Almost a dozen people were poisoned, but no one died, and imports of Israeli citrus temporarily plummeted.

For the terrorist looking for public sympathy, biological weapons are tricky to use and so taboo that they may backfire, literally and politically. "You have to have an idea of what you're doing. You have to plan. The untutored individual stands a good chance of infecting himself. Most people have neither the scientific training nor the tactical training," says McWright. "If terrorists turn to this, they'll turn the world community against them. They risk worldwide condemnation."

Dr. Robert Kupperman, terrorism expert at the Center for Strategic and International Studies at Georgetown University in Washington, D.C., sees biochemical terrorism as a low-probability, high-consequence threat. "To use any biological is a vast escalation over what they have done," he says. "If terrorists start to use them, there is no end to which a nation would not go to stop them."

According to a State Department official in the Office of Counter Terrorism and Emergency Planning, "Most of the effort has been directed at nuclear, but we are directing more and more attention to chemical and biological, moving in the direction of domestic prevention." If the bioterrorist uses a human disease, the FBI would investigate and enlist the help of the Centers for Disease Control. In a letter to the State Department's Office of Counter Terrorism in 1984, CDC's director James Mason wrote: "The cause of an event, whether it be a naturally occurring disease outbreak, an industrial toxic accident, a highway spill, an environmental emergency (such as Mount Saint Helens), or a hostile act which involves the use of microbiological or chemical materials as weapons, is largely irrelevant. CDC has responded in the past and will continue to respond in the future."

Responsibility for investigating diseases that affect livestock and crops belongs to the Animal and Plant Health Inspection Service (APHIS) of the Department of Agriculture. Like CDC, its main purpose is to track the introduction of foreign pests and prevent their entry into the United States. (For example, APHIS blocked the importation of pig heart valves used for transplants until the country of origin could prove that the valves did not harbor African swine fever.) But APHIS pays no particular attention to the problem of deliberate introductions. "We've not given any consideration to terrorists," says Harvey Ford. "There is enough breaking out without worrying about that too. If an individual wanted to bring in a disease, there would be no way we could stop that from coming in."

Indeed, in a paper entitled "Biological Terrorism: A Direct Threat to Our Livestock Industry," two veterinarians at Ohio State University, John Gordon and Steen Bech-Neilsen, conclude that the United States is ill prepared to deal with a massive attack against its livestock. If intentionally introduced, three diseases—African swine fever, rinderpest, velogenic viscerotropic Newcastle disease—could, they argue, wipe out 90 percent of the country's domestic livestock population, hitting the pork, dairy, beef, and poultry businesses.

By all accounts, vigilance is the best defense against the biological saboteur. Countries around the world already share a great deal of information through the World Health Organization and the Food and Agriculture Organization on outbreaks and occurrences of human, animal, and plant diseases. To monitor and deter the use of biological weapons would require a neutral, respected, international organization with access to public health information and professionals around the world. But in the United States, defense against biological warfare remains the province of the military, where top priorities do not go to building an international network but to a small aerosol test facility in the high desert of Utah.

SEVENTEEN

Proving Ground

Once a year, across the nation, leaders in the government, the community, and the military meet for a breakfast at which they seek divine guidance from a higher authority. In Salt Lake City, Utah, the 1986 National Prayer Breakfast was held in a club with a low ceiling of varnished tongue-and-groove planks and antler racks that alternate with rifle racks decorating the walls. It looks like a hunting lodge, except for one small item that gives it away. Stashed in a wall niche, like an icon in an Orthodox church, stands a mannequin garbed in the uniform of soldiers past. Duty, not sport, reigns at the Fort Douglas officer's club.

Senator and Mrs. Orrin Hatch, Congressman and Mrs. David Monson, representing nearly half of the state's Washington, D.C., delegation, as well as Governor and Mrs. Norman Bangerter, sit at the head table along with a creative coupling of religious leaders. In this mecca of Mormons (72 percent of the state's population), the organizers of the breakfast have also found a Catholic priest, a Jewish rabbi, and even a Scots-accented Presbyterian. The rest of the room looks as cramped as a bingo hall, a quip the Catholic priest can't resist making even though Mormons have banned bingo and all

forms of gambling from the state. Utah's civic and military
leaders squeeze their shoulders at four long rows of banquet
tables.

Nearly everyone is seated when Dugway's commander,
Lieutenant Colonel David Nydam, pulls into the parking lot in
his midnight-blue Audi, which looks as if it was acquired in
Germany while he did a tour of duty there as head of the
army's nuclear-chemical division. By the time he parks, the
digital clock reads 7:15. The soldiers who direct the now dwindling traffic snap salutes as he walks in, and, in turn, Nydam
salutes back, all as automatically as the Japanese bow. What
the soldiers don't know is that Nydam expects to be promoted
to general in a few months.

With the tables packed and a few catching the overflow on
the dance floor near the bar, Nydam sees the last seats left. He
inches in, excusing himself while scrunching past four or five
people. As he sits down, he introduces himself to his neighbors.
The dour-faced, elderly man directly across the table says in a
booming voice, "General Fairbourn." They nod. For the rest
of the breakfast, the two do not speak. Not only do they sit on
opposite sides of the table, they sit on opposite sides of a lawsuit, disagreeing about the importance and utility of the proposed aerosol testing laboratory at Dugway Proving Ground.
Since it is a small world out here, there is not a whole lot more
to say.

After pledging allegiance to the flag, digging into eggs,
sausage, and sweet rolls, and listening to a young woman who
bursts into song midway through the meal, Governor Bangerter leads the gathering with a prayer that sounds uncannily
like a pitch for the defense budget. "Last year, I had the privilege of attending President Reagan's inauguration in Washington, D.C.," he says. "Despite what you heard about the cold
weather in Washington, there was a reassuring warmth in the
words of our president when he said: 'There are those in the
world who scorn our vision of human dignity and freedom.

One nation, the Soviet Union, has conducted the greatest military buildup in the history of man, building arsenals of awesome, offensive weapons. There must be no wavering by us, nor any doubt by others, that America will meet her responsibility to remain free, secure, and at peace.' "

While the coffee cups rattle, Bangerter's voice resounds through the club. "I am not yet ready to follow anyone who is not fully committed to the preservation of this Republic with all of their energy, resources, and time. I am thankful that our great leaders have set the example for us. I can not imagine Washington disarming against the British or Lincoln hesitating to commit less than all of the resources available to him to preserve a nation."

At the prayer's end, Bangerter sits down while the audience claps long and hard. To the military commanders here, he is a welcome relief, a man who sees things their way. He would not suggest, as some experts do, that if you compare the total military expenditure of the United States and its NATO allies with that of the Soviets and the Warsaw Pact countries, the Western alliance has been outspending the Soviet bloc for the last decade in all areas related to national security. No, this governor does not question military spending the way the last one did.

To understand how the people of Utah view the aerosol lab, you need to understand how the Mormon Church dominates people's lives and how the military, as the state's largest employer, dominates the economy. Although the membership of the Mormon Church today is largely conservative and Republican, that was not always the case. "Our people are persecuted people, forced out of Ohio and Missouri, forced to give up our teachings," explains Ed Firmage, professor of law at the University of Utah, and a great-grandson of Mormon patriarch Brigham Young. "When a fiercely independent people make terms with the government, they have the convert's

zeal to prove their orthodoxy. After being abrasive, cantan-
kerous dissenters, they prove superpatriots."

For the last forty years, superpatriotism has meant supporting the nation's program for defense at almost any cost.
But Firmage and other Mormons believe that the church membership should be more willing to dissent when the government's military plans collide with the church's fundamental
values. In the late 1970s, President Carter proposed building
racetracks throughout Utah and Nevada for the MX missile. It
was a shell game, a decoy ploy that involved building 4,600
silos in the desert, in which only 200 missiles would be hidden,
forcing the Soviets to strike all the silos in order to destroy all
the missiles. Firmage and six of his students formed Utahns
United Against the MX because they did not like the idea of
the military playing nuclear cat and mouse in the desert. At the
time, polls showed the state in favor of the MX by three to one,
with the senators and congressmen in Washington giving the
plan their strong support. "It was a big post office. More
dough," says Firmage, a former White House Fellow who
served on Hubert Humphrey's staff.

Firmage began to stump and lobby the elders of the Mormon Church. Return the MX to the Rube Goldberg cartoons
where it belongs, he said. Its $60–100 billion price tag was a
"rathole without bottom." It would destroy the ranching and
farming in Utah's Great Basin and transform the citizens of
Utah into sitting ducks in the event of a nuclear holocaust. By
Christmas 1980, a tenuous coalition of ranchers, environmen-
talists, and taxpayers rallied, and the opinion polls shifted
against the MX. Then, in a radical step for the church's elders,
they spoke out against the MX in three sermons, insuring its
demise.

Firmage believes there are other small signs of disenchant-
ment with the military within the Mormon Church since the
MX. According to a recent lawsuit, the atmospheric tests of nuclear weapons in the 1950s, certified as safe by the government,

contributed to a higher incidence of cancer in southern Utah. The findings seeded a sliver of doubt. "Maybe the government is not always true blue," says Firmage. But the doubt was not strong enough for the church to get involved with the BL-4 lab. When the controversy erupted, the Mormon Church kept its traditional silence, even after General Fairbourn, also a Mormon, spoke to the church's elders about his concerns.

Former governor Scott Matheson first learned about the proposed lab not from the commander at Dugway, but by reading about Senator Sasser's decision to blow the whistle in the newspapers. As governor from 1976 to 1984, Matheson was highly regarded by his peers, popular—despite the fact that he was one of the few Democrats in the state—and willing to take on the military when its agenda conflicted with the state's. "Look at Utah from the perspective of carrying out national public policy, especially defense," he explains. "First, the population is so sparse it is easy to put a federal program here. You don't get much protest. Then, 66 percent of the land is federal public land. Our state is irresistible for solving problems of national defense." To Matheson, the lab seemed like another case of the military dumping a controversial, potentially dangerous program on Utah without any public debate. He offered to join Rifkin's lawsuit, but by the time it was filed, Matheson was on his way out of office. After two terms and a heart attack, he had chosen not to run again.

Norman Bangerter, the new and Republican governor, did not join the lawsuit, but seems to have found the military just as bossy as his predecessor. An aide to the governor specializing in military affairs says, "We have seven military installations in Utah. We don't have a lot of impact on what they do or don't do. The trend is to inform us after the decision is made." Since the membership of the Mormon Church is reluctant to dissent, and the state government is reluctant to interfere with the money and jobs that the military brings with it, Utahns know little about the military's plans or activities in Utah. For example, Tooele, a small town 46 miles from Salt Lake City, stores almost half of the free world's stockpile of chemical weapons, a fact with which few people seem acquainted. "My guess is that the public does not know that biological testing goes on at Dugway," says the aide.

The public does, dimly sometimes, associate Dugway with an accident that occurred many years ago. On March 13, 1968, the army conducted a secret test with nerve gas, a type called VX, at Dugway. Something failed. A gate didn't close on one of the spray tanks, so the plane released the 320 gallons of nerve gas at an abnormally high altitude. Freak winds carried it even higher, and rain brought it down 27 miles away on Skull Valley, a broad, high desert valley where sheep and cattle grazed. Within a day, five herds of sheep started to act strange.

The governor of the state called Dr. Jerry Osguthorpe, a veterinarian in Salt Lake City and one of the herd's owners, to ask him to look into the mysterious disease that was killing the sheep in the west desert. When Osguthorpe arrived, he found the sheep dazed, uncoordinated, frightened, suffering, and dying. The army denied any responsibility and wondered if the sheep had eaten a local poisonous weed called halogeton. But Osguthorpe's autopsies showed that the animals had suffocated. On March 22, when the governor told the Dugway commanders that he held them responsible, they finally admitted holding nerve gas tests in the area but expressed skepticism that the test actually killed 6,400 sheep. Why didn't dogs, horses, cows, birds, or rabbits show any signs?

One year later, a congressional subcommittee investigated the incident and concluded that army officials had impeded the investigation, denied testing lethal weapons, delayed supplying nerve gas samples, withheld needed data, and furnished fake and misleading information. If the army had admitted its role up front, some of the sheep could have been saved. And to add insult to injury, the army ended up paying more money in damages than the sheep-owners had initially requested.

In August 1969, the Senate moved to ban the secret open-air testing of chemical and biological weapons without congressional authority. But this time, the army suspended tests on its own. Although Dugway's life sciences director said at the congressional hearing that he thought the nerve gas had something to do with the sheep deaths, the army continued to waffle. In 1975, another director of life sciences at Dugway was quoted in the local newspaper as saying, "We didn't lie when we said we didn't do it. We just didn't know if we killed the sheep. We never had any baseline data on the effects of VX nerve agents on local animal populations to see how far it dispersed. We probably got the Russians wondering how we got VX to travel 29 miles. The furthest it ever drifted before was 8 miles."

Whether the army willfully denied its responsibilities or failed to recognize the nerve gas's lethality, it lost credibility with a small group of Utahns who did not feel that the Department of Defense put their interests first. Stephen Gillmor, a sheep rancher and head of the National Woolgrower's Association who served as Governor Matheson's secretary of agriculture, explains why he is leery of the BL-4 lab. "The feds have been devious. The fallout, the nerve gas, boy, it hits home. To say the least, we are a little nervous about experiments with toxicants."

The directions to Dugway are fail-safe. From Salt Lake City, drive 40 miles west on Interstate 80. Just after the Stansbury Mountains and long before the Nevada state line, turn left. Follow the deserted, unnumbered blacktop 37 miles across Skull Valley until it dead-ends at Dugway's front gate. You'll pass one or two working ranches, an Indian reservation, and more sagebrush than you care to count. Pay attention to speed limits when fog clutches the valley, as it often does, and watch for Black Angus and stray sheep; they wander across the road from time to time.

Ecologists call this part of the state high mountain desert. Against a rocky horizon, the dusty scrub is tinged green in spring and summer and turns brown in the fall and winter. Telephone poles intrude on the rugged, breathtakingly barren expanses, but otherwise the uncluttered stillness suggests a land of exile. Out of sight, just beyond Skull Valley, lie the vast salt flats, remnants of an ancient saline ocean that covered the West during the days of the dinosaurs. After one of the ice ages, the ocean dried and shrank, leaving the Great Salt Lake and the salt flats in its retreat. If the high desert is barren, then God has forsaken the salt flats. They stretch for eternity—miles and miles of nothing but miles and miles. Once considered as a suitable landing strip for the space shuttle, nature's wasteland now belongs to the Utah Test and Training Center, an area the size of Rhode Island, dedicated to testing more conventional armaments, and to the adjacent Dugway Proving Ground, an area twenty times the size of Washington, D.C., dedicated to testing chemical and biological weapons.

Once a year, Jim Coyner, a biologist with the Utah State Fish and Wildlife Service and head of a local Audubon chapter, flies over the salt flats to count eagles. Even Coyner admits that not much lives out there. "You see half a dozen eagles sitting on Wildcat Mountain in the winter, but you rarely see a coyote or a jackrabbit," he says. Although he does not see eye to eye with the military on the subject of biological weapons, he guesses that it picked the most lifeless place in the country to do the work.

Dugway has few if any neighbors. To the north of the proving ground and test center, race car drivers set landspeed records at the Bonneville Salt Flats. To the south, migrating birds and ducks take cover at Fish Springs Wildlife Refuge, and to the west a few hardy ranchers, like Cecil Garland, carve out a living, Garland lives without a telephone in a town so small the post office does not even bother with a zip code. In a letter, Garland answers inquiries about Dugway this way.

I'll try to give you an idea of how people here feel about Dugway. For as long as anyone can remember, and even going back to Pony Express days [Cecil's town was a stop when the Pony Express took the mail across the country in 1864], the military has been hereabouts. During World War II, it really got going as troops trained for the desert and B-29s practiced here for the A-bomb drops over Japan. As you probably know, even today, the military is by far the largest employer in the state, so Dugway was in its beginning welcome. I'm not sure that has changed much.

I've heard that we all have sleeping sickness immunity here from testing and the mosquitoes. I've heard that they contaminated a large parcel of ground on the salt flats with anthrax and that they had a hard time and it took many years to get rid of it. I've heard that they experimented with many more different kinds of diseases and bacteria, etc. I can prove none of it as I never go to Dugway and rarely even talk to anyone in the military.

Nonetheless, their presence is always here and I believe that most of us feel a vague uneasiness toward them. It is sort of like knowing that there are rattlesnakes around, only with a rattler there is usually some warning. I doubt that if something goes wrong at Dugway there will even be a warning. Much like the sheep kill over in Skull Valley. So we shove it in the back of our minds and tend not to think about it too much.

To the outside world, Dugway keeps a profile that is low to the vanishing point. Even though the drive from Salt Lake City takes an hour and a half, a distance that Los Angelenos would consider reasonable to travel for dinner, the only people who take the time are those who live and work there. "There are a lot of people in the Department of Defense who don't even know Dugway exists," says Dugway's commander, Lieutenant Colonel David Nydam. Of course, Dugway does not do much to advertise its presence either to the military or to the public.

Like all Department of Defense installations, Dugway's public affairs office handles media calls, and, depending on who is asking and who is overseeing, the requests get handled differently. Local reporters find it easier to visit than national reporters, for example. On the whole, the army is committed to being open and talkative, but public controversies, like Rifkin's lawsuit, bring out its fighting spirit and memories of Vietnam, a debacle for which many top brass still hold the media responsible.

Colonel Nydam has been designated to take the responsibility and the heat for articulating the army's views on the BL-4 lab, which he begins to do at the end of the prayer breakfast. It is a gentle February day, and with a new snowfall in the mountains Nydam, who is fit, youthful-looking, and in his fifties, admits that he would really rather be skiing. He was born in Oak Park, Illinois, went to a small college in New England, and has spent all of his professional life in the biological and chemical side of the military. He started at Fort Detrick, eventually becoming deputy chief of special operations during the early days of the Vietnam War. Nydam does not elaborate on what he did in that position except to say he visited Dugway once. He worked his way up, serving for many years in Europe before taking the post as Dugway's commander in 1984, just in time for the BL-4 debacle.

Nydam's job is to modernize Dugway, bring it out of the "Dark Ages," pay attention after thirteen years of "dire neglect," and get it back into state-of-the-art testing in chemical and biological weapons. At the end of the fiscal year in 1984, the army had some money left over in one of its budgets for military construction. A call went out from Washington to the base commanders: Submit a wish list of new projects you want funded fast. Nydam listed twelve projects, including the BL-4 lab. "Why not start a year ahead?" he said. "We thought we could get ahead on the power curve. It was as innocent as that."

He contends that the lab would have been requested in the usual way the following year. Subversion, surreptitiousness, catching Congress before vacation—none of these things played a role, Nydam says. Apparently, neither did the sensitivity of the project and the appearance that might be conveyed to the world at large by making a request under emergency funding procedures.

Senator Sasser's indignant public announcement, the media's stabs and pokes, and especially the nuisance of a lawsuit came out of the blue. While Nydam calls Fairbourn a "rascal" in a mildly irritated voice, he seems more than irritated by Rifkin's legal crusade. He dismisses the idea that the army use simulants. "You can not use a simulant on a biological alarm," he says, referring to a device the army is currently developing that would signal the presence of germ weapons prior to attack. The fuss over genetic engineering sounds like academic hairsplitting. "I wouldn't know if an organism is a normal mutant or a genetically engineered one," he says. And finally, Nydam is frankly skeptical about what purpose will be served by doing an environmental impact statement. "What's going to come out of an EIS?" he wonders, after all the data that Dugway has collected over the years on the impact of microbes on its environment.

Nydam counters Rifkin's claim that the lab will be used to make weapons. "We're not talking about offensive. I remember working very hard to weaponize biologicals," he says. "There is so much misunderstanding." He cites Rifkin's often repeated example that one gram of botulinum toxin is potent enough to kill every person on earth. The Dugway Lab does possess this amount and, theoretically, the calculation is accurate. But in practice, it is impossible, short of lining everyone up and giving them an injection, to distribute the tiny lethal dose.

Defending a small laboratory has become more of a job than Nydam ever anticipated, and he is not sure why. "In downtown Atlanta, they work on some of this same stuff," he says, genuinely surprised. He has a point—no one in the well-heeled Atlanta neighborhood complains about the BL-4 labs at the Centers for Disease Control. But at CDC, the scientists do not create aerosols; in fact, they go to great lengths to avoid them. No one imagines that the knowledge gained by the Centers for Disease Control will further a biological arms race. But at a military outpost like Dugway, scientists working on defense inevitably gain knowledge and form opinions about offense. Only the treaty blocks the development of those ideas and opinions into weapons.

Out of nowhere, an F-16 swoops low and menacing out of the sky, then wheels like a hawk beyond the horizon. It is the only vehicle visible until the road ends at Dugway's gate.

Inside the gates, Dugway looks more like a small frontier town (population 2,700) than a military base, and Nydam begins to sound more like the mayor than a commander. He talks about the dry lightning that knocks out the electricity every so often, the urgent need to insulate the base's cinder-block houses, and the need for a crafts shop—to help keep the drinking down. "That is very hard to explain to people who have never been here," he says. The residents of this sleepy community do not seem concerned about the lab that could be built at the edge of the salt flats, 18 miles away from town. Out of sight, its activities would be out of mind, and besides, it takes a certain scientific bent to keep track of what they do out there.

The car rattles up a deserted road, passing makeshift stables where families tame and keep wild mustangs that are culled from a nearby herd and sold once a year. Tumbleweed skips across the landscape. In the middle of the sagebrush, sand dunes shift their shapes. Halfway to the site proposed for the BL-4 lab, the car stops at the chemical labs, a cluster of low-slung buildings where masks and suits are tested against nerve gas and other chemical weapons. The facility proclaims its deadly importance with a chain-link fence topped with concertina wire and big signs warning that the use of deadly force is authorized. To tour the lab, a visitor is outfitted with a gas mask and given an antidote injector, with instructions on how to use it, just in case. The message lingers: You can never be too vigilant with invisible weapons.

After the chemical labs, the paving becomes even bumpier. Off in a foggy distance are broad, flat test grids where weapons explode on top of a tower and instruments placed on a circular grid on the ground record the stealthy drift of the gas. In the old days, before 1969, the army exploded the real chemicals and biologicals, not just on the test grids but by releasing weapons from airplanes. There is a plot of ground over which anthrax was tested in the 1950s, marked on all maps as permanently contaminated, even though Nydam says that tests show no presence of the spores. There is an area where they once tested the cloud of germs that a helicopter would kick up taking off and landing on a disease-filled battlefield.

"Our records do not substantiate any infection during open air testing," says a Dugway spokesperson. But Joel Trupin, professor of microbiology at Meharry Medical College in Nashville, Tennessee, says that infections with tularemia occurred while he was at Dugway in the late 1950s. Now, by law, the army tests only biological simulants—*Bacillus globigii,* an enfeebled strain of *E.Coli,* the bacteriophage virus, but not *Serratia.* Many believe that open-air tests of real biological weapons, even in the name of defense, would be against the treaty.

The road seems to go no father than the Baker Lab, Building #2028, where biological research takes place. It sits on the fringe of the desert, facing the desolate salt flats. Unlike at the chemical weapons testing facility, no guards check for passes, no fence seals it off, and no signs spell out the consequences to an intruder who stumbles upon it. The vigilance associated with chemical weapons is dropped.

The slightly ramshackle laboratory building could be a large repair shed for heavy equipment. A light snow begins to fall and the desert closes in. "These people feel neglected," says Nydam. Inside, the lab's director, Dr. A. Paul Adams, offers coffee in his office. With pure white hair and a wine-colored V-neck sweater, he looks like an off-season Santa Claus. Adams came here in 1953, a year or two after the building's completion, left to teach biology at North Dakota State, and came back for good in 1963.

"When we signed the treaty, the money just sort of dried up. Even for work in biological defense. We went along at a low level of funding with a skeleton crew until 1979. And then they had that incident at Sverdlovsk where five hundred to a thousand people were reported to be killed," Adams says, disparaging the Soviet explanation that anthrax is endemic and was caused by tainted meat. "If you're a microbiologist, you know that's a crock. We knew the amounts involved were greater than that allowed by treaty. A lot of concern was expressed in high circles that we should get our defense ready."

After Sverdlovsk, and after Yellow Rain, the money started to flow again for testing germs, viruses, and toxins that have been identified as a threat.

What does the United States believe to be threats?

"I don't know what we'll be asked to test," says Adams. "We haven't gotten the Russians to send us a shopping list. We've looked more at viruses than we used to."

What else?

"We're still studying the same ones," says Adams.

Which ones?

"For an ideal biological agent, it should aerosolize well, store well, and it should have a low rate of decay as it travels downwind and little lethal effect, but great incapacitating effect. It should be easy to make in large quantities."

For example? Brucellosis? Brucellosis was one of the first candidates studied and is rarely mentioned these days.

"Brucellosis had a rapid decay rate. It was unpredictable," says Adams.

But Nydam counters, "That's the reason they threw it out. But that's also the reason I might use it as a Russian commander."

What about genetically engineered organisms?

"There is a lot of concern about genetically altered organisms. We haven't dealt with them out here. That is one thing potentially," says Adams.

Which ones are you immunized against?

Biological warfare researchers are immunized against the diseases they test, but Adams will not say what they are. Although twenty-eight people work here, including eight Ph.D.s besides Adams, only three can open the locked room and locked deep-freeze where the biological materials feared as weapons are stored. Documents released by Sasser's inquiries and Rifkin's lawsuit show that in the deep-freeze are one gram of botulinum toxin, half a gram of food poisoning toxin, and fourteen grams of the toxin alleged to have been supplied by the Soviets in Southeast Asia. There are also microbes, including tularemia, Q-fever, and Venezuelan equine encephalitis.

The researchers have been conducting experiments with dangerous aerosols inside a glass glove box, a totally encased laboratory bench accessible only through long-armed rubber gloves. It is clumsy and resembles the setup for handling plutonium or kids born without an immune system. They want the BL-4 lab as a replacement. Since Baker is too ramshackle, the plan is to construct it in an adjacent building, #2026, just two or three steps away.

The new structure is nothing but a hollow shell—utilitarian, windowless, and cold, with a concrete slab for a floor. Through the peaked spine of rafters, thin prefab roof and walls, the wintry desert wind seeps in. In the still quiet, Adams and Nydam flick on the light bulb and seem curiously sheepish about this empty, 1,300-square-foot place, as if they can't quite fathom the controversy that has overtaken it. This is after all only a building, and Dugway is in the business of working with deadly aerosols. They want better and safer facilities than those next door. What is the big deal?

"The shell has always been here," says Nydam, walking around to stay warm.

"The big ticket item is the lab itself." Adams points down. Drawn on the floor, like chalk outlines at the scene of the crime, is the plan of the new facility. Adams and Nydam point out what will go where, acting like real estate agents who are showing a client through a house that just won't sell. There will be two areas for regular lab-bench research, changing rooms for the workers to get inside their space suits, showering rooms for workers to shower in and shower out, a room for caged experimental animals—mice, rats, and guinea pigs—and a room where the aerosols will be sprayed.

The tightly enclosed aerosol chamber will only be 400 square feet, just big enough to test a few pieces of equipment or the reactions of a few test animals. Since the military argues that it needs the lab for testing equipment against the real thing, why the animals? Adams says it is for information on the lethality, virulence, and infectivity of the aerosols. But critics say this information has no bearing on protective equipment and hold it up as another disturbing way for the army to build its knowledge base for offense.

The BL-4 lab has become a symbol of something that enters Dugway's daily life infrequently if at all—the innate terror of biological weapons. Over the years, Adams and Nydam have acquired knowledge that protects and shields them from the fear. And, perhaps, familiarity breeds a little contempt. They know the germs, their attributes and failings, their modes of infection and routes of destruction, too well; and they have forgotten the irrational fear that biological weapons unleash in most people. While the isolation of the desert provides the necessary margin of safety, it also breeds an insularity.

"Very few commanders understand BW," says Nydam, who, unlike some of his colleagues, did not desert the Chemical Corps when it was disestablished in 1973. "A lot of people say that biological weapons are not predictable. The people I talk to say if you know the characteristics of biologicals and apply them to the right tactical situation, they are. They're not as predictable as putting a hole in someone's chest, but a casualty is better than a death."

Adams shrugs. "I'd like to write a book, *A Strange Sense of Chivalry*," he says. "If you can say war is humane—and that is a question—then what is more humane? Giving somebody a disease from which they recover or shooting them?"

Indeed, not all biological or chemical weapons cause instant death. Some—like food poisoning—only cause temporary suffering. In the mid-1950s, the Chemical Corps decided to capitalize on the idea that chemical and biological weapons did not always kill. With an unprecedented publicity campaign dubbed "Operation Blue Skies," launched in 1959, dozens of articles written by Chemical Corps members praised CBW as "humane." General Stubbs told a congressional committee that "we are attempting to completely separate these [incapacitating] agents from the lethal agents so that any castigation normally given to toxic agents will not be associated with these agents since they do not maim or kill. As a result, we hope to have a weapon which will give the commander much freer rein in its use, as compared with toxic agents. It is my hope that through incapacitating agents the free world will have a relatively cheap and rapid means of both fighting and deterring limited warfare, which has come to the forefront in the international political scene in the last several years." To the Department of Defense, an incapacitating agent is one that kills no more than 2 percent of those affected.

By the 1960s, incapacitants became the darlings of the biochemical arsenals—from VEE to tear gas, defoliants, and BZ. The United States manufactured at least 50 tons of BZ, quinuclidinyl benzilate, a chemical cousin to LSD that was envisioned as the perfect humane weapon. While a typical dose of LSD sends the user on a trip for eight hours, the same dose of BZ lasts for over three days. The army believed that BZ would make soldiers so crazy that they would be easy to subdue. What they learned was that BZ made soldiers angry, not docile, and that with guns in their hands, BZ created an even more awesome adversary.

Stockpiles of BZ wait to be destroyed in Pine Bluff, Arkansas, but the myth of the humane weapon, which propelled the army to develop it in the first place, stays alive. There is no such thing as a harmless chemical or biological weapon. Even with so-called incapacitants, someone will always be at risk, whether from age, debilitation, illness, malnutrition, or stress. On a battlefield, the dosage of a biological or chemical weapon cannot be controlled to keep it within humane limits. More important, the context in which biological and chemical weapons are used is not humane, nor will it ever be. Chemical and biological weapons may be used initially to incapacitate, but, except for a few highly unusual situations, they will always be used in tandem with more conventional weapons.

Hastening to counter what may be a wrong impression, Nydam adds, "BW is not even considered to be something that will come back. It is over the hill as far as the United States is concerned."

What about the intelligence agencies? Do you do any work for them?

"Haven't done any work for intelligence. Would be good if we did, in the sense of getting more customers," Nydam says.

But the public affairs officer, who has been notably silent, pipes up. "Not that I know of. Those guys scare me."

Has the United States ever used biological weapons in clandestine operations?

"To my knowledge, the United States has never used biological weapons covertly," says Adams strongly.

On this subject, Nydam is silent.

Afterword

We are poised on the threshold of a frightening new arms race. What Winston Churchill called "an unspeakable method of warfare" is now being openly, widely, even eagerly discussed. The menace of biological warfare, once dormant, if not moribund, has been revived. And thanks to genetic engineering and the biotechnology business, which is advancing the knowledge and marketing some of the technology that the Biological Weapons Convention dismantled, it is potentially more devastating now than when it was laid to rest over fifteen years ago.

I'm left with unsettling questions about the future. Will the treaty restrain the menace of biological warfare? Or will the momentum of scientific advances help unleash it? These questions will continue to be debated in the public arena, if only because Jeremy Rifkin filed yet another lawsuit, this one in September 1986, charging that the Department of Defense accelerated and expanded its biological defense program without the appropriate environmental impact statements. In February 1987, the army agreed to do the environmental impact statements. He also set up a $100,000 fund to protect any scientist who had seen a violation of the Biological Weapons Convention and wanted to blow the whistle.

Despite heated claims about Soviet activities, there are signs that the treaty will prevail. I'm encouraged by efforts to bolster the international consensus that biowar is too dangerous, too uncontrollable, for anyone to pursue. In September 1986, representatives from over forty countries met for a three-week-long conference on disarmament in Geneva, Switzerland, to discuss the health and future of the Biological Weapons Convention. The contentious fireworks expected between the United States and the Soviet Union did not materialize. Ambassador Donald S. Lowitz, head of the U.S. delegation, said that the United States believed that the Soviet Union "has been involved in the production and use of toxins for hostile purposes in Laos, Kampuchea, and Afghanistan," but he did not dwell on it.

The Soviet Union's ambassador, Victor Issraelyan, countered that the U.S. claims were "inventions from beginning to end" and that its charges about treaty violations were "ungrounded and far-fetched." But in a turnaround from its previous belligerent and uncooperative behavior, the Soviets gave Western delegates the chance to ask Moscow's minister of public health, Nikolai Antonov, questions about the mysterious outbreak of anthrax in Sverdlovsk. According to *Science* magazine, Antonov "presented what some of those present later described as the most complete version of the Sverdlovsk events. He pointed out that there had been at least 150 outbreaks of anthrax in the Soviet Union in 1978 and provided detailed descriptions of the medical care provided to victims and the cleanup techniques that were subsequently used." Antonov told *Science* that victims came down with anthrax over a seven-day period and that the government had decontaminated streets in Sverdlovsk because "undisciplined workers" had discarded tainted meat in open garbage containers.

For most of the three-week conference, the participants focused not on Yellow Rain nor on Sverdlovsk, but on ways to cope with the temptations created by science. The solution to the new temptations was not, as some conservative commentators had argued, a treaty that could be verified. By their nature, the facilities needed to produce biological weapons are unverifiable by satellite or on-site inspection and, in fact, in the Gene Age are even more so. Ironically, delegates rejected a Soviet verification proposal for fear that it could be used to conceal secret work. Instead, delegates decided by consensus that the treaty could best be strengthened by cooperation: exchanging information on BL-4 labs, on the outbreak of infectious and toxin-related diseases, and fostering publication of research results and the active exchange of scientists in efforts related to BW.

I'm also encouraged by the efforts to pass a bill in Congress making it illegal to produce biological weapons in the United States. The treaty requires the passage of such domestic legislation and, while it has taken place in other countries, it has never taken place in the United States. In 1980, New Jersey congressman Peter Rodino introduced a bill, but it died before passage. In August 1986, he introduced it again, at the behest of the Committee for Responsible Genetics, a Boston-based group of scientists concerned with the social aspects of biotechnology. Like the British Biological Weapons Act, it would stipulate that anyone "who develops, produces, stockpiles, transfers, acquires, retains or possesses any agent, toxin, weapons, equipment or delivery systems for a prohibited purpose" would face a $10 million fine and life imprisonment.

The treaty is still not as strong as it could be. Many Third World countries have not yet signed it. And of course, it is only as powerful as the mutual interests that it reinforces. Despite these shortcomings, I'm troubled by voices claiming that the treaty is an utter failure. On September 15, 1986, the *Wall Street Journal* ran an editorial dubbing the treaty a "bioanachronism." In the concluding paragraph, it said, "Ever since the Hague Convention of 1899 and the Geneva Protocol of 1925, governments have been trying to ban chemical and biological warfare. But the treaties alone have never worked—not in Europe in World War I or in China in World War II. History teaches the lesson that the only credible deterrent is the fear of biochemical retaliation. That is the key issue that the diplomats in Geneva prefer to avoid."

It would be folly to resume production of biological and toxin weapons, in the name of deterrence or anything else. The logic behind Nixon's renunciation is even stronger today than it was in 1969. Biological weapons are too cheap and too powerful. To some degree, the proliferation of nuclear weapons can be controlled because it is difficult and costly to obtain the raw materials, the expertise, and the infrastructure needed. But biological weapons pose no such problems. The only way to control their proliferation is to outlaw them altogether.

I'm disturbed by the Pentagon's recent change of heart about the military utility of biological weapons. Now, it appears that Pentagon officials believe that biotechnology and genetic engineering might overcome some of the problems that handicapped biological weapons in the past. But I wonder if the change of heart does not reflect the changes in military thinking over the last eighteen years. With or without the new breakthroughs in biotechnology, biological weapons are still uniquely suited to sabotage, to panic-instilling surreptitious operations aimed at civilians, to low-intensity conflicts (in the current jargon), to the types of war that can be waged covertly, outside Congressional oversight and the media's glare.

What I fear is that the future of biowar will be dictated not by pragmatic analysis but by irrational momentum, the never-ending race to milk advantage out of the latest laboratory breakthrough.

The United States vows that it does not intend to break the treaty. But actions speak louder than words, and budget allocations have a way of influencing policy more than any public declarations. Since biological weapons are so laboratory intensive, so scientifically based, it does not take much money to lay the foundation for a biological weapons capability. And the reality is that, in the initial stages, it can be done without compromising anyone's conscience.

In a country in which chemists made decisive contributions to the weaponry of World War I and physicists built the decisive weapon of World War II, the military is now eagerly knocking at the biologists' door. It is the first time that the military has actively solicited the biologists' knowledge. In exchange for funding, bio-scientists are now asking and answering intellectually fascinating questions and, at the same time, building up laboratory capabilities, an infrastructure that meets the peculiar needs of the military's biowar efforts, not the needs of, say, a public health program.

It is hard to grasp just how extensive the military's sphere of influence has become. We live in a country in which 50 percent of each tax dollar (after you subtract entitlement programs like Social Security) goes to the Department of Defense. We have what Columbia University economist Seymour Melman calls a permanent wartime economy, geared up to keep the country in a state of permanent readiness to fight an all-out war. There is a great temptation for the military to do something simply because the technology now permits it. This technological imperative fuels its research and development programs more than any analysis of the Soviet threat. It is exceptionally powerful, and I wonder how easily it can be stopped.

Consider that scientists are on the verge of mapping the human genome, all of the genes that make up the DNA in a human being, an exploration that on its scale could prove as momentous as the European discovery of the New World. Only the naive would believe that such spectacular advances could occur without some abuse. In the future, scientists expect to be able to identify a person's predisposition to certain diseases by looking at his or her genes. Predispositions may then be correlated with a person's racial or ethnic heritage. While there is no such thing as a pure racial or ethnic group (with the exception of a few small, isolated island communities), there may be statistical tendencies. This knowledge could then easily be used to make a sinister weapon.

The desire to find a biological weapon that discriminates between the attacker and the enemy goes back to the beginning of modern biological warfare when Ishii used POWs to investigate the susceptibility of different groups of people to disease. In 1971, the army's professional journal, *Military Review*, ran an article by a Swedish geneticist who raised the possibility that weapons could be created that exploited the differences in enzyme systems between two populations. During the offensive years, the army experimented with a spore-forming fungus, *Coccidioides immitis*, found in the soil of California's Central Valley and other arid parts of the Southwest, Mexico, and Central America. When inhaled, it causes only a mild lung infection, but if it progresses to other parts of the body, the disease is deadly. Even with antibiotic treatment, the mortality rate can reach 50 to 60 percent. Although no one knows why, it turns out that 20 to 25 percent of blacks develop the deadlier form as compared to 1 percent of whites. The deadly form of the fungus could be a biological weapon with an ethnic bias. It was found by trial and error, but what if others could be designed, tailor-made?

I believe that we've come to a critical crossroads and that although there are formidable pressures, it is not too late once again to subdue the specter of biological warfare. In the pursuit of evil, human ingenuity knows no limits. But it seems to me that we have a choice. We can assume fatalistically that the advances in biotechnology mean an inevitable proliferation of biological weapons. Or we can assume that our actions can make a crucial difference, and we can refuse to sanction — in any way — biological warfare in the Gene Age.

Notes

CHAPTER ONE

PAGE

4   "the rare politician": "Evolution of a Stand: Memphis, Marines, Managua," *New York Times*, 18 March 1986.

5   "Dear Mr. Chairman": Military Construction, Army, Reprogramming request. Project 0817300, Aerosol Test Lab, Class 4 (no date given).

5   "another reprogramming request": Military Construction, Army, Reprogramming Request. Project 0817200, Toxic Agent Test Support Facilities (no date given).

7   "none of these projects": Letter from Senator James Sasser to Senator Mack Mattingly, 31 October 1984.

7   "article in *Science*": "New Army Biowarfare Lab Raises Concern," *Science*, 7 December 1984.

8   "Weinberger moved quickly": Letter from Caspar Weinberger to Senator Jim Sasser, 2 November 1984.

9   "I have been castigated": Rifkin, Jeremy, *Declarations of a Heretic* (Boston: Routledge and Kegan Paul, 1985).

9   "the first time I heard": Interview with J. Rifkin, 18 March 1986, Washington, D.C.

10   "rah-rah fraternity member": "Jeremy Rifkin Usually Infuriates—and Often Bests—Biotech Industry," *Wall Street Journal*, 12 May 1986.

12   "you could not aim them": Telephone interview with G. LaRoque, 3 June 1986.

13   "Rifkin called to ask me": Interview with W. Fairbourn, 13 February 1986, Salt Lake City, Utah.

281

PAGE

14 "the intentional production": Declaration of David Dubnau, 17 December 1984. Filed with Civil Action 84-3542, U.S. District Court for the District of Columbia.

14 "if there has been an attack": Reponse to Environmental Assessment of Proposed Dugway Biowar Laboratory. Statement made by Richard Novick. No date given. Filed with Civil Action 84-3542. US District Court for the District of Columbia.

15 "paint a fictitious picture": Statement filed by defendant 17 April 1985. Civil action 84-3542. US District Court for the District of Columbia.

16 "an Environmental Assessment, she wrote": Memorandum Opinion and Order. Judge Joyce Hens Green. Civil Action 84-3542. Filed 31 May 1985. US District Court for the District of Columbia.

CHAPTER TWO

18 "Armis Bella Non Venenis Geri": Cited in "The Threat of Biological Weapons," *Technology Review,* May/June 1982.

18 "It's not too often": Interview with Genieveve Bell. 17 March 1986. Washington D.C.

19 "Each state party": Convention on the Prohibition of the Development, Production and Stockpiling of Bacteriological (Biological) and Toxin Weapons and on their Destruction. Signed in Washington, London and Moscow, 10 April 1971.

20 "Since Greco-Roman times": Jensen, Lloyd B. *Poisoning Misadventures.* Springfield, Il: Thomas, 1970.

21 "the earliest, and one of the few": cited in Geissler, E. Ed. *Biological and Toxin Weapons Today.* Stockholm: Sipri. New York: Oxford University Press, 1986.

21 "another oft recounted case": Ibid.

22 "various types of biological weapons": Biological Weapons. ADIU Factsheet. University of Sussex, Brighton, England. 15 March 1984.

23 "experimented with the following human and animal diseases": Harris and Paxman. *A Higher Form of Killing.* New York: Hill and Wang, 1982.

24 "produced and/or standardized": Biological Weapons, ADIU Fact sheet. Also, Miller, D., History of Air Force Participation in the Biological Warfare Program, 1944–1951 and 1951–1954. Historical Section, Wright-Patterson Air Force Base.

24 "Anthrax": Christie, A. *Infectious Diseases: Epidemiology and Clinical Practise* (Edinburgh: E. and S. Livingstone, 1969).

25 "Botulinum": *Ibid.*

25 "Brucellosis": *Ibid.*

26 "Q-Fever": *Ibid.*

PAGE

26 "Saxitoxin": Halstead, B., and Schantz, E., *Paralytic Shellfish Poisoning* (Geneva: World Health Organization, 1984).

27 "Staphylococcus enterotoxin": Christie, A., *Infectious Diseases.*

27 "Tularemia": Felsenfeld, O., *The Epidemiology of Tropical Diseases* (Springfield, IL: Charles C. Thomas, 1966).

28 "VEE": Hoeprich, P., Ed., *Infectious Diseases* (Hagerstown, Md: Harper and Row, 1982).

28 "Yellow Fever": *Ibid.*

29 "Wheat Rust" and "Rice Blast": Large, E.C., *The Advance of the Fungi* (New York: Henry Holt and Co., 1940), Van Der Plank, J. E., *Plant Diseases: Epidemics and Control* (New York: Academic Press, 1963), Rohm and Haas Compendium of Plant Diseases (Philadelphia: Rohm and Haas, 1959).

30 "to an army field manual written in 1966": Proceedings of the conference on Chemical and Biological Warfare, sponsored by the American Academy of Arts and Sciences and the Salk Institute, 25 July 1969.

30 "a panel of experts": quoted in Livingstone, N., and Douglass, J., CBW—The Poor Man's Atomic Bomb (Cambridge, MA: Institute for Foreign Policy Analysis, 1985).

31 "poor man's atomic bomb": *Ibid.*

33 "Gerhard Schrader": Harris, R., and Paxman, J., *A Higher Form of Killing* (New York: Hill and Wang, 1982).

33 "that produces pesticides": "Nerve gas and pesticides: Links are close." *New York Times,* 30 March 1984.

34 "I can say that I have seen chemical warfare": mayor of Bhopal quoted in "Bhopal Report," *Chemical and Engineering News,* 11 February 1985.

35 "total budget for biological warfare": Letter from Chuck Dasey, Public Affairs Specialist, Fort Detrick, Frederick, MD, 24 July 1986.

35 "Convention has failed": Finder, J. "Biological Warfare, Genetic Engineering and the Treaty That Failed." *Washington Quarterly,* Vol. 9, #2 (Spring 1986).

CHAPTER THREE

36 "Russia's Secret": "Russia's Secret Germ Warfare Disaster," *NOW!,* 26 October 1979.

36 "similar article had run earlier in *Possev*": *Possev,* October 1979. Cited by Zhores Medvedev in "The Great Russian Germ Warfare Fiasco," *New Scientist,* 31 July 1980.

36 "*Possev* ran another article": *Possev,* January 1980. Cited by Medvedev in "The Great Russian Germ Warfare Fiasco."

PAGE

37   "some sort of lethal": "Soviet Mishap Tied to Germ-War Plant,"
     New York Times, 19 March 1980.

37   "Soviets answered the query": "Soviet Lays Outbreak of Illness
     to Bad Meat, Not Germ-war Plant," *New York Times*, 21 March
     1980.

37   "Soviet Foreign Ministry": Reuters (London), 20 March 1980. Re-
     printed in Foreign Broadcasting Information Services (Soviet
     Union), 21 March 1980.

37   "journalist Richard Burt": *New York Times*, 29 March 1980.

37   "Carter was apparently told": "Death at Sverdlovsk: A Critical
     Diagnosis," *Science*, 26 September 1980. Also, Interview with
     M. Meselson, 23 July 1986, Cambridge, MA.

38   "was blown by the way": Interview 27 May 1986, Philadelphia, PA.

38   "according to a Defense Department official": Interview 17 March
     1986, Washington, D.C.

38   "It took the British": Harris, R., and Paxman, J., *A Higher Form of
     Killing* (New York: Hill and Wang, 1982).

39   "anywhere from ten to a thousand": Washington Post, 29 June 1980.
     Also, Gelb, L. "Keeping an Eye on Russia," *New York Times Maga-
     zine*, 29 November 1981.

39   "It didn't seem reasonable": Telephone interview with P. Brachman,
     1 May 1986.

39   "unscheduled arrival": Gelb, L. "Keeping an Eye on Russia."

40   "yes, there was an explosion": Telephone interview with S. Turner,
     22 April 1986.

40   "a meat factory next to Compound 19": Gelb, L., "Keeping an Eye
     on Russia."

40   "professor Donald Ellis": Telephone interview with D. Ellis, 4 June
     1986.

41   "average intelligence officer": Telephone interview with T. Davies,
     29 May 1986.

41   "totally unconvinced": Interview with M. Meselson, 23 July 1986,
     Cambridge, MA.

41   "Zhores Medvedev": "The Great Russian Germ Warfare Fiasco."
     1980.

42   "two million vaccines": F.A.S. Public Interest Report, June 1980.
     Cited in E. Harris, CSIA, Harvard University. "Sverdlovsk and Yel-
     low Rain: Two Cases of Soviet Non-Compliance?" June, 1986, un-
     published paper.

42   "in 1923": From a Soviet medical text, *A Course in Epidemiology*,
     published in 1947 and translated into English in 1961. Cited in
     "Death at Sverdlovsk: A Critical Diagnosis."

42   "an article submitted for publication": Bezdenezhnykh, I., and Niki-
     forov, V., "An Epidemiological Analysis of Incidences of Anthrax in
     Sverdlovsk" (translation). *Russian Journal of Microbiology, Im-*

PAGE

   munology and Epidemiology, May 1980. (Submission date is given as 29 August 1979).

42 "article that appeared in a Russian": Telephone interview with T. Davies, 29, May 1986.

43 *"Russkaja Mysl,* an émigré": Published in July 1980 issue of *Russkaja Mysl*, cited in *New York Times*, 3 July 1980.

43 "House Subcommittee on Intelligence": "The Sverdlovsk Incident: Soviet Compliance with the Biological Weapons Convention?" Hearing before the Subcommittee on Oversight, Permanent Select Committee on Intelligence, House of Representatives, May 29, 1980.

CHAPTER FOUR

45 "the international community": Haig, A. "A Certain Idea of Man: The Democratic Revolution and Its Future," address before the Berlin Press Association, Berlin. 13 September 1981, State Department press release.

46 "over fourteen countries": "US finds 14 nations now have chemical arms," *New York Times,* 20 May 1984.

47 "the Hmong emigrated": Hendricks, G, Downing, B., Dienard, A., editors, *The Hmong in Transition* (Staten Island, NY: The Center for Migration Studies, 1986).

47 "average life spans thirty-five years": Ember, L. "Yellow Rain." *Chemical and Engineering News*, 9 January 1984.

48 "organized a secret army": Marchetti, V., and Marks, J. *The CIA and the Cult of Intelligence.* New York: Dell, 1980.

48 "drops of food": Chagnon, J., and Rumpf, R., "Decades of Division for the Lao Hmong." *Southeast Asia Chronicle,* October 1983.

49 "Hmong used several different words": *Ibid.*

49 "2 million tons of bombs": "Yellow Rain: The Case Is Not Proved," *The Nation,* 10 November 1984.

49 "Montagnards also told": "The Effects of Herbicides in South Viet Nam," Part A; Summary and Conclusions, National Academy of Sciences, Washington D.C. 1974.

50 "refugees told many stories": *Asia Week,* 2 October 1981; "Political Science," *Atlantic Monthly,* October 1985; Evans, G. *The Yellow Rainmakers* (London: Verso Editions, 1983); Interview with J. Chagnon and R. Rumpf, 18 March 1986. Washington D.C.

50 "the *Bangkok Post*": *Bangkok Post,* 24 October 1976.

50 "two French relief doctors": Evans, G. *The Yellow Rainmakers.*

50 "the *International Herald Tribune*": "Poisonous gases reported used on Laos tribe," *International Herald Tribune,* 23 October 1979; Thomas Stearns, AKA given in "Information Paper," DAMO-NCC;

PAGE

8 Novemer 1979. Subject: Purported Use of Chemical Warfare Amongst the H'mong People in Laos.

51 "regularly raised the issue": Telephone Interview with L. Moser, 21 March 1986.

51 "penny-ante game": Telephone Interview with A. Townsend, 29 May 1986.

52 "we didn't know what": Telephone Interview with E. McWilliams, 15 May 1986.

53 "I'm one of those": Telephone interview with S. Turner, 22 April 1986.

54 "the Reagan administration felt": Telephone interview with S. Schwartzstein, 1 May 1986.

55 "perceived as a threat": Interview with D. Bunner, 20 February 1986, Frederick, MD.

55 "alimentary toxic aleukia": Chemical Warfare in Southeast Asia and Afghanistan. Special Report #98, Report to the Congress from the Secretary of State, Alexander Haig, U.S. Department of State, 22 March 1982.

56 "When Mirocha": Telephone interview with C. Mirocha, 5 June 1985.

57 "Bazell": Interview with M. Meselson, 15 November 1985, Cambridge, MA.

58 "Senate Committee on Foreign Relations": Yellow Rain, Hearing before the Subcommittee on Arms Control of the Committee on Foreign Relations, U.S. Senate, 97th Congress, 10 November 1981.

58 "thirty-two-page white paper": Chemical Warfare in Southeast Asia and Afghanistan. Special Report #98.

58 "food scientist at Rutgers": "Rain of Terror," ABC-News documentary, aired 21 December 1981.

59 "Committee on Foreign Affairs": Hearings before the Subcommittees on International Security and Scientific Affairs and on Asian and Pacific Affairs of the Committee on Foreign Affairs of the House of Representatives, 97th Congress, 2nd session, 30 March 1982.

59 "one of the 'bases' ": Letter from Fred Schwartzendruber, 28 May 1986.

60 "Soviets appear to be": *Boston Globe*, 3 December 1982.

60 "to help plead their case": Chemical and Bacteriological (Biological) Weapons, Report of the Secretary-General, United Nations document A/37/259, 1 December 1982.

CHAPTER FIVE

61 "to analyze for trichothecenes": Chemical and Bacteriological (Biological) Weapons; Report of the Secretary-General, United Nations document A/37/259, 1 December 1982.

PAGE

61 "the group could not state":

61 "no canisters, shells, grenades": "Yellow Rain," *Chemical and Engineering News,* 9 January 1984.

62 "Jerry Barker Daniels": Telephone interview with E. McWilliams, 15 May 1986.

62 "most U.N. organizations": Telephone interview with E. McWilliams, 15 May 1986.

63 "If the stories were true": Chagnon, J., and Rumpf, R., "Search for Yellow Rain," *Southeast Asia Chronicle* (June 1983). Also, interview with Chagnon and Rumpf, 18 March 1986, Washington, D.C.

63 "Saul Hormats": "A Chemical Weapons Expert Who Doubts the Soviets Used Yellow Rain," *Washington Post,* 26 February 1984. Also, telephone interview with S. Hormats, 16 May 1986.

64 "released a study": "Protection Against Trichothecene Mycotoxins," Committee on Protection Against Mycotoxins, National Academy of Sciences, 1983.

64 "palynologist": Interview with J. Nowicke, 6 February 1986, Washington D.C.

65 "I knew for sure": Interview with M. Meselson, 26 November 1985, Cambridge, MA.

65 "perfect description": Interview with T. Seeley, 18 November 1985, New Haven, CT.

66 "meeting of the AAAS": Ashton, P.; Meselson, M.; Nowicke, J.; Robinson, J. P.; Seeley, T., "Comparison of yellow rain and bee excrement," paper presented at the AAAS meeting, Detroit, MI, 31 May 1983.

66 "Great Bee Caper": Phrase used by Alan Romberg, State Department spokesman, at State Department press conference, Washington, D.C., 1 June 1983.

66 "according to Kucewicz": "One Scientist's Crusade: A Profile of Matthew Meselson," *Technology Review* (April 1986).

66 "mycotoxin residues in attack area": *Wall Street Journal* editorial, 30 March 1984.

67 "It would seem that in order to accept": T. Seeley, J. Nowicke, M. Meselson, J. Guillemin, Akratanakul, P., "Yellow Rain," *Scientific American* (September 1985).

67 *"Science"*: "The Apology of Yellow Rain," *Science,* 15 July 1983.

67 "I certainly had not realized": Interview with M. Meselson, 26 November 1985.

68 "from 1981 to 1986": Interview with members of the Chemical Research Development and Engineering Command, 13 June 1986, Edgewood, MD.

68 "internally, we've elected": Interview with Joe Vervier, 13 June 1986, Edgewood, MD.

69 "Army's Defense Science Board": Cited in "New Data Weaken U.S. Yellow Rain Case," *Chemical and Engineering News,* 9 June 1986.

PAGE

69   "a Lao pilot": "Flight into Controversy," *Far Eastern Economic Review,* 8 October 1982.

69   "Nyuyen Quan": Memo from Amos Townsend to Volags, I.O.'s JOC/SC, RTA. Chemical Department, AFIRMS, Bangkok, 8 October 1982.

69   "Canadians disputed": "An Epidemiological Investigation of Alleged CW/BW Incidents in Southeast Asia" prepared by Directorate of Preventive Medicine, Surgeon General Branch, National Defense Headquarters, Ottawa, 11 August 1982. Also, Final Summary Reports on the Investigation of Yellow Rain Samples from Southeast Asia. Norman, J. and Purdon, J., Defense Research Establishment, Ottawa, February 1986.

69   "Lois Ember": "Yellow Rain," *Chemical and Engineering News.*

70   "in eighteen out of sixty blood and urine samples": *Ibid.*

70   "reservoir in the body": *Ibid.*

70   "Richard Kenley": *New York Times,* 15 May 1984.

71   "It fell everywhere": Interview with M. Meselson, 15 November 1985, Cambridge, MA.

71   "If the Hmong failed": "Yellow Rain," *Scientific American,* September 1985.

72   "the truth of an idea": James, William. *Pragmatism and Other Essays* (New York: Washington Square Press, 1963).

72   "the British Ministry of Defence": House of Commons Official Report, Vol. 98, #117. Written Answers to Questions. 19 May 1986.

72   "from Thais who were *not* exposed": Final Summary Report on the Investigation of Yellow Rain from Southeast Asia. Canada's Defense Research Establishment. February 1986.

72   "summaries of about two hundred": Interview with J. Guillemin, 4 June 1986, Cambridge, MA.

73   "if a clan leader": Interview with J. Guillemin, 4 June 1986.

75   "in a lead editorial": "Still Caught in the Yellow Rain." *New York Times,* 16 June 1986.

76   "element of fear": Telephone interview with S. Schwartzstein, 1 May 1986.

76   "something too overt": Interview with G. Crocker, 6 February 1986, Washington D.C.

76   "no convincing evidence": Interview with J. Leonard, 27 May 1986, Philadelphia, PA.

76   "cost the U.S. taxpayer": Sources: Jim Allingham, public affairs specialist, Chemical Research Development and Engineering Center, Edgewood, MD; Chuck Dasey, public affairs specialist, U.S. Army Medical Research and Development Command, Frederick, MD.

76   "bee feces and hysteria": Interview with M. Meselson, 23 July 1986, Cambridge, MA.

77   "utter nonsense": Telephone interview with T. Davies, 29 May 1986.

PAGE
77 "ego and stupidity": Telephone interview with Richard Kenley, 12 September 1986.
77 "yellow drops fell": Tsung-Eng, C., Wuee-Ming, C., Shio, C., Min, L. "A study of the origin and the pollen analysis of the 'Yellow Rain' in northern Jiangsu" (translation), Kexue Tongbao, Vol. 22, pages 409–412, 1977.

CHAPTER SIX

78 "From the military point of view": Report of the Chemical Warfare Review Commission (Washington D.C.: Government Printing Office, June 1985).
79 "5,000 men and women": "Army Training exercise to use live nerve gas,"*Atlanta Journal and Constitution,* 17 November 1985.
79 "in World War I": Harris and Paxman, *A Higher Form of Killing* (New York: Hill and Wang, 1982).
79 "phrase of the day": *Ibid.*
81 "didn't appreciate": Interview with Lt. Colonel Morris. 4 December 1986. Anniston, Alabama.
82 "logistical nightmare": *Ibid.*
82 "Army's 'Field Manual for NBC Operations' ": Army Field Manual for NBC Operations, available through U.S. Army Chemical School, Anniston, AL.
84 "proposed strike targets": Interview with Evan Koslow, 6 March 1986, New York, NY.
85 "increased spending on NBC protection": Statement of Dr. Thomas Welch, deputy assistant to the secretary of defense before the Strategic and Nuclear Forces Subcommittee of the Senate Armed Services Committee, 10 April 1986.
85 "the first issue infuses": *Nuclear, Biological and Chemical Defense and Technology International,* Vol 1, #1 (April 1986).
86 "in its second issue": "Yellow Rain Report," *Nuclear, Biological and Chemical Defense and Technology International,* Vol 1, #2 (May 1986).
87 "would use a seven-dollar bill": Interview with M. Meselson, 23 July 1986, Cambridge, MA.
89 "relatively small group of specialists": Interview with Joseph Douglass, 7 February, 1986. McLean, VA.
90 "rated a low priority": Kestin, H., "The C Team," *Playboy* (May 1986).
90 "cull leads, 80 percent by one estimate": Statement made by Roscoe Hillenkoeter, director of Central Intelligence in 1948, cited in Richelson, J., *The U.S. Intelligence Community* (Cambridge, MA: Ballinger, 1985).
91 "In 1986 testimony": Testimony by Douglas Feith, deputy assistant secretary of defense for negotiations policy, on Biological and Toxin

PAGE

Weapons before the Subcommittee on Oversight and Evaluation of the House Permanent Select Committee on Intelligence, 8 August 1986.

91 *"Breaking with Moscow"*: Shevchenko, A., *Breaking with Moscow* (New York: Ballantine Books, 1985).

92 *"Boston Globe"*: *Boston Globe,* 28 September 1975.

92 "first anniversary": Associated Press, 15 June 1976. Carried by CBS-TV Morning News and, following day, *Christian Science Monitor.*

92 *"Soviet Military Power"*: *Soviet Military Power* (Washington D.C.: Government Printing Office, 1984).

92 "John Birkner": "Biotechnology may be used against U.S., Official says," *New York Times,* 28 May 1984.

92 "Soviet Non-Compliance": U.S. Arms Control and Disarmament Agency, Washington D.C., "Soviet Non-Compliance." Released March 1986.

93 "Feith told the House": 8 August 1986.

94 "this portrayal": Julian Perry Robinson, "Chemical and Biological Warfare: Analysis of recent reports concerning the Soviet Union and Viet Nam," March 1980, ADIU, Occasional Paper #1. Science Policy Research Unit, University of Sussex, England.

94 "very little evidence": Andrew Cockburn, *The Threat: Inside the Soviet Military Machine.* (New York: Random House/Vintage Books, 1983).

95 "bomber gap": Ranelagh, J., *The Agency* (New York: Simon and Schuster, 1986).

95 "missile gap": *Ibid.*

CHAPTER SEVEN

97 "the technological imperative": Interview with R. Sinsheimer, 7 October 1985, Santa Cruz, CA.

98 "military utility of BW": Douglas Feith, quoted in "Biological Weapons Reweighed," *Washington Post,* 17 August 1986.

98 "rational arguments": "Chemical and Bacteriological Weapons in the 1980s," editorial, *The Lancet,* 21 July 1984.

98 "Outlandish, crazy things": Susan Wright, paper presented at meeting of the American Association for the Advancement of Science, Philadelphia, 27 May 1986.

100 "Janet Mertz": Krimsky, S., *Genetic Alchemy* (Cambridge, MA: MIT Press, 1982).

100 "in terms of the atomic bomb": Janet Mertz quoted in Krimsky, *Genetic Alchemy.*

100 "interest in biological warfare": Interview with D. Baltimore, 16 December 1985, Cambridge, MA.

PAGE
102 "BW would not be discussed": Interview with S. Krimsky, 31 October 1985, Medford, MA.
102 "according to Novick": Interview with R. Novick, 19 November 1985, New York, NY.
103 "potential for biohazard": Plasmid Working Group, Proposed Guidelines on Potential Biohazards Associated with Experiments Involving Genetically Altered Microorganisms. Asilomar Conference, 24 February 1975, Recombinant DNA Controversy Collection, MIT.
103 "keep them from developing": Interview with S. Krimsky, 31 October 1985.
103 "potential for misuse": Interview with R. Goldstein, 3 and 10 January 1986, Boston, MA.
104 "the sick imagination": Erwin Chargaff, quoted in "Research with Recombinant DNA: Academy Forum," March 7–9, 1977, National Academy of Sciences.
104 "not now using recombinant DNA": Unnamed DOD official, quoted in "BW and Recombinant DNA," Science, 18 April 1980.
104 "funded twenty-seven recombinant DNA projects": Recombinant DNA Research Projects Funded by the Department of Defense as of 8 September 1983. List compiled by Department of Defense.
105 "grown to sixty": Institutional Biosafety Committee Approved and "Guideline Exempt" Recombinant DNA Research Projects, performed and/or funded by Department of Defense, as of 21 March 1985. List compiled by DOD.
105 "$50 million in funds": Susan Wright, "The Military and the New Biology," Bulletin of the Atomic Scientists (May 1985).
105 "in North Africa, not North Roxbury": Jonathan King quoted in "Controversy grows over Pentagon's work on biological agents," Wall Street Journal, 17 September 1986.
105 "credible research group in biological toxin defense": Department of the Army, Walter Reed Institute of Research. Subject: Recent Personnel Decrements. To: All WRAIR personnel, 6 December 1985.
105 "RAC guidelines": Notice published in the Federal Register, Vol. 7, #102, 26 May, 1982.
106 "Baltimore led the discussion": Department of Health and Human Services, Public Health Service, National Institutes of Health, Recombinant DNA Advisory Committee. Minutes of meeting, 28 June 1982.
106 "innocuous but reasonable": Interview with R. Goldstein, 3 and 10 January, 1986.
107 "clone the Shiga": "Gene Cloning Could Further Biological Warfare," New Scientist, 16 Feburary 1984.
107 "you have to look at this": Interview with R. Sinsheimer, 7 October 1985.

PAGE

107 "over two hundred companies": Telephone interview with Alan Goldhammer, Industrial Biotechnology Association, 4 March 1986.

108 "nine contracts": "Nine firms get $2.5 million to develop anti-biowar kits," McGraw-Hill's *Biotechnology Newswatch,* 20 August 1984.

108 "be talking to DOD": Telephone interview with Ms. Trantolo, spokesperson for Dynatech, Cambridge, MA, August 1985.

109 "to clone tetanus toxin": Interview with M. Nelson, 7 January 1986, Beverly, MA.

110 "potential Pandora's box": Letter written by James Larrick, Published in *Nature,* Vol 301: 651 (1983).

110 "singled out microbiology": Fred Ikle, quoted in "Commercial Biotechnology—An Institutional Analysis," Office of Technology Assessment, 1984.

110 "Alfred Hellman": Interview with A. Hellman, 27 January 1986, Washington D.C.

111 "manufactured in this country": Telephone interview with A. Goldhammer, 4 March 1986.

111 *"Soviet Military Power": Soviet Military Power* (Washington D.C.: Government Printing Office, 1984).

112 "eight-part series": "Beyond Yellow Rain—The Threat of Soviet Genetic Engineering," *Wall Street Journal,* From 23 April 1984 to 18 May 1984.

112 "no real evidence": Telephone interview with Elkan Blout, September 1986.

113 "the flu virus": Interview with N. Zinder, 6 March 1986, New York, NY.

113 "worse pathogen": Interview with R. Novick, 19 November 1985.

113 "in terms of deadlines": Interview with S. Falkow, 8 October 1985, Stanford, CA.

114 "too much smarts": Interview with D. Huxsoll, 20 February 1986, Frederick, MD.

114 "need for BL-4 Lab": Department of Defense, Biological Defense Program, Report to the Committee on Appropriations, House of Representatives, May 1986.

115 "stunning advances": Testimony by Douglas Feith on Biological and Toxin Weapons to House Intelligence Committee, 8 August 1986.

116 "nuclear path": Interview with Richard Falk, 20 November 1985, Princeton, NJ.

117 "potential adversary": Testimony by R. Novick on the impact of genetic engineering technology on the development and use of biological weapons to the Subcommittee on Oversight and Investigations of the House Committee on Energy and Commerce, 18 December 1985.

117 "might be exploited": Remarks on Biological Warfare by Dr. Joshua Lederberg to the Conference of the Committee on Disarmament.

PAGE

Documents on Disarmament, U.S. Arms Control and Disarmament Agency, 5 August 1970.

CHAPTER EIGHT

121 "Regarding BW Training": National Archives, Science Branch/Research Unit, 15 January 1945.

122 "Some veterans today": Statement by Congressman Pat Williams before the House Veterans' Affairs Compensation Subcommittee, 17 September 1986.

122 "one of those POWs": Testimony of Frank James, House Committee on Veterans' Affairs, Subcommittee on Compensation, Pension and Insurance, 17 September 1986.

124 "had waved feathers": Interview with Greg Rodriguez, Jr., 17 September 1986, Washington, D.C.

124 "Dr. John Hatcher": Statement by Dr. John Hatcher, Chief of Army Records Management, Department of the Army, House Veterans' Affairs Committee, Subcommittee on Compensation, Pension and Insurance, American prisoners of war in Manchuria, 17 September 1986.

125 "delegation from Poland": Harris, R., and Paxman, J., *A Higher Form of Killing* (New York: Hill and Wang, 1982).

125 "a number of sabotage operations": *Ibid.*

126 "demon seed": *Ibid.*

126 "Russo-Japanese War": McNeill, W., *Plagues and Peoples* (Garden City, NY: Anchor Press/Doubleday, 1976).

126 "took a greater toll": *Ibid.*

127 "Kyoto Imperial University": Thompson, Arvo, Report on Japanese Biological Warfare Activities, Army Service Forces, Camp Detrick, Frederick, MD, 31 May 1946.

127 "told his higher-ups": Tsuneishi, K., "The Research Guarded by Military Secrecy," *Historia Scientarium*, Vol. 30 (1986). History of Science Society of Japan.

127 "blamed an outbreak of disease": General Headquarters, U.S. Army Forces Pacific, Scientific and Technical Advisory Section. Subject: Biological warfare. Date: 8 November 1945. Interviewed: General Yoshijiro Umezo. Interviewers: Lt. Col. Murray Sanders and Lt. H. Young. Also from the same set of interviews, Date 10 November 1945. Interviewed General Shimomura. Interviewers: Lt. Col. Murray Sanders and Lt. H. Young.

128 "yearly budget": BW Activities at Pingfan. Appendix 29-F-b. Subject: Japanese Activities in Biological Warfare. Date: 16 October 1945. Interviewed: Lt. Col. Masuda and Lt. Col. Niizuma. Interviewers: Sanders and Young.

PAGE
128 "empire stretched": Japanese BW Activities (Offensive and Defensive). Appendix 29-E-a-1. Subject: Japanese Offensive Activities in Biological Warfare. Date: 6 October 1945. Interviewed: Dr. Ryoichi Naito. Interviewer: Lt. Col. Murray Sanders.

128 "guinea pigs": General Headquarters, Far East Command, Military Intelligence Section, General Staff, 17 January 1947. Subject: Bacteriological Warfare Experiments by Japanese.

129 "to promote my study": Interview with Akimoto, cited by Tsuneishi, K., in "The Research Guarded by Military Secrecy."

129 "used in experiments as 'monkeys' ": Report of Investigation Division, Legal Section, General Headquarters, SCAP, 4 April 1947. Synopsis of Facts: Report of Investigation Division, Case #330 to date. Experiments conducted on POWs at Kwantung Army Stables and Army Water Purification and Supply Unit reflect plan of bacterial warfare. Also, "Germ Tests: Manchurian Mask Lifted," *Los Angeles Times*, 19 December 1982.

129 "epidemic hemorrhagic fever": Tsuneishi, K., "The Research Guarded by Military Secrecy."

129 "accidental death": BW Activities at Pingfan. Appendix 29-F-a. Subject: Biological Warfare. Date: 11 October 1945. Interviewed: Col. Tomosada Masuda and Lt. Col. Seiichi Niizuma. Interviewer: Lt. Col. Murray Sanders.

129 "eight different types of bombs": Report of the Scientific Intelligence Survey in Japan, Vol. V., Biological Warfare, 1 November 1945. General Headquarters, U.S. Army Forces, Pacific; Scientific and Technical Advisory Section.

130 "bombs against the Chinese": G-2, China Theater Report. Subject: Bacterial Warfare. From: Chungking, China. Source: Japanese prisoners of war. 4 December 1944. Also, Confidential Memo #336. Subject: Allegations of Japanese bacteriological warfare in China. To the Secretary of State from American Embassy in Chungking, 11 April 1942.

130 "grains from heaven": quoted from Japanese Attempt at Bacterial Warfare in China. Report of Dr. P. Z. King, Director-General of the Chinese National Health Administration, 31 March 1942.

130 "Dr. Politzer": Powell, J., "Japan's Biological Weapons," *Bulletin of Atomic Scientists*, October 1981.

130 "Unit 731": "Unit 731—What Did the Emperor Know?" Documentary film produced by Peter Williams for TV South, Southhampton England. First broadcast in England, 13 August 1985.

131 "wartime intelligence reports": Secret Bacteriological Warfare Summary Report, Japan's Intentions and Capabilities, 2 February 1944. Also, Secret Digest of Information Regarding Axis Activities in the Field of Bacteriological Warfare, 8 January 1943.

PAGE

131 "no lack of desire": Tsuneishi, K., Japanese Biological Warfare Activity and Investigation on It. Compilation of original documents from the U.S. National Archives. Note on page 102 of the documents.

131 "destroyed all evidence": Japanese BW Activities (Offensive and Defensive). Appendix 29-E-d-1 to Report of Scientific Intelligence Survey in Japan. Subject: Biological Warfare. Date: 9 October 1945. Interviewed: Lt. Col. Saichi Niizuma and Col. T. Masuda. Interviewer: Lt. Col. Murray Sanders.

132 "appointed Dr. Ryoichi Naito": "Unit 731—What Did the Emperor Know?"

132 "contact before the war": Confidential memorandum for Col. Simmons, Office of the Surgeon General, War Department General Staff. Military Intelligence, Division G-2, Washington D.C., 3 February 1941.

132 "to see that I didn't learn too much": Murray Sanders in "Unit 731—What Did the Emperor Know?"

133 "hand-written note": Private (secret) information to Colonel Sanders. Twelve-page hand-written letter from Dr. Naito to Col. Sanders. Xerox obtained from Dr. Sanders through office of Congressman Pat Williams.

133 "immunity from war crimes": Murray Sanders in "Unit 731—What Did the Emperor Know?"

133 "Scientific Intelligence Survey Report": Report of Scientific Intelligence Survey in Japan, Vol V. Biological Warfare.

134 "Arvo Thompson": Thompson, Arvo, Report on Japanese Biological Warfare Activities, 31 May 1946.

134 "outpost of Ishii's operation": Headquarters, U.S. Army Forces, China Theater. SINTIC Item #213. Subject: Japanese Preparations for Bacteriological Warfare in China. 12 December 1944.

134 "the tribunal's president": International Military Tribunal for the Far East. Trial transcript, 29 August 1946.

134 "anonymous letter-writer": Report of Investigation Division, Legal Section, General Headquarters, SCAP. 4 April 1947.

134 "the emperor knew": "Unit 731—What did the Emperor Know?"

135 "to interrogate Ishii": Memorandum for Record. Subject: Request of Russians to arrest and interrogate Japanese Bacteriological Warfare Experts in Whom U.S. had prior interest. 27 March 1947. Also, State-War-Navy Coordinating Committee for the Far East. Request of Russian prosecutor for permission to interrogate certain Japanese. 28 February 1947.

135 "top secret cable": Radio message. From CINFE Tokyo. To War Department. 6 May 1947.

135 "the War Department answered immediately": State-War-Navy Coordinating Committee, 15 July 1947.

PAGE

136 "eight thousand slides": Interview with Norm Covert, public affairs specialist, U.S. Army Medical Research and Development Command, Fort Detrick, 20 February 1986.

136 "pragmatic terms": State-War-Navy Coordinating Subcommittee for the Far East. Interrogation of Certain Japanese by Russian prosecutors, 1 August 1947.

136 "deal split the Americans": State-War-Navy Co-ordinating Subcommittee for the Far East. Interrogation of Certain Japanese by Russian Prosecutors. 29 September 1947.

137 "Dr. Edwin Hill": To: General Alden Waitt, Chief Chemical Corps. Subject: Summary Report on BW Investigations. Written by: Dr. Hill and Dr. Victor. 12 December 1947.

138 "the smoking gun": Statement by Congressman Pat Williams, POW Press Conference, 6 December 1985.

138 "I was the gun": Sanders quoted in "MD–US Hid Japan's Experiments on POWs," *Miami Herald,* 7 December 1985.

CHAPTER NINE

139 "Friday night": Interview with A. Olson, 21 February 1986, Frederick, MD.

141 "almost 4,000": Rosebury, T., *Peace or Pestilence?* (New York: McGraw-Hill, 1949).

141 "more priority": Speech given by Dr. Ira Baldwin at Fort Detrick's Silver Anniversary Luncheon, La Scala Restaurant, New York City, 2 May 1967.

141 "test the camp's sewage": Rosebury, T., *Peace or Pestilence?*

141 "in the 1920s and 1930s": Fox, L., "Bacterial Warfare—The Use of Biological Agents in Warfare," *The Military Surgeon,* Vol. 72, #3 (March 1933).

142 "committee of twelve scientists": Brophy, Miles, and Cochrane. The Chemical Warfare Service: From Laboratory to Field. Office of the Chief of Military History, U.S. Army, Washington D.C., 1959.

142 "debatable question": Cochrane, R., Biological Warfare Research in the U.S. History of the Chemical Warfare Service in World War II, July 1940–August 1945. Historical Section, Office of Chief, Chemical Corps, November 1947.

142 "colonel posed the question": Speech given by Dr. Ira Baldwin at Fort Detrick's Silver Anniversary.

142 "appointed George Merck": U.S. Army Activity in the U.S. Biological Warfare Programs, Vol I. Department of the Army. 24 February 1977.

143 "other than typical respiratory": Speech given by Dr. Ira Baldwin at Fort Detrick's Silver Anniversary.

PAGE
143 "aerosols of infectious disease": Rosebury, T., *Peace or Pestilence?*

144 "tests at Horn Island": Harris, R., and Paxman, *A Higher Form of Killing* (New York: Hill and Wang, 1982).

144 "biological warfare intelligence": Brophy, Miles, and Cochrane, The Chemical Warfare Service.

144 "rockets with anthrax": Harris and Paxman, *A Higher Form of Killing.*

144 "never intended": *Ibid.*

145 "Operation Paperclip": Outgoing classified message from Joint Chiefs of Staff to Commander in Chief, Europe. Berlin, Germany. 8 October 1947. Also, Memo from Joint Chiefs of Staff, Joint Intelligence Objectives Agency. To: Commander in Chief, European Command. Subject: Detention of German Scientific Personnel. 15 October 1947.

145 "press release": Report to the secretary of war by Mr. George Merck, special consultant for biological warfare. For release at 7:30 P.M. EST, 3 January 1946.

145 "closed hearing": Rosebury, T., *Peace or Pestilence?*

145 "more frightful": *Ibid.*

145 "representative boasted": *Ibid.*

146 "shrouded in secrecy": Interview with A. Langmuir, 30 January 1986, Cambridge, MA.

147 "rose to $4 million": Miller, D., History of Air Force Participation in the Biological Warfare Program, 1944–1951. Historical Division, Wright-Patterson Air Force Base, September 1952.

147 "silence was lifted": "Forrestal Scouts Germ War as Army Says U.S. Is Ready," *New York Times,* 13 March 1949.

147 "Committee on Biological Warfare": Letter from Secretary of Defense James Forrestal to Dr. Caryl Haskins, 16 March 1949.

148 "Here Is What": "Here Is What You Need to Know About Biological Warfare." Pamphlet published by the Federal Civil Defense Administration, February 1951.

148 "20 percent of his time": A. Langmuir quoted in "Disease Expert Sees Threat of Germ Warfare," *New York Times,* 21 March 1977.

149 "all of Europe": Miller, D., History of Air Force Participation in the Biological Warfare Program, 1944–1951.

149 "most secret place": Marks, J., *The Search for the Manchurian Candidate* (New York: McGraw-Hill, 1980).

149 "largest intelligence organization in the world": Ranelagh, J., *The Agency: The Rise and Decline of the CIA* (New York: Simon and Schuster, 1986).

149 "Professor Moriarty": Marks, J., *The Search for the Manchurian Candidate.*

PAGE
150   "utterly uninhibited": Stanley Lovell in speech to the Harvard Club,
        7 November.
150   "deepest respect": Harris and Paxman, *A Higher Form of Killing.*
150   "props and gadgets": Marks, J., *The Search for the Manchurian Can-
        didate.*
150   "Gottlieb arranged": *Ibid.*
151   "ultra-sensitive": *Ibid.*
151   "paid SOD $3 million": *Ibid.*
151   "weekend retreat": *Ibid.*
152   "the Agency had a technical agenda": Memorandum for the Director
        of Central Intelligence. Subject: CIA Activities at Fort Detrick, Fred-
        erick, MD, 20 May 1975.
153   "potent Red Tide poison": Senate Select Committee to Study Gov-
        ernmental Operations with Respect to Intelligence Activities (usually
        called the Church Committee, for its head, Senator Frank Church),
        15, 16, 17 September 1975.
153   "ten seconds": *Ibid.*
153   "Powers was shot down": *Ibid.*
153   "microbioinoculator": *Ibid.*
154   "bemoaned the fact": *Ibid.*
154   "planned to assassinate": Ranelagh, J., *The Agency.*
154   "the president and dictator": *Ibid.*
155   "target for wild ideas": *Ibid.*
155   "Cuban economic sabotage program": The Church Committee. Also:
        "Canadian Says U.S. Paid Him $5,000 to Infect Cuban Poultry,"
        Washington Post, 21 March 1977.
156   "biological warfare against Cuba": "Cuban Outbreak of Swine Fever
        Linked to CIA," *Newsday*, 9 January 1977.
156   "equally nasty devices": Livingstone, N., and Douglass, J., *CBW—
        The Poor Man's Atomic Bomb* (Cambridge, MA: Institute for Foreign
        Policy Analysis. 1985).
156   "defense consultants": *Ibid.*
157   "I screamed": Interview with Alice Olson, 21 February 1986.

CHAPTER TEN

158   "strong emotional appeal": Miller, Dorothy *History of Air Force Par-
        ticipation in the Biological Warfare Program, 1944–1951.* Prepared by
        Historical Office, Wright-Patterson Air Force Base, September
        1952.
158   "five thousand biological cluster bombs": *Ibid.*
159   "$64,000 question": *Ibid.*
159   "Cover and Deception Plan": "Deception in the biological warfare
        field." Memorandum by the Chief of Staff, U.S. Army. References to
        JCS 1927/JCS 1927–31 (Plan Schoolyard). No date. Also, Memoran-

PAGE

dum for the Secretary, JCS, Subject: Deception in the Biological Warfare Field. 30 January 1952.

159   "born in 1919": Kutler, Stanley, *The American Inquisition* (New York: Hill and Wang, 1982).

160   "some knowledge": Interview with Bill Powell, 8 October 1985, San Francisco, CA.

160   "Justice Department authorized": Kutler, S., *The American Inquisition.*

161   "San Francisco grand jury": *Ibid.*

161   "mock horror": Interview with Bill Powell, 8 October 1985.

162   "mistakenly referred": Kutler, S., *The American Inquisition.*

162   "Powell broke the story": Powell, J., "Japan's Germ Warfare: the US Cover-up of a War Crime," *Bulletin of Concerned Asian Scholars,* Vol. 12, #4 (1980).

163   "on June 21, 1950": The Stevenson Report. Secretary of Defense's Ad Hoc Committee Report, JCS, 30 June 1950.

163   " 'Germ Warfare in Korea' ": "Germ Warfare in Korea?" *Science News Letter,* 8 July 1950.

163   "Ellis Zacharias": "Bacteriological Warfare," *Journal of Contemporary Asia,* Vol 7, #2 (1977).

163   "bacteriological weapons research labs": *New York Times,* 13 April 1951; *Newsweek,* 13 April 1951.

164   "Sams revealed": "Special Operations in North Korea." 17 March 1951. Report #TB-1005-51. Department of Defense. Cited in Kutler, S., *The American Inquisition.*

164   "lodged a protest": Kutler, S., *The American Inquisition.*

164   "newspaper dispatch from Rangoon": "Bacteriological Warfare," *Journal of Contemporary Asia,* Vol 7, #2 (1977).

164   "General Ridgeway angrily denied": *Ibid.*

165   "really leaflet bombs": "Reds' Photographs on Germ Warfare Exposed as Fakes," *New York Times,* 3 April 1952.

165   "General Bullene": Associated Press dispatch, 5 April 1952, quoted by Robert Sikes, chairman of the House Appropriations Subcommittee, which had received secret testimony from Bullene on 4 April 1952.

165   "top secret memo": From Department of the Air Force, staff message division. HQ, USAF. To: CGFE, Tokyo, Japan. Personal to Smart from Burns. 17 April 1952. Also, From CINCFE Tokyo, to: DEPTAIR, Washington, D.C., for JCS. September, 1952.

166   "Walker Mahurin": Stephen Endicott "Germ Warfare and Plausible Denial," *Modern China,* Vol 5, #1 (January 1979).

166   "unofficial policy": *Ibid.*

166   "In Canada, James Endicott": Stephen Endicott, *James Endicott: Rebel Out of China* (Toronto: University of Toronto Press, 1980).

167   "much more extensive investigation": Report of the International

PAGE

Scientific Commission for the Investigation of Facts Concerning Bacterial Warfare in Korea and China (Peking, 1952).

169   "97 percent sure": Correspondence from Joseph Needham, The Needham Research Institute, East Asian History of Science Library, Cambridge University, 20 July 1986.

169   "brainwashed": "Germ warfare: Forged Evidence," *Time*, 9 November 1953.

169   "to condition the Russian people": Miller, D., History of Air Force Participation in the Biological Warfare Programs.

CHAPTER ELEVEN

170   "unwarranted luxury": Miller, Dorothy, History of Air Force Participation in the Biological Warfare Program, 1951–1954. Prepared by the Historical Division, Wright-Patterson Air Force Base, January 1957.

170   "antilivestock diseases": *Ibid.*

170   "$5 million/year": *Ibid.*

170   "Maryland's state penitentiary": "Army Paid UM to do Germ Study," *Baltimore Sun*, 1 April 1977.

170   "Operation White Coat": Hersh, S., *Chemical and Biological Warfare: America's Hidden Arsenal* (Indianapolis: Bobbs-Merrill, 1968).

171   "only ten to twenty-five microbes": *Ibid.*

171   "When Nevin remembers": Interview with E. Nevin, 7 October 1985, San Francisco, CA.

172   "originally written by John Cummings": *Newsday*, 21 November 1976.

172   "Meselson had heard": Interview with M. Meselson, 23 July 1986, Cambridge, MA.

173   "a 1939 Chevy": Interview with Nevin.

173   "listed the cause": Wheat, Zuckerman and Rantz, "Infection Due to Chromobacteria," *Archives of Internal Medicine*, Vol. 88. 1951.

173   "Lord knows": "Bacterium Like One Army Used Caused Infection After Germ Test," *New York Times*, 13 March 1977.

176   "The genesis": U.S. Army Activities in the United States Biological Warfare Programs, 1942–1977.

176   "large-scale field tests": *Ibid.*

176   "turned to the coast": *Ibid.*

177   "overt or covert operations": *Ibid.*

177   "overlook the potential": Civil Action C-78-1713-SC. *Mabel Nevin vs. USA.* U.S. District Court for the Northern District of California. Findings of Fact and Conclusions of Law, 13 March 1981.

177   "by secret letter": U.S. Army Activities in the United States Biological Warfare Programs, Vol. II Annexes, Department of the Army, 24 February 1977.

PAGE
178 "vainly to calculate": Biological Warfare Trials at San Francisco, CA, 20–27 September 1950. Special Report #142. Chemical Corps, Biological Laboratories, Camp Detrick, Frederick, MD, 22 January 1951.
178 "labeled the seventh test inconclusive": *Ibid.*
178 "we used *Serratia*": George Connell, quoted in Civil Action C-78-1713-SC.
179 "five cases": "Bacterium Like One Army Used Caused Infection After Germ Test," *New York Times*, 13 March 1977.
179 "it was a coincidence": Interview with A. Langmuir, 30 January 1986, Cambridge, MA.
179 "security clearance": Interview with E. Nevin, 7 October 1985.
179 "we and other bacteriologists": Dr. Rantz quoted in "Bacterium Like One Army Used Caused Infection After Germ Test."
180 "the army argued": Civil Action Number C-78-1713-SC.
181 "I was pleased": Interview with E. Nevin, 7 October 1985.
181 "testing was foolish": Interview with M. Meselson, 23 July 1986, Cambridge, MA.
181 "line officers": Interview with A. Langmuir, 30 January 1986.
182 "Documents released": U.S. Army Activity in the U.S. Biological Warfare Programs, Vols. I and II. Department of the Army. 24 February 1977.
183 *"Newsday"*: "Germ Weapons Tested in Eight Locales," *Newsday*, 20 December 1976.
183 "citizens of Winnipeg": "Weapons of War," *Goodwin's Premier* (Spring 1983).
183 "Dr. L. Arthur Spomer": Spomer, L. Arthur, "Fluorescent Particle Atmospheric Tracer: Toxicity Hazard," *Atmos. Environ.* 7 (3) 353:355 (March 1973).
184 "real diseases": U.S. Army Activity in the U.S. Biological Warfare Programs, Vol. II. 24 February 1977.
184 "basic principle": Interview with Telford Work, 30 September 1985, Los Angeles, CA.
184 "special oversight committee": U.S. Army Activity in the U.S. Biological Warfare Programs, Vol. II. 24 February 1977.
184 "subsequent oversight committee": *Ibid.*
185 "fire broke out": *NBC News*, "First Tuesday: Chemical and Biological Warfare," 4 February 1969.
185 "targeted against livestock": U.S. Army Activity in the U.S. Biological Warfare Programs. Vol. II. 24 February 1977.
186 "Fort Greely": Hersh, S., *Chemical and Biological Warfare.*
186 "remote, isolated, tropical island": SIPRI *Yearbook of World Armaments and Disarmament 1968/69* (New York: Humanities Press, 1970).

PAGE
186 "pathogenic organisms": U.S. Army Activity in the U.S. Biological
     Warfare Program, Vol II. 24 February 1977.
187 "Sidney Galler": Quoted in "The Smithsonian Secret Contract: The
     Link Between Birds and Biological Warfare," *Washington Post Magazine*, 12 May 1985.
187 "bird bombs": Feathers as Carriers of Biological Warfare Agents. Biological Department, Chemical Corps, SO and C Divisions. Camp
     Detrick, Frederick, Maryland. Special Report #138. 15 December
     1950.
187 "CIA had also funded": Role of Avian Vectors in Transmission of
     Disease. MKULTRA Subproject #139. October 1961.
187 "National Airport": Miscellaneous publication #7. Prepared by
     Study Group composed of representatives of U.S. Army Biological
     Laboratories. U.S. Army Biological Laboratories, Fort Detrick,
     Frederick, MD. July 1965.
188 "most notorious biological": Church Committee, 16–17 September
     1975.
188 "if 30 percent of the city was sick": Harris, R., and Paxman, J., *A
     Higher Form of Killing* (New York: Hill and Wang, 1982).

                           CHAPTER TWELVE

189 "far-ranging review": Hersh, S., *Chemical and Biological Warfare:
     America's Hidden Arsenal* (Indianapolis and New York: Bobbs-Merrill, 1969).
189 "drop rice blast": Interview with USDA plant research scientists, 20
     February 1986, Frederick, MD.
189 "VEE": Hersh, S., *Chemical and Biological Warfare.*
190 "to use tularemia": "Germ Warfare," *Ramparts,* December 1969.
190 "okayed the secret use": Gettleman, Franklin, Young, Franklin, eds,
     Vietnam and America (New York: Grove Press, 1985).
190 "a hundred million pounds": *Ibid.*
190 "deeper into the jungle": Herbicide and Military Operations. Office
     of the Chief of Engineers, Department of the Army, Engineer Strategic Studies Group. February 1972.
191 "wanted to see what the world": Interview with M. Meselson, 23 July
     1986, Cambridge, MA.
191 "grew up with laboratory": "One Scientist's Crusade: A Profile of
     Matthew Meselson," *Technology Review* (April 1986).
193 "describes in his memoirs": Dyson, F., *Disturbing the Universe* (New
     York: Harper and Row, 1979).
194 "not the low military utility": M. Meselson, remarks at the AAAS
     meeting, Philadelphia, PA, 27 May 1986.
195 "Richard McCarthy": McCarthy, R., *The Ultimate Folly: War by
     Pestilence, Asphyxiation and Defoliation* (New York: Knopf, 1969).

PAGE

195 "Grab what you can": Interview with J. Leonard, 27 May 1986, Philadelphia, PA.

196 "Nixon explained": Remarks of the president on announcing the chemical and biological defense policies and programs. Office of the White House Press Secretary, 25 November 1969.

197 "*Washington Post* editorial": Interview with M. Meselson, 23 July 1986.

197 "submitted a paper": "What Policy for Toxins?" unpublished paper by M. Meselson, 22 January 1970.

198 "had to be a supplement": Interview with I. Bennett, 6 March 1986, New York, NY.

198 "took two years": Interview with J. Leonard, 27 May 1986.

200 "proposed an alternative": Memorandum for director of Central Intelligence. From Thomas Karamessines, deputy director for plans. Subject: Contingency Plan for Stockpile of Biological Warfare Agents. Included in the Church Committee hearings.

200 "congressman observed": Senator Frank Church, Hearings of the Senate Select Committee to Study Governmental Operations with Respect to Intelligence (also known as the Church Committee), 16 and 17 September 1975.

CHAPTER THIRTEEN

204 "safety officer": Interview with Larry Ware, 21 February 1986, Frederick, MD.

205 "423 cases": Wedum, A., The Detrick Experience as a Guide to the Probable Efficacy of P4 Microbiological Containment Facilities for Studies on Microbial Recombinant DNA Molecules. Unpublished manuscript. 20 January 1976.

205 "since 1969": Source: Chuck Dasey, public affairs specialist, U.S. Army Medical Research and Development Command, Frederick, MD. Letter, 3 October 1986.

205 "Howard Dinterman": "Army Admits '64 Bacteria Accident at Detrick," *Frederick Post,* 14 October 1982.

206 "another type of lab accident": "Suit Charges Army Misplaced a Virus," *New York Times,* 24 September 1986.

207 "days of the Vietnam War": "Detrick Birthday: Dispute Flares Over Biological Warfare Center," *Science,* 19 April 1968.

208 "AIDS being a biological weapon": "Soviets Say CIA Created AIDS to use in Biological Warfare," *San Francisco Examiner,* 31 October 1985.

208 "Detrick received 95 percent": Letter from Chuck Dasey, 24 July 1986.

208 "two-thirds of Detrick's budget": *Ibid.*

PAGE

209   "only other scientific research": Telephone conversation with Gale
       Lloyd, public affairs specialist, Centers for Disease Control, Atlanta,
       GA, 26 September 1986.

209   "USAMRIID has the responsibility": Interview with D. Huxsoll, 20
       February 1986, Frederick, MD.

211   "small percentage of the total": Letter from Chuck Dasey, 24 July
       1986.

212   "declined his invitation": Dean Fraser of Indiana University, quoted
       in "Detrick Birthday."

212   "various annual reports": Every year the Department of Defense
       publishes an annual report on chemical warfare and biological de-
       fense.

213   "shallow depth of field": Telephone interview with J. Leaning, 5 Au-
       gust 1986

213   "the military is not": Interview with J. King, 3 October 1986, Cam-
       bridge, MA.

CHAPTER FOURTEEN

214   "Men go into this branch": Zinnser, H., *Rats, Lice and History* (Bos-
       ton: Little, Brown, 1934).

214   "experimental animals": USDA/APHIS. VS Form 18–23. Annual
       Report of Research Facility, USAMRIID, 1984.

216   hemorrhagic fevers: Belshe, R., ed. *Textbook of Human Virology*
       (Littleton, MA: PSG Publishing). Strickland, T., *Hunter's Tropical
       Medicine,* Fourth Ed. (Philadelphia: W. B. Saunders, 1984).; Wil-
       cocks and Manson-Bahr, ed., *Manson's Tropical Diseases* (Baltimore:
       Williams and Wilkins Co.). Nnochiri, E., *Textbook of Imported Dis-
       eases* (Oxford: Oxford University Press, 1979).; Hoeprich, P., ed., *In-
       fectious Diseases* (Hagerstown, MD: Harper & Row, 1982); "Rift
       Valley Fever: An Emerging Human and Animal Problem" (pam-
       phlet) (World Health Organization, Geneva, Switzerland, 1982).

218   "arboviruses": *Ibid.*

220   "prep my suit": Interview with J. Dalrymple, 20 February 1986,
       Frederick, MD.

221   "Slammer has seen": Interview with Chuck Dasey, 20 February
       1986, Frederick, MD.

222   "increasing recognition": Interview with J. Middlebrook, 27 March
       1986, Frederick, MD.

223   "50 percent of USAMRIID's research program": Interview with D.
       Bunner, 20 February 1986, Frederick, MD.

223   "batrachotoxin": "Dart Poison Frogs," *Scientific American* (February
       1983).

224   "Tetrodotoxin": Davis, W., *The Serpent and the Rainbow* (New York:
       Simon and Schuster, 1985).

PAGE

225   "other low-molecular-weight toxins": U.S. Army Medical Research and Development Command. Broad Agency Announcement, August 1986.

227   "forty thousand die": Arena, J., *Poisoning,* Fourth Ed. (Springfield, IL: Charles C. Thomas, 1979).

227   "contrary to popular opinion": *Ibid.*

CHAPTER FIFTEEN

229   "$27.2 million contract": Letter from Chuck Dasey, 24 July 1986.

230   "eradicate smallpox": The Global Eradication of Smallpox. Final Report of the Global Commission for the Certification of Smallpox Eradication (World Health Organization: Geneva, Switzerland, 1980).

232   "army has ten vaccines": Interview with Colonel Thomas Cosgriff, 20 February 1986, Frederick, MD.

234   "in the late 1970s": Interview with D. Anderson, 27 March 1986, Frederick MD.

234   "stockpiled enough vaccine": Anderson, W. C., and King, J. M., Vaccine and Antitoxin Availability for Defense Against Biological Warfare Threat Agents. U.S. Army Health Services Command, Fort Sam Houston, TX. Report 83-002, September 1983.

235   "rational defense": Interview with R. Goldstein, 3 and 10 January 1986, Boston, MA.

235   "shortcomings of its vaccine program": Anderson, W. C., and King, J. M., Vaccine and Antitoxin Availability.

236   "National Institute of Medicine": New Vaccine Development, Establishing Priorities, Vol. II, Diseases of Importance in Developing Countries. Appendix A, Selection of Vaccine Candidates for Accelerated Development (National Academy of Sciences, Washington, D.C., 1986).

238   "Furthermore, aerosol vaccines": Research in aerosol immunization. Contract #DA-49-193-MD-2588. Illinois Institute of Technology. June 1964–July 1967.

238   "initial contracts": Interview with J. King, 3 October 1986, Cambridge, MA.

239   "Molecular Genetics": Telephone interview with C. Moscoplat, president of Molecular Genetics, 8 October 1986.

239   "few antiviral drugs have yet been found": Interview with P. Canonico, 27 March 1986, Frederick, MD.

240   "Why should DOD do it?" Interview with R. Sinsheimer, 7 October 1985, Santa Cruz, CA.

240   "president of the Salk": American Men and Women of Science, 14th Ed. (New York: R. R. Bowker, 1979).

PAGE

240   *"San Diego Union":* "Salk Institute Studies Germ Warfare Defense," *San Diego Union,* 7 August 1984.

241   "Delbart Glanz": Interview with Delbart Glanz, 2 October 1985, La Jolla, CA.

242   "leaves me cold": Telephone interview with J. Salk, 29 October 1985.

CHAPTER SIXTEEN

243   "according to the Swedes": Wallin, L., *Doctrines, Technology and Future War, a Swedish View,* Stockholm: National Defense Research Institute, undated.

244   "It has been hoped": Testimony by Douglas Feith, deputy assistant secretary of defense for negotiations policy, on biological and toxin weapons before the Subcommittee on Oversight and Evaluation of the House Permanent Select Committee on Intelligence, 8 August 1986.

245   "Nicaraguan minister of health": "U.S. Biological War Menace," *Daily World,* New York, NY, 12 November 1985. Also, "U.S. plans to conduct CBW Against Nicaragua," TASS, 2 February 1986.

245   "Soviets alleged": First appeared in *Literaturnaya Gazeta,* 3 February 1982. Reported the following day by UPI.

245   "Fidel Castro": U.S. Denies It Caused Dengue Fever in Cuba," *New York Times,* 28 July 1981.

246   "two hundredth anniversary": Interview with M. Gregg, 5 December 1985, Atlanta, GA.

246   "Dave Fraser": Letter from Dave Fraser, 25 March 1986.

247   "salmonella food poisoning": "Rajneeshees to pay millions for poisonings," *The Oregonian,* 16 August 1986.

248   "David Knapp": Press release, U.S. Department of Justice, U.S. Attorney, District of Oregon, 22 July 1986.

249   "confirmed the bad news": Citrus Canker, short form chronology, revised 15 November 1985, Published by USDA. Also, Fruit Crops Fact Sheet, Citrus Canker. Florida Co-operative Extension Service, University of Florida.

249   "There have been suspicions": Telephone interview with H. Ford, 28 February 1986.

250   "Leonid Rvachev": "Averting Genetic Warfare," *Environmental Action* (June 1984). Also, Longini, Fine, and Thacker, "Predicting the Global Spread of New Infectious Agents," *American Journal of Epidemiology,* Vol 123, #3, 1986.

251   "mucking around": Interview with M. Gregg, 5 December 1985.

251   "most epidemiologists": Telephone interview with I. Longini, 11 March 1986.

PAGE

252 "state-sponsored terrorism": Telephone interview with T. Thompkins, September 1986.

252 "so insidious": Interview with J. Douglass, 7 February 1986, McLean, Va.

252 "poor man's atomic bomb": Livingstone, N., and Douglass, J., *CBW—The Poor Man's Atomic Bomb,* National Security Paper #1. (Cambridge, MA: Institute for Foreign Policy Analysis, February 1984).

253 "alarming fact": *Ibid.*

254 "nut fringe": Telephone interview with C. G. McWright, 1 August 1986. Also, McWright, C. G., *DNA Warfare—Perspectives on Biological Weapons* (Center for Strategic and International Studies, Georgetown University, Washington D.C.), work in progress.

254 "cache of ricin": Telephone interview with J. McGeorge, Public Safety Institute, McLean, VA, 22 January 1986.

254 "ATCC": "FBI Investigates Attempt to Buy Deadly Germs," *Washington Post,* 25 November 1984.

254 "equally few but frightening": Livingstone and Douglass. *CBW—The Poor Man's Atomic Bomb.*

254 "have an idea": Telephone interview with C. G. McWright, 1 August 1986.

254 "vast escalation": Telephone interview with R. Kuppermann, 6 June 1986.

255 "in a letter": Letter from James Mason, director of Centers for Disease Control, to Robert Oakley, director of Office for Counter Terrorism and Emergency Planning, State Department, 19 November 1984.

255 "any consideration to terrorists": Telephone interview with H. Ford, February 1986.

255 "Biological Terrorism": Gordon, J., and Bech-Neilsen, S. "Biological Terrorism: A Direct Threat to Our Livestock Industry." Unpublished paper. Available from Department of Veterinary Preventive Medicine, College of Veterinary Medicine, Ohio State University, Columbus, OH.

CHAPTER SEVENTEEN

258 "I had the privilege": Governor Norman Bangerter's remarks to the National Prayer Breakfast, Fort Douglas Military Club, Salt Lake City, 12 February 1986.

259 "as some experts do": Franklyn Holzman, professor of economics at Tufts University and fellow at the Russian Research Center at Harvard University, is one expert.

259 "persecuted people": Telephone interview with E. Firmage, 13 March 1986.

PAGE

261 "Scott Matheson": Telephone interview with S. Matheson, 7 April 1986.

261 "Look at Utah": *Ibid.*

261 "seven military installations": Interview with Ruth Ann Story, aide to Gov. Bangerter, 13 February 1986, Salt Lake City, UT.

262 "free world's stockpile": *Ibid.*

262 "associate Dugway with an accident": "600 sheep stricken near CBW Center," *Science,* 29 March 1969.

262 "Osguthorpe": Telephone interview with J. Osguthorpe, 13 February 1986.

262 "congressional subcommittee": Investigation by Conservation and Natural Resources Subcommittee of the House of Representatives, Released September 1969.

263 "in 1975": Dr. J. Clifton Spendlove, quoted in "Dugway Still Not Sure It's to Blame in Sheep Deaths," *Deseret News,* 20 December 1975.

263 "feds have been devious": Interview with S. Gillmor, 13 February 1986, Salt Lake City, UT.

264 "to count eagles": Interview with J. Coyner, 11 February 1986, Salt Lake City, UT.

264 "in a letter, Garland": Letter from Cecil Garland, 6 March 1986.

265 "who don't know Dugway exists": Interview with D. Nydam, 12 February 1986, Salt Lake City and Dugway, UT.

270 "signed the treaty": Interview with P. Adams, 12 February 1986, Dugway, UT.

271 "1,300-square-foot place": Information Paper. DAMA-PPM-T. Subject: Modernization of Dugway Proving Ground. 8 November 1984.

273 "Operation Blue Skies": Hersh, S., *Chemical and Biological Warfare: America's Hidden Arsenal.* (Indianapolis: Bobbs-Merrill, 1969).

Index